Praise for *Collaboration and Co-creation*

In today's customer-empowered world, collaboration and co-creation competencies are critical to the future growth of a company. Execution skills will be at a premium. Gaurav Bhalla offers a concrete framework and specific examples that managers can use to implement value co-creation programs with their customers. A must-read for companies not wishing to get left behind!

> Vijay Govindarajan, Earl C. Daum 1924 Professor of International Business, Tuck School of Business, Dartmouth College

Collaboration and co-creation are the sweet spots for rethinking how companies should practice marketing and innovation. I personally am very passionate about co-creation; it creates real competitive advantage. It is the foundation of IFF's customer-centric thinking, and guides every aspect of our new product development creative process. Gaurav Bhalla's book is very timely, and offers readers an effective way for building businesses around customers.

> Nicolas Mirzayantz, Group President, Fragrances, International Flavors and Fragrances

Companies can't afford to fake it. Customer-driven innovation has moved from the edge to become a core business practice. Gaurav Bhalla helps you understand what it takes to make this shift, and not a moment too soon.

> John Hagel III, Co-Chairman, Deloitte Center for the Edge, and co-author, *The Power of Pull*

If running your business seems more difficult lately, reading this book will help you understand why. It will also provide insights into how collaboration and co-creation can improve your company's performance.

> Vince Barabba, Author, *Meeting of the Minds*, and Founder and Chairman, Market Insight Corporation

Gaurav Bhalla is after big game: how the world's leading institutions are connecting and collaborating with their most important asset — their customers — in novel and important ways. Understanding this space as few do, he shows how this new form of customer interaction leads to game changing business decisions. This book is an important one to read for any marketing, market research, or product innovation professional.

Steve Howe, CEO, Passenger

Based on my research, it is clear that user co-creation is a strong driver for transforming the marketing and innovation programs of those companies that dare to listen and respond. Gaurav Bhalla provides a solid framework to guide this process and a rich set of case stories to explain why and how. In particular, I must credit him for taking the challenge of implementing user-driven innovation inside the company seriously — it's no easy task, but highly rewarding!

Jacob Buur, Professor of Participatory Innovation, Research Director of SPIRE, University of Southern Denmark

Gaurav Bhalla

Collaboration and Co-creation

New Platforms for Marketing and Innovation

 Springer

Gaurav Bhalla
Knowledge Kinetics, Inc.
Reston, VA
USA
gaurav.bhalla@knowledgekinetics.com

ISBN 978-1-4419-7081-7   e-ISBN 978-1-4419-7082-4
DOI 10.1007/978-1-4419-7082-4
Springer New York Dordrecht Heidelberg London

Printed on acid-free paper

Springer is part of Springer Science+Business Media (www.springer.com)

To Mothers

*consummate practitioners of collaboration
and co-creation*

Foreword

Business can sometimes be accused of promoting new techniques and practices that have more to do with jargon and theory than with action. Fortunately, this is not the case with *Collaboration and Co-creation*.

In today's networked world, power has irrevocably shifted to the consumer. This has significantly altered the nature of interactions between companies and consumers, especially in the areas of marketing and innovation. Traditional methods of fueling growth through thirty-second commercials and products developed exclusively by in-house R&D departments have run out of steam. They are increasingly being replaced by a collaborative, co-created view of value that emphasizes the individual's needs rather than the "one-size-fits-all" model of mass marketing.

Gaurav Bhalla's book is about this new customer-centric model of value-creation. It is a book about transformation: the need to rethink customer value — what it is and how it should be created. The book recommends that readers think of value not as "what companies *do to* their brands in their factories," but as "what consumers *do with* brands to make their lives better and more fulfilling." Consequently, value lies not in building more features into products and services, but in providing more and varied opportunities to consumers for co-creating personalized experiences, much like the Ponds Institute does in helping a diverse set of consumers co-create individualized beauty and skin care experiences.

Implementing new business practices is not always obvious. A common quandary that most companies find themselves in is where to begin. How does a company make collaboration and co-creation a core capability? How does it sequence this capability-building process? Fortunately, the book is up to this challenge. It lives up to its promise of taking the reader beyond theory to implementation. By presenting a simple, easy-to-understand framework, it takes the intimidation factor out of adopting these new value-creation platforms. The book stresses that new mindsets and new cultures are prerequisites to broadening one's horizons and promoting creativity.

The "Listen-Engage-Respond" framework for implementation should appeal to both sides of the reader's brain. It is simultaneously intuitive and rational. It is an obvious reality that to get consumers to pay attention, you have to first listen to them. Listening is even more important when dealing with consumers at lower levels of the pyramid, where engagement cycles tend to last months, and sometimes years, before positive business outcomes are experienced. Additionally, engaging and responding to the whole consumer and not just her wallet is the best way to ensure that a company's current offerings and future innovations will be crowd favorites.

The book makes a compelling case for rethinking marketing, not as a department or as a function, but as an ingrained pattern of behavior that leads to an obsession about creating and nurturing consumer value. The author also urges the reader to rethink innovation, not as something that a company does on its own with its proprietary R&D resources, but as an activity it undertakes in collaboration with other stakeholders operating in its ecosystem.

Both these themes merit serious attention. The world is far too complex and multifaceted for any company, no matter how large, to ignore the interests and well-being of other stakeholders — consumers, customers, suppliers, NGOs, and regulators. Also, since our businesses and brands have impacts at every stage of their lifecycle — in sourcing raw materials, packaging, manufacture, distribution, consumer use — shared value-creation must involve the full spectrum of stakeholders. Unilever's own experience with the sustainable sourcing of palm oil bears this out. We partner with Greenpeace, Oxfam, WWF, and an industry coalition comprising over 20 global retailers and manufacturers. Without this level and range of collaboration, it would be impossible for us to meet our public commitments — to draw all our palm oil from certified sustainable sources by 2015.

The book offers a timely reminder that collaboration does not happen automatically and spontaneously; it requires an investment in effort and resources. Collaborating across the entire value chain is complex and time-consuming. It challenges everyone. But it can be very — rewarding, resulting as it does in faster and more relevant innovations.

Very few business books venture beyond the business world, even though a lot of good ideas and projects are implemented by nonprofit organizations. This book does and deserves credit for it. The discussion on how Denmark, Norway, Scotland, Ireland, Sweden, and Chicago are collaborating with their citizens to co-create value in the areas of health, education, clean air, and reducing urban congestion is very instructive.

The book uses a rich array of examples to illustrate the key concepts of collaboration and co-creation. The diversity of companies, organizations, and individuals featured in the book — Hallmark, Nike, President Obama, Robert Redford, Phoenix Suns, IBM, GE, P&G, Coca-Cola, Mini Cooper, Dell, Audi, Nokia, Marico — is impressive. There is much to reflect on and learn from these case studies.

Let me turn you over now to the pages of this book. We are all beneficiaries of Gaurav Bhalla's decision to tackle this difficult subject. Marketing and innovation have and will continue to be two of the strongest drivers of margin and revenue growth. The concept of customer value is central to both of them. How that value is created will determine which companies will win in the future. If companies want to get enduring competitive advantage, they will need to master the skills of collaboration. Embracing and implementing the new models of value co-creation, discussed in the book, will help companies make that transition.

Paul Polman
Chief Executive Officer, Unilever

Prologue

Businesses and organizations today face a complex and rapidly changing landscape. Three aspects stand out. First is the emergence of a new, empowered customer, very skilled at using the new digital information commons for a variety of vocational, recreational, and creative purposes. Second is the inevitability of a linked, interconnected global economy. Third, "people, planet, and profits" is the new performance imperative; companies can't ignore the interests of people – especially those living at the bottom of the pyramid – and of the planet in setting their own growth agendas. It is the first aspect that focuses our energies and attention.

In the last five to ten years, several books have been written applauding the emergence of the empowered customer. Books like *The Cluetrain Manifesto* (Levine, Locke, Searls, and Weinberger), *The Future of Competition* (Prahalad and Ramaswamy), *Groundswell* (Li and Bernoff), *Crowdsourcing* (Howe), *Here Comes Everybody* (Shirky), *Wikinomics* (Tapscott and Williams), and *We-Think* (Leadbeater) have very successfully and skillfully established how empowered customers — meaning better-educated, better-informed, and more creative customers — armed with ubiquitous and Internet-enabled information and communication technologies, are not just consumers of value, but also its co-producers. This new handshake, depicting a radically different way in which customers interact with companies and organizations is not just trendy fashion, here today, gone tomorrow. Rather, the new handshake represents a fundamental and irrevocable shift in the way traditional, firm-centric, customer value-creating activities, like marketing and innovation, are implemented.

The wall of intimidation has been breached. With every passing day, businesses and executives get increasingly more comfortable with the world and ideas realized by collaborative innovation. Consequently, it is not surprising that collaborating with customers to co-create new customer value is a hot item on the strategic agendas of most companies. But as with most things that require a change in behavior, migrating from recognizing the importance of something to actually doing something about it is not trivial.

To borrow a phrase from Eric Berne, author of *What Do You Say After You Say Hello?*, What do companies do after they get all excited and motivated about collaborating with customers? How do they engage their customers in collaborative innovation efforts? How do they rethink and reshape their marketing and innovation efforts? A few companies have figured it out through a mix of experimentation and trial and error; some are muddling through, but the majority of the companies have questions. They would like to know how companies like Unilever, IBM, Nike, P&G, and Hallmark do it. More importantly, they are keen to learn how they can implement co-creation programs in their own companies.

It is this need that our book fills. Our goal is to take the reader beyond applause and appreciation to implementation. In a manner of speaking, we start where the books mentioned earlier leave the reader. We assume that the reader is convinced that collaboration and co-creation is a game-changing business practice. We also assume that the reader is convinced that debating on whether or not to adopt this emerging business practice may not be a wise option, as today's new, empowered customers may not offer them that choice. Accordingly, we focus our energies on helping the reader reach a deeper understanding of implementation. We do so with the help of a simple framework, which as Mr. Paul Polman, CEO of Unilever, says in his Foreword, should appeal to both sides of the reader's brain. We agree. The Listen-Engage-Respond framework has both emotional and rational appeal. Its emotional appeal stems from its simplicity. It is at once intuitive and obvious. Its rational appeal derives from its structural integrity. It is a system for transforming a transactional approach to relating with customers to achieving ongoing and sustainable relationships with them.

All companies today want to have conversations with customers; there is nothing wrong with that. However, it is impossible to have a conversation with anybody, let alone customers, without first listening to them. Wives, husbands, children, parents can all attest to that. In families across the world, the objection — *you are not listening to a word of what I am saying* — is screamed out thousands of times a day. However, listening is not enough. Conversations, in order to be sustained, need fuel; they need the fuel of attention and engagement. They also need an agenda and an investment in resources. Finally, for conversations to be transformed into ongoing relationships, people need a response, a commitment to action. Companies that are not committed to following through, that are unwilling to respond with concrete, tangible actions that create mutual value for the customer and the company, are unlikely to find customers who would want to maintain a relationship with them. It is the sum of all these aspects and the interrelationships between them that make the Listen-Engage-Respond framework an effective system for designing and implementing collaboration and co-creation programs.

Poets never tire of admonishing — *Show, Don't Tell* — meaning demonstrate, illustrate, don't simply narrate. As authors, we have taken this admonition to heart. We have used numerous case studies from a number of different companies, representing a number of different sectors, including nonprofit organizations, to illustrate the various implementation concepts discussed in the book. Each decision, every aspect of the framework is amplified, not through definitions and explanations, but through examples and case studies. In selecting case studies and examples, we were careful not to just go after well-publicized examples. We have tried our best to research and showcase examples of companies and organizations that have a lot to teach us, even though previously they may not have been featured widely, companies like Electrolux and organizations like Susan G. Komen for the Cure®.

A few more points on our choice of words and phrases before we leave you with the text to make it your own. Mindful that our readers are likely to have diverse backgrounds and represent different industries, we have used the more general term — customer — throughout the book to refer to people who would ordinarily be referred to as consumers. Our friends who work in the consumer-packaged-goods (CPG) sector were not entirely convinced, since for them "customer" is an intermediary that buys and distributes their product – companies like Wal-Mart, Tesco, Carrefour, and Big Bazaar. Consumers are end-users, who buy their products and services. CPG companies are more likely to collaborate and co-create value with consumers than with customers. We understand and respect this point of view. In instances where companies shared their stories and case studies with us and wanted us to maintain this distinction, we have done so and used the word "consumers" instead. Additionally, as is becoming increasingly customary, we have mainly used the feminine pronoun, she or her, in referring to the customer, rather than the more cumbersome he/she.

Thank you for picking up our book. We hope you will enjoy reading it and find it useful. We also hope that as you are reading, or after you finish reading the book, you will join us at www.gauravbhalla.com/co-creation to share your thoughts and achievements related to the design and implementation of collaboration and co-creation programs with your fellow readers from around the world.

Contents

Chapter 1
Collaboration and Co-creation

Meet the Deckers — John Decker Jr., his younger brothers Josh and Tyler, his sister Tessa, and his parents Donna and John Decker Sr. For the past 20 years, the Deckers' lives have had a singular focus, how best to cope with and conquer Wiskott-Aldrich syndrome (WAS), a primary immunodeficiency disease involving both T- and B-lymphocytes.[1] Their story and experiences in these past 20 years are also a microcosm of the principal themes of this book.

WAS is an inherited disorder that is passed on from mother to son. Mothers are carriers, but the disease affects only males. It is difficult to diagnose and even more difficult to treat. WAS patients are usually diagnosed as children, when symptoms like recurrent infections, bruising, lymphoma, and leukemia present themselves. Unfortunately, there is no simple way to cure WAS. The best chance for recovery requires a bone marrow transplant, but transplants can be done only if a donor with an identical human leukocyte antigen (HLA) can be found. Unfortunately for John and the Deckers, a potential donor could not be found. When a bone marrow transplant is not possible, treating the symptoms and preventing injuries, especially among children, is the only remaining course of action to cope with the disease effectively.[2]

John and his parents had a choice. They could either stay with the hope-and-pray mindset, or become pilgrims in search of a deeper understanding of the disease, of alternative treatments available, and advances in medicine that could potentially help cure John's condition in the near future. They chose to become pilgrims — a pilgrimage that is still ongoing and one that continues to evolve in rich and unpredictable ways. It is through the choices and behaviors exhibited by John and his family during this pilgrimage that we would like to illustrate the rise of a new type of consumer and the changing dynamics of customer value-creation. John Decker's story is a story of exceptional courage and resourcefulness. It is also an excellent case study of the changing relationship between customers and companies, of the rise of new platforms of collaboration and co-creation, and the role that these platforms play in the creation and consumption of customer value.

A few years ago, before the dawning of the digital age, John Jr. and his parents (hereafter referred to simply as John, or the Deckers) would have visited a hospital

G. Bhalla, *Collaboration and Co-creation: New Platforms for Marketing and Innovation*, DOI 10.1007/978-1-4419-7082-4_1, © Springer Science+Business Media, LLC 2011

acclaimed for its treatment of WAS, sought the advice of resident experts, and after asking a few polite questions to assure themselves would have followed the prescribed treatment regimen to the best of their ability.

But the Deckers live in a digital, highly connected, and networked world. They have the Internet, which provides them access to vast amounts of information related to the disease and its treatment, to expert advice, and to the opinions and experiences of other patients. Their goal was not merely to find a hospital with the most sterling reputation for treating WAS. Instead, their goal was to educate themselves, to immerse themselves in the wealth of information available and learn all that they could about the disease, before meeting any doctors. A major part of this self-education also involved searching for the most appropriate team of physicians for John. Medical talent and reputation were not the only factors important to the Deckers. Of course, they wanted a group of physicians who were the best in their field. Who would not want the best affordable care for their children? But they also wanted physicians who would be sensitive to John's unique needs and requirements, both as a patient and as a human being. They were unwilling to assign John to a mass collective category called "patient." They wanted physicians who would respect his uniqueness, and tailor their treatment to meet his unique needs.

Sensing that they were not alone in their quest for understanding and answers, the Deckers decided to open themselves up to other connections and influences. Consequently, they traveled to medical conferences coordinated by organizations such as the Immune Deficiency Foundation to learn of advances in medical science, and of new treatments likely to be available in the coming years.[3] There, they met other families and patients like themselves, who had children suffering from WAS. They made a conscious effort to forge connections with them. Over time, as their involvement with WAS patients, parents, and support groups increased, they found themselves playing dual roles. In addition to seeking answers to their own questions, their experience also became a source of information and solutions for others.

As a result of their efforts, the Deckers were able to connect with two experts in hematology-oncology at the University of Michigan: Doctor Raymond Hutchinson, a medical researcher, and Doctor Dan Wechsler, a practicing specialist. This collaboration between a full-time researcher and a medical practitioner proved extremely beneficial for John. While collaboration between two doctors with complementary skills is not new, what is new is the role John played in this collaboration. John was not merely a passive recipient of the treatment offered by the medical team of Hutchinson and Wechsler. He was actively helping them shape his own treatment by investing effort in monitoring his own condition, keeping meticulous records, and offering insights on how he was responding to medication, especially to adjustments and changes that the physician team would make.

Unwittingly, John was setting in motion the dynamics of collaboration and co-creation. The more effort and energy he invested in his own treatment, the more useful he became to companies, institutions, and individuals involved in treating and providing care to WAS patients. Using his own empirical data, recorded diligently and chronologically in a journal, John offered to help doctors find the right dosing regimens for their patients. His data, coupled with his understanding of medical terminology, allowed him to reach out to influential scientists and medical doctors working in leading institutions, such as Immune Deficiency Foundation, National Institutes of Health (NIH), and National Human Genome Research Institute. Over time, John formed a virtual team with WAS specialist Dr. Han Ochs at the Immune Deficiency Foundation and Dr. Fabio Candotti at the National Human Genome Research Institute. Although technically a patient, John was not just a patient. He was also a respected and valued resource, co-creating health and well-being not just for himself, but for other WAS patients as well.

John's collaboration with the medical establishment has produced several valuable outcomes. Two are especially noteworthy:

- Determining optimal dosages and frequency of treatments: Baxter International, Inc., a leader in immune deficiency pharmaceuticals, collaborated with John and his doctors in designing an experiment to find the optimal dosages and frequency of treatments for people battling WAS.
- Developing treatment standards for other WAS patients: John also served as a quasi-subject for a Baxter and NIH study. He diligently monitored and documented his weight, hemoglobin levels, platelet counts, and treatments. He also documented his health status corresponding to these indicators. Baxter and NIH used the information provided by John to develop treatment standards for other WAS patients.

By proactively confronting WAS through a mix of knowledge, collaboration, and personal initiative, John has become a WAS spokesperson and activist. He routinely reaches out to other patients and their families to provide support and advocacy. John has also discovered the power and influence of new Web 2.0 technologies in helping him connect and communicate with a wider audience. He relies on social networking sites like Facebook to build communities, network, and communicate with collaborators. He also uses micro-blogging tools like Twitter to disseminate calls to action, coordinate events, and send alerts to other WAS patients.

Introducing a New Type of Customer

John's story is unique, but his behaviors are not; they are exhibited every day to thousands of customers around the globe in a number of different environments, not just health care or medicine. While all of John's behaviors make compelling reading, four in particular deserve to be highlighted. They are the essence of customer collaboration and co-creation and represent the changing face of customer value.

- Active participation and involvement: To begin with, John proactively confronted his condition; he did not passively accept it. This required him to put in effort and give time, to work hard at learning, and to work with the health care system to find the right treatments, and to stubbornly persist when things were not going his way. He was not content with the outside world to take care of him and his needs; he was willing to work with them so he could help himself.

- Balancing expert opinion with personal judgment: John engaged experts. He accepted their expertise, but not to the blind subordination of his own beliefs, values, and preferences. Throughout his ordeal he never once gave up his right to understand, to question, and to push the experts to think deeper about his condition and his unique treatment needs. He was never just one of many patients; he was always one unique patient.
- Connecting and networking: Contact with other WAS patients, caregivers, and institutions not only gave John and his family a wider support base, but also established reciprocal relationships for information and knowledge-sharing. More importantly, this collaboration grew organically, was tacit, and was guided by a set of mutually shared expectations. There were no formal rules or contracts.
- Individual as both producer and consumer: John was both a producer and a consumer. He was not just a WAS patient, consuming his share of medical care; he was also a producer of valuable data that were used to customize and tailor medical care for him and other patients. He was a co-creator of WAS treatment protocols and standards. In addition to consuming the output of modern medicine, he was also a living laboratory shaping the future of WAS treatment.

Companies today are dealing with a new type of customer — one that is better educated, more collaborative, and infinitely more resourceful than at any time in the past. Comparisons on several key dimensions between the old and new customer realities are presented in Table 1.1. The implications of information-armed, interlocked customers are quite profound. Today's customers are not content with being mere spectators. They want to be heard; they want to have a say in how customer value is created and what they would like to consume. Given the opportunity, they are willing and unafraid to use their initiative and resources to back themselves and their own agendas against the agenda of large corporations.

Table 1.1 A Profile of the New Customer

	Old Reality	New Reality
Identity	Consumers, respondents	Real people, creative partners
Role	Passive; consumers of value	Active collaborators; co-producers of value
Source of insights	Surveys, dispassionate objective observation	Conversations, stories, impassioned immersion
Handshake with company	Transactions-based	Interactions and experience-based
Location	Fixed and invisible; at one end of a long value chain	Adaptive and very visible; anytime, anyplace
Information and influence	Company advertising and messages; expert opinion	Word-of-mouth; peer-to-peer; social media
Concept of value	Company offers; one size fits all	Customer determines; tailored and unique
Primary source of value	What's in the brand; attributes and features	What customers do with the brand; unique solutions and customized experiences

In order to better understand the new customer, it is important to reflect on how we got here. Context is the key to understanding the emergence of new customer behaviors, so that companies can design new ways of responding to them in a mutually fulfilling and satisfying manner. Since the early 1900s, when formal theories of modern business firms first started appearing, the dominant tendency has been to treat companies and consumers as distinct and separate entities. This is not surprising because the business function that most enables companies to understand customers is marketing, and marketing is an offspring of economics. In economics, producers and consumers are always distinct and separate. Producers produce goods and services, and consumers buy and consume them. As companies have access to greater amounts of resources, they wield more power. The rest of the actors comprising the market — wholesalers, retailers, and consumers — simply follow along.

A direct consequence of this power imbalance is the process by which customer value has been created and consumed. Until very recently, customer value was created in company factories, mainly by R&D departments. Consumers were passive recipients of what companies offered them, even if it was not what they actually wanted. Much like Oliver in Dickens' *Oliver Twist*, you either ate the institutionalized watery gruel or you went hungry. It is not as if companies were blind or insensitive to customers' needs, or what customers regarded as value. It is just that the company's agenda — what it liked to and could produce at a targeted level of profit — always took precedence over the customers' agenda. Management ideas, like customer centricity and market orientation, provided useful sound bytes, but companies seldom shared power with customers, and customer-centered thinking rarely drove their operations.

For several decades, the firm-centric, product-oriented way of thinking produced very successful businesses. However, in the last ten to fifteen years, a new and separate reality has arisen to question the status quo. Tired of being disenfranchised, customers want to be part of the game. They want to have a say in what companies produce for them, how they produce it, what raw materials they use, and how much they charge for it. They are no longer willing to be passive recipients at the end of a long impersonal value chain, playing solely according to rules made up by companies. Customers feel that companies should be talking to them because they believe they can help companies figure out what they really want. They do not like being valued only for their eyeballs or their share of wallets, or being herded into nameless, faceless segments, even if those segments have interesting names like loyalists, apostles, and terrorists!

This new, separate, and emerging reality is not merely a spur-of-the-moment, Ralph Nader–style protest launched by a bunch of angry consumers that will blow away next autumn. Instead, it is a tectonic shift that carries within it the seeds of how commerce and community will cohabit and converge in the future. Its message is simple and compelling:

Dear Company, When was the last time you read the folk tale, "The Emperor Has No Clothes," by Hans Christian Andersen? Let us in, we can be like the little boy in the story who shouted, "But the emperor has no clothes!":
Don't you think you owe it to yourself to hear us tell it like it is, to help you see yourself as we see you? You may not like what we have to say, but at least you will not be surprised.

*Face it, despite several rounds of reorganizations, agency changes, and raises in promotion
and advertising budgets, the sales needle on your corporate dashboard hasn't moved.
Why? Because we, the customers, still see you as you are, naked!*[4]

Collaboration and Co-creation in Action

There are a few better seats in the house from which to view the new dynamics of
value-creation in action than the development of the open source movement and the
creation of the mountain biking industry. Both case studies offer excellent perspectives on customer-driven innovation: on how value was created outside the reach of
the formal and organized new product development processes and departments of
companies.

Open Source Movement

The open source movement, best known for its achievements in software development, typifies the reality and potential of collaboration and co-creation. Before the
open source movement, the dominant way in which value was created in the software world was through proprietary software. Sponsoring companies released versions of the software that they believed were the best for its customers. Periodic
updates were issued mainly in response to market pressures, like customer impa-
tience and increased competitive activity. Occasionally, spurred on by emerging
new technologies, developers within a company would push for new releases and
introduce better-performing products.

In this traditional model of software development, roles were rigid and formally
defined. Different groups of people would be responsible for managing the
product's architecture, its development, and its implementation. Eric Raymond in
his essay and book, *The Cathedral and the Bazaar*, likens the traditional approach
to that of building cathedrals — a small band of individual wizards and mages
working in splendid isolation.[5] Developers and end-users had little choice but to
accept what was offered, even if they had better ideas than the company's software
engineers. Activities considered desirable by them, such as code modification,
improving end-user experience, and fixing bugs, were not always undertaken, as
often they did not meet the company's objectives of cost containment and adher-
ence to long-term R&D schedules.

All that changed with the emergence of the open source movement. Raymond
likens the open source movement to a bazaar — a babbling of different agendas and
approaches. Another word that builds on Raymond and captures the spirit of the
bazaar model perfectly is *libre*, Latin for free.[6] The open source movement liberated
users and developers from the shackles imposed on them by companies and laws
associated with proprietary software. They now became co-developers and co-creators
with equal access to the source code of the software. They were no longer merely
end-users or developers; they also became the software's producers, proposing

modifications, suggesting code fixes, generating bug reports, and producing relevant documentation. Their collaborative efforts fed off one another, as developers took turns playing doctor and patient, to use a metaphor from a different field; alternating between complaining about problems and prescribing remedies and solutions to solve them.

Not every programmer has equal programming skills; some are more skilled than others. That's okay. Not every application is equally demanding; some are more demanding than others. Not every machine on which the software runs is the same; some are more powerful than others. Further, they may not all be configured identically. That's okay too. Complexity of the end-use environment — namely, the presence of a multitude of users, implementing different applications, on machines with different operating capabilities — previously a problem, now became an opportunity. What was formerly an obstruction to the implementation of improvement and innovation initiatives became a reason for creating new value in the open source world. This has been observed repeatedly, and in several different environments. The impetus for innovation, so essential for the development of the next generation of products and services, is more likely to be provided by bazaars than cathedrals. A quick glance at Java, Linux, Firefox, and the GNU compiler will demonstrate that this is no empty claim.[7]

Mountain Biking

Themes of collaboration and co-creation so evident in the open source movement can also be found in the birth and growth of an unrelated industry: mountain biking. Mountain biking started as a fringe recreational pastime among a few teenagers in the hills and mountains of Marin County, California, in the early 1970s. Today, it is an Olympic sport, a $100 billion global industry, and a form of recreation for millions around the world.

New value and a new market were created not through a single *eureka* moment experienced by a lone R&D specialist at an established bike company, but through the shared passion and obsessive tinkering of a bazaar of mountain bikers. In the initial years, the staple of the recreational off-road bikers was the 1940s-type, single-speed, fat-tired bicycle, typically used by newspaper delivery boys. However, as the pioneers got more adventurous and ventured farther from their regular trails, they found that their old bikes couldn't take the extra punishment. Nor could they deliver the extra performance the bikers hungered for.

It is this need that fueled an ever-increasing cycle of modification, improvisation, and innovation that eventually led to the birth of the modern-day mountain bike: a machine specifically built to meet the rigors and demands of mountain biking and the performance expectations of those pursuing it either as a sport or as recreation. A ninety-minute video named *Klunkerz* traces the Darwinian evolution of the mountain bike in the most compelling way, using the words, emotions, and experiences of the pioneers of mountain biking — people like John Finley Scott, Joe Breeze, Gary Fisher, and Tom Ritchey.[8]

From the perspective of this book, what is most gripping about the mountain biking saga is not the homespun ingenuity, the amputation of old bikes, their subsequent reconfiguration, and metamorphosis. What is most gripping is the spirit and vocabulary of collaboration and co-creation that existed even then. A sampling of comments shared by the pioneers in the video are compelling testimony to the role the bazaar model played in the evolution of the Klunker to the modern-day mountain bike.

> always exchanging ideas about these new bikes in an open, informal, and ongoing way
> brotherhood — absence of competition when it came to knowledge and sharing — we were like one extended family
> communal spirit of the times dictated that they share their discoveries
> this process of continual modification, each riffing off each other's innovations was a critical factor in the evolution of the mountain bike
> the real innovation acceleration took place when it spilled out of Marin county became something bigger than just the obsession of a small group of people and became a movement.
> across the board, everybody was collaborating with each other, there was no enmity, no jealousy, there was no rivalry.

Everybody wanted a better bike: a machine built specifically for the purpose of mountain biking. To fulfill their desire, amateur mountain bikers were willing to put in the effort and time, share their expertise, and learn from the expertise of others in building a special-purpose mountain bike. In their willingness to network, collaborate, and share, the mountain bikers were acting as both customers and producers of mountain bikes.

Collaboration and Value Co-creation Go Mainstream

The terms customer collaboration and co-creation may be new, but the dynamics they represent are not. Rewind several thousand years to the time of hunter-gatherer societies. Do you think it would have been possible for people living in that economic system to survive without collaborating and co-creating value? Or, if you prefer more recent times, fast forward to Adam Smith's world of division and specialization of labor. Would the staple of most economic textbooks — the butcher, the baker, the tailor, and the candlestick maker — have been able to survive without collaboration and co-creation?

A more recent and striking example concerns the making of the Oxford English Dictionary (OED), a story told brilliantly in *The Professor and the Madman*.[9] The vision for the OED, articulated on Guy Fawkes Day by Richard Trench, Dean of Westminster, and adopted formally as a resolution in 1859 by the Philological Society, materialized as a dictionary only in 1928, when the last of the original ten volumes was published. Seventy years in the making, it still is one of the grandest examples of global collaboration and co-creation. Realizing that the work was beyond the capacity of a single individual or even a small group, no matter how expert, a global appeal was issued in April 1879, asking for volunteers from the British Isles, the Americas, and the British colonies to donate their time. The original appeal issued in 1879 can be found in its entirety on OED's website.[10] Thousands of volunteers offered their services, reading books, noting words, and the context within which they were used, on slips of paper, and mailing them to Dr. James Murray (the Professor). If the present day system of peer reviews, awarding stars and rating points, to discriminate between individual contributors had existed then, Doctor William C. Minor (the Madman) would be the proverbial Gulliver among Lilliputians. Among the thousands of volunteers whose efforts formed the core of OED's creation, Dr. Minor was the most prolific, contributing over 10,000 entries to the total of 400,000 words contained in the original ten volumes. Since a dictionary is a living, evolving body of knowledge, the work of continuously updating it never ends, especially as today we have not just one, but several different "Englishes," as John Simpson's appeal issued in 1999 so charmingly reminds us (Box 1.1).

Box 1.1 Appeal for Readers: Your Language Needs You!

John Simpson, Chief Editor of the Oxford English Dictionary, issued the following appeal in 1999:[11]

> I would like to invite readers to contribute to the development of the Dictionary by adding to our record of English throughout the world. Everyone can play a part in recording the history of the language and helping to enhance the Oxford English Dictionary.

One hundred and twenty years ago, James Murray, original editor of the OED, launched an "Appeal to the English-Speaking and English-Reading Public of Great Britain, America, and the British Colonies" for words for the dictionary. The appeal proved that dictionary-making is an exception to most fields of scholarship; anyone can make a valuable contribution. From Minnesota to Melbourne, scholars and readers came to Murray's aid. Without their help, the dictionary would never have been published. Since that time, many more people have made valuable contributions to the dictionary. They have been of all ages and from all walks of life (among them writers, teachers, a stevedoring superintendent, a Nobel laureate, a retired businessman, a cryptographer, and, perhaps most famously, Dr William C. Minor, inmate of Broadmoor Asylum). Now, Murray's appeal is being relaunched to mark one of the most important events of the start of the new millennium — the creation of a record of the English language unlike any other.

Lexicographers at Oxford University Press are now engaged in the huge task of completely revising the OED. The first complete revision in its history, it is projected to cost £34 million (US$55 million). Oxford has taken a big step towards that goal by publishing the OED online, which will incorporate at least 1,000 new and revised entries every quarter. According to John Simpson: "There is no longer one English — there are many Englishes. Words are flooding into the language from all corners of the world. Only a dictionary the size of the OED can adequately capture the true richness of the English language throughout its history, and the developments in world English. Now that the online edition has been launched, I would be delighted to have a host of new readers helping us to map the past, the present, and the future of English."

So, if the dynamics represented by the terms collaboration and co-creation are not new, what is new? In modern, post industrialized economies, as small and local gave way to gigantic and global, a tremendous distance developed between the proverbial butchers and bakers, and their customers. Commerce and community became irrevocably separated. What is new is how a combination of modern information and communication technologies (ICT) and customer empowerment is challenging incumbent ideas of company-customer separation. Companies no longer have a monopoly on ideas or resources. In many fields, like software, computer games, and product design, social approaches to creativity and innovation often perform better than hierarchical corporate bureaucracies. Consequently, value-creation activities that once could mainly be found in small, relatively informal commercial settings are increasingly gaining attention at several large companies. Traditional, company-centered mindsets are becoming increasingly wary of consigning customers to the invisible end of a long value chain. With everyday customers eager, willing, and able to use their knowledge, resources, and creativity in value-creation activities that often rival the capabilities of the world's richest organizations, confining customers to a limited economic role, namely consumption, is just not a smart idea. That awareness and realization, among even some of the most hardened product-centric companies, is what is new.

We would now like to discuss how one company, Hallmark Cards, Inc., is acting on this awareness, and expanding its century-old tradition of customer caring, by seeking to deepen its understanding of the new consumer, and looking for ways to collaborate with them to co-create innovative products and services.

Hallmark's Collaboration and Co-creation Journey

On January 10, 2010, Hallmark celebrated its one-hundredth birthday. Started in January 1910 by Joyce C. Hall, the Kansas City-based company is virtually synonymous with greeting cards, wherever its products are sold. The company's self-perception is more formal. Its website and public relations materials introduce Hallmark as a leader in the "personal expression" industry. Today, the company has a global footprint, operating in over 100 countries, and publishing in more than 30 languages. In addition to several different lines of greeting cards, personal expression products, and Keepsake Ornaments (Box 1.2), Hallmark's portfolio of offerings also includes television programming, through *Hallmark Hall of Fame* and the Hallmark Channel cable network, and creative experience products for children, offered through its Crayola subsidiary.[12]

Specialty stores, like Hallmark's Gold Crown retail outlets, and mass retailers account for the greatest share of Hallmark revenue. The company also offers e-cards, mobile greetings, and party products through its online channels. By the late 1990s, this traditional growth strategy, fueled by in-store sales of greeting cards and other personal expression products, had started showing signs of slowing down.

Box 1.2 Hallmark's Keepsake Ornaments: Co-creating Christmas Experiences[13]

From *Sideline to Sensation* is how a special release book, *A Century of Caring*, tells the Hallmark Keepsake Ornaments story. Decorated with original designs and artwork, Hallmark's Christmas ornament line was launched in 1973 with 18 ornaments, and was received with great enthusiasm by both consumers and retailers. These days, the Keepsake ornament line introduces about 300 Christmas ornaments each year. Everything from miniatures to ornaments with motion, they depict a range of characters, like Tinker Bell, classic American cars, sports stars, and characters from Star Wars. Even the Beatles joined the line in 1994, when Keepsake celebrated the thirtieth anniversary of the Fab Four's first appearance on The Ed Sullivan Show.

The ornament series are especially popular with collectors. Around the mid-1980s, several ornament and collector clubs sprung up across the United States. Members would meet regularly to share stories and decoration tips — or in the language of this book, co-create memorable Christmas experiences. In 1987, Hallmark built on this grassroots movement and formed a Hallmark national Keepsake Ornament Club. The club has a dedicated staff within Hallmark that provides over 100,000 national members with information through newsletters and web updates, on events like new series, Keepsake artists, and club-exclusive ornaments. The staff also organize artist-signing events and large annual conventions where enthusiastic collectors dressed up as their favorite ornament characters swap ornaments and treat Hallmark artists like rock stars.

The commitment of Hallmark's Keepsake ornaments line to creativity and craftsmanship and its connection with the company's fundamental mission make it a perfect fit in the company's portfolio. In the words of CEO Don Hall, Jr.:

> Keepsake ornaments are more than decorations. Like greeting cards, they speak to what's universal in the human heart by helping people preserve memories, commemorate milestones, and nurture relationships.

Externally, the company was confronted by a significant change in consumers' shopping preferences, card-buying behavior, and greeting habits. Time-constrained, busy life-styles, coupled with adoption of new interactive technologies that allowed consumers to connect with one another through emails and phone text messages (Short Message Service, SMS), were beginning to exert pressure on the greeting card market, compelling Hallmark to seek additional, innovative ways to grow its business.

Internally, Hallmark was beginning to sense that if it wanted different results in the market place, it had to conduct business differently. The company had seen several of its mass-marketing approaches play themselves out, and it was time to try something new. Hallmark felt that the most logical place to look for additional sources of growth was innovation and innovative new products. Additionally, the company believed that the innovation charge should not be led by its own artists, designers, and creative thinkers, but by consumers. Hallmark felt that consumer-led innovation had a better chance of succeeding than company-led innovation, even though the company had some of the brightest and most gifted minds in the self-expression industry.

To meet the needs of future growth, Hallmark decided to explore new and different ways to interact internally, across various departments, and externally, with their customers. While the company has always been close to its customers — at the heart of Hallmark is its foundational belief that its products must enrich people's lives — the company was keen to leverage emerging technologies, like the Internet and Intranet. The company believed this would allow them to get even closer to its customers externally, and to stimulate interaction and information-sharing across departments internally.

Hallmark was becoming increasingly aware that ideas were the new capital of growth. Since ideas were to be found everywhere, especially among the company's customers, Hallmark was keen to connect with them, and subsequently develop the ones most attractive to the company's future growth. To its credit, Hallmark did not follow the traditional script of forming committees and embarking on endless rounds of meetings. Instead, it did what few companies dream of and even fewer have the courage to implement. It let "tempered radicals" like Jay Dittman and Tom Brailsford, upper-level managers in the customer insights group of the company, experiment with initiatives to help Hallmark explore new platforms for interacting and collaborating with customers (Box 1.3 presents a thumbnail sketch of tempered radicals).[14]

Box 1.3 Tempered Radicals: A Thumbnail Sketch

Debra Meyerson's book, *Tempered Radicals: How People Use Difference to Inspire Change at Work,* is about succeeding at work without selling out. Nearly everybody feels at odds with the company they work for at one time or the other.[15] Rather than leaving, or assimilating, Meyerson suggests a provocative alternative: use the tension between the desire to express our whole selves, and building careers in companies that leave little room for difference to learn, lead, and bring about positive change.

Tempered Radicals are individuals who exhibit this third type of response. These individuals are committed professionals who have learned to walk the tight rope between conformity and rebellion. When faced with threats to their ideas, suggestions, and identities, tempered radicals don't resort to drama and heroics. They eschew the revolutionary in favor of the incremental; they work toward transformational ends with conviction, patience, and courage. These "everyday leaders" know the value of small wins, quietly asserting their agendas without jeopardizing hard-won careers.

An early initiative to achieve this goal involved the creation of an online community of retailers. In 1998, 100 Hallmark Gold Crown Retailers were invited to form the Hallmark Gold Crown Retailer Knowledge Sharing Community. Since the retailers represented the front line of customer interactions, Hallmark hoped that this initiative would help foster extensive sharing of retailer best practices, and lead to penetrating insights into the needs and shopping behaviors, of customers visiting the company's flagship stores. The experiment was a valuable learning experience for Hallmark. First, it demonstrated that online communities worked, and that the company had the capability to design and implement them. Second, it showed that it is possible to ignite creativity in online communities; several creative and commercially useful ideas were generated and shared with Hallmark.

Despite its success, the retailer community initiative did not provide the breakthrough that Hallmark was looking for, to engage its consumers in a manner different from what it had done in the past. However, since the experiment had reinforced the company's faith in online communities as a platform for learning and sharing, Hallmark decided to persist with it. This time the company invested in an online community of consumers.

Hallmark's Customer Collaboration Initiatives

Hallmark's online consumer community initiative has been operating continuously since November 2000. Called IdEx (an acronym created by combining the first two letters of the words Idea and Exchange), the initiative has evolved from being an additional accessory in the company's marketing research tool chest to offering the company an ongoing, always-on platform for engaging customers. Today, engagement activities with the IdEx consumer communities offers Hallmark the opportunity to collaborate with customers on a variety of innovation activities, ranging from idea sharing to refining the benefits and designs of current products, to developing new additions to the company's portfolio of products and services.

Over the years, Hallmark has experimented with a variety of consumer communities, such as communities for Hispanics, for extremely creative individuals, and for male consumers. However, in its current incarnation, in place since 2005, IdEx consists of two main communities: moms under 45 with kids at home, and moms over 45 with no kids at home.

A few examples illustrating how IdEx has helped Hallmark engage and collaborate with consumers in a more effective and productive way are described below:

- IdEx allows Hallmark to have richer ongoing conversations with consumers (moms), partly because neither the company nor the community members feel the need to force the pace of the conversation. The continuous nature of the community, in contrast to the episodic nature of traditional marketing research methods like focus groups, permits both the company and its customers to explore issues along multiple dimensions, and from a number of different perspectives. A good example of this is Project "Ha Ha," where Hallmark's goal was to develop a deeper understanding of humor, the imagery, and vocabulary surrounding it, and its various applications in consumers' lives. An unexpected insight that emerged during the course of this conversation involved the power of humor in healing; helping people get over temporary downers, like injury and illness, and even coping with serious adversities. Having listened, Hallmark responded. It changed the editorial content in several of its humor cards to reflect the healing aspects of humor. It also launched several new card variations in its Shoebox line to help readers laugh and recover. For example, one get-well-soon card shows a very worried turtle lying on its back. A tiny beetle is trying to push the turtle back up. Open the card and it reads, "Hope you're back on your feet again soon." The turtle has a smile on its face, and the beetle, comfortably seated on the turtle's back, is happily hitching a ride!

- IdEx also offered Hallmark the opportunity to hear and build on consumers' ideas. One such exchange concerned gift-wrap, and the role that gift-wrapping plays in gift giving. A new insight that particularly impressed Hallmark was that the role of gift-wrapping was not merely limited to protecting or wrapping the gift, but that gift-wrapping also helped prolong and add to a person's gift-receiving experience. This led to the development of the concept of gift presentation. Several rounds of conversations and prototypes later, zip boxes, a new Hallmark product line, was born. Named ƒUNZIP, the product promises to make unwrapping gifts fun. Shaped as animals or objects — a baby elephant for baby gifts, a crocodile for children's gifts, a birthday cake for birthday gifts — zip boxes are large enough to store the gift, and are opened by operating a paper zip. Unlike gift wrap paper, which either tears or crumples on unwrapping, the zip box retains its shape even after the gift is unwrapped, thereby enhancing the overall experience of both the gift giver and the person receiving the gift.

IdEx communities have also proved to be an excellent platform for listening, and for building trust and loyalty. Consumers participating in the community tend to form mini social networks within the community. This allows Hallmark to listen, when participants interact and speak with one another, and even when the company is not part of the conversation. Additionally, the degree to which IdEx has helped Hallmark earn the trust, loyalty, and sponsorship of community members is truly enviable, and well beyond the reach of conventional marketing and promotional campaigns. Community participants do not get paid for their participation. Their main reward, apart from occasional gift coupons and sweepstakes, is recognition and respect. When Hallmark invites community members to share their thoughts, feelings, and suggestions, they feel worthy and respected because their ideas are heard and accepted. They reciprocate by becoming personally and emotionally invested in Hallmark and all that the company stands for. Not only do they fulfill their basic contractual obligations by offering their time and effort, they do more. They underwrite their participation by becoming brand ambassadors, increasing their own spending on Hallmark products and strongly recommending the company and its offerings to family and friends.

Participation in the IdEx consumer communities is by invitation only. Even though community membership changes annually, Hallmark can engage only a small number of consumers at a time (only moms) through community activities. To widen its base of collaboration, Hallmark uses its website to engage consumers in co-creation activities. Through its website, Hallmark offers print-on-demand cards, card contests, personalized party products, augmented reality cards, and Hallmark Card Studio software for consumers to co-create unique social expression experiences.

- Print-on-Demand: This service enables consumers to co-create cards by uploading their own photos, writing their own messages, and adding sound clips. Once the consumer is satisfied, Hallmark professionally prints the card and can even stamp and send it to the recipient if the consumer desires. Consumers can use the print-on-demand tool kit to co-create cards for a variety of events and special occasions, such as birthdays, anniversaries, and Valentine's Day.
- Consumer-created Card Contests: These contests invite consumers to exercise their creativity and be a Hallmark star. Started in 2007, competitions are theme-based. Themes used for past competitions have included Pets, Holidays, Parenthood, and A Girl's Gotta Laugh! The website offers detailed instructions for consumers to create and submit their entries. Participants can win $250 plus the admiration of others if their entry is selected for sale on Hallmark.com, and another $250 if the card is sold in stores.
- Hallmark Card Studio 2010: This software-based option lets consumers create and personalize greeting cards. It is available in standard or deluxe versions. The deluxe option comes with 100,000+ Hallmark cards, 17,000+ premium images, 7,500+ sentiments, exclusive Hallmark fonts, and a digital photo editor. After creating their card using the software's features and options, consumers have a choice of either printing or emailing their creation.

In addition to the online co-creation initiatives discussed above, approximately five years ago Hallmark also invested in a physical collaboration and co-creation space, called Consumer Place at its corporate headquarters in Kansas City. A large open area, it can be configured in a variety of ways to stimulate collaboration and conversations with consumers. A regular feature at Consumer Place is Consumer Thursdays. One Thursday a month, consumers are invited to engage with Hallmark staff on innovative ideas and products. For example, consumers may collaborate with Hallmark staff to help refine a prototype created by them. Self-adhesive giftwrap, launched in 2009, was co-created at Consumer Place. It took several rounds of refinement and improvement before consumers and Hallmark development professionals agreed on the final offering.

All the initiatives discussed above — IdEx, Print-on-Demand cards, Consumer-Created Contests, Consumer Place, and Consumer Thursdays — represent an ongoing journey and are the expression of Hallmark's desire to build on its one hundred year tradition of customer caring. In 2009, Hallmark's consumer communities were rebranded as Circles of Conversation. The intent of the rebranding is not merely symbolic; it is to signal that Hallmark wants to deepen its conversations with consumers and build on the collaboration and co-creation momentum it has generated in the last ten plus years.

Other companies have also heard the applause for collaboration and co-creation and are eager to launch their own collaboration and co-creation programs. Chapter 2 describes and discusses the Listen-Engage-Respond implementation framework that will be used throughout the book to explore ways in which collaboration and co-creation programs can be designed and implemented by a variety of organizations, large and small, public and private, for-profit and nonprofit.

Notes and References

1. Details of John Decker's story were shared graciously by John and his family and were gathered through personal interviews conducted with them between December 2008 and February 2010.
2. Website: National Marrow Donor Program. (2009, September). *Causes of Wiskott-Aldrich Syndrome*. Retrieved September 4, 2009, from http://www.marrow.org
3. Website: Immune Deficiency Foundation. (2008). *About the Immune Deficiency Foundation*. Retrieved February 12, 2010, from http://www.primaryimmune.org/about/about.htm
4. We would like to thank and credit Professor Jacob Burr for spurring this line of thinking. Professor Burr is the head of research at "The Mads Clausen Institute, at University of Southern Denmark" (http://www.sdu.dk/staff/buur.aspx). His primary focus is on the study of people and technology, design collaboration, and design learning.
5. Raymond, E. (2001). *The Cathedral and the Bazaar: Musings on Linux and Open Source by an Accidental Revolutionary*. Sebastopol: O'Reilly Media.
6. Gehring, A.R. and Lutterbeck, B. (2004). *Open Source Jarhrbuch*. Berlin, Germany: Technical University of Berlin Press.
7. Crammond, T. (2010, February 8). Top 10 Areas where open source leads the way. *IT Pro Fit For Business*. Retrieved February 13, 2010, from http://www.itpro.co.uk/620266/top-10-areas-where-open-source-leads-the-way/3
8. Savage, B. (2007, September). *Klunkerz A Film about the Development and Birth of Mountain Bikes*. William Savage Studio. See also the official *Klunkerz* website (http://www.klunkerz.com), which carries additional details related to the film, and a link for purchasing the DVD.
9. Winchester, S. (1999). *The Professor and the Madman: A Tale of Murder, Insanity, and the Making of the Oxford English Dictionary*. New York: Harper Perennial.
10. Website: *Oxford English Dictionary*. (1879). Archived documents. *Help is Urgently Needed in the Eighteen Century*. Retrieved February 13, 2010, from http://oed.com/archive/appeal-1879-04/p3.html
11. Ibid (Ref. # 10).
12. Details of the Hallmark case were obtained mainly through the contributions of Tom Brailsford and his colleagues; the company's website (http://corporate.hallmark.com) and several links contained therein; personal visits to Hallmark Gold Crown Retailers, and Patrick Regan's *Hallmark: A Century of Caring* (Reference 13).
13. Regan, P. (2009). *Hallmark: A Century of Caring*. Kansas City: Andrews McMeel Publishing, LLC.
14. Meyerson, D. E. (2003). *Tempered Radicals: How Everyday Leaders Inspire Change at Work*. Boston: Harvard Business Press.
15. Ibid (Ref. # 14).

Chapter 2
A Framework for Implementation

The Phoenix Suns may not have the most impressive record on the basketball court, but they are outpacing their competition in building relationships with their fans. The Suns, a National Basketball Association (NBA) team based in Phoenix, Arizona, do not have an NBA title yet, though they have had their spotlight moments. The team did exceptionally well in the 2004–05 season. During that period, which came to be known as the third greatest turnaround in League history, the team had the best scoring record: 62–20. In the same season, one of their key players, Steve Nash, won the Most Valuable Player award. The team also boasts of a number of Hall-of-Famers, most notably Charles Barkley.

There is a reason why NBA teams, including the Suns, are obsessed with winning titles and awards. Professional sports teams need large and loyal fan followings to survive and there is no greater insurance to retaining fan loyalty and commitment than winning. But while "Winning is everything" may be a time-tested Hollywood formula, professional sports teams like the Suns work hard both on and off the court. Their on-court performance is what fills basketball arenas on game day. Off the court, they work just as hard to earn the attention and praise of their fans by supporting social causes and participating in community activities, such as teen development, education, and personal health.[1]

While the Suns have yet to win a championship, just listen to their fans talk, and feel their passion and enthusiasm, and you will think the team has been undefeated for the past several years. The Suns have one of the strongest fan followings in the League. Their home games are perennially sold out. Based on our conversations with trailblazers like Amy Martin, the Suns' former Digital Marketing Director, no tickets are available through normal box office channels for the next several years.[2]

The character and strength of the team's fan following is mirrored even in the current ownership structure of the Suns. Robert Saver, a lifelong team fan and a banking entrepreneur, led the investment group that purchased the team in 2007. Steve Kerr, a seasoned basketball NBA champion, is also part of the owner manager team. In short, the owners have an emotional and financial investment in the club that goes beyond the officialdom of job titles. Their ability to relate to the team and the fans is rooted in who they are as individuals and in their love for the game. Their involvement with the team's affairs extends beyond on-court involvement demanded by their organizational roles. Both Saver and Kerr are well known in Arizona as

G. Bhalla, *Collaboration and Co-creation: New Platforms for Marketing and Innovation*,   17
DOI 10.1007/978-1-4419-7082-4_2, © Springer Science+Business Media, LLC 2011

strong community leaders who are deeply involved in social and humanitarian initiatives, like education.

Based on fan feedback and their personal observations, the management team recognizes that the playing arena is not enough to satisfy fan hunger for contact with the game, the team, and its stars. They have noticed and heard the surge in fan voices, on the Internet and in traditional media, demanding greater access to the team, to the locker rooms, and to their favorite stars, beyond what they traditionally get on game days. It was against this backdrop that the Phoenix Suns decided to launch their first major fan collaboration effort to co-create and enrich the total fan experience with the Suns.

Planet Orange: Creating Value with Fans

The Suns' fan collaboration effort goes by the name *Planet Orange*. The name was deliberately chosen to create a world where all inhabitants share one common trait — they are all fiery, fervent, and forever Suns' fans! Within this world, fans are not merely members or fans, they are *citizens*. Planet Orange is an online community whose citizens create their own personal profile pages for blogging, photo uploads, and video streaming. In addition to interacting with the Suns, the citizens interact freely with one another and create their own preferred subgroups, such as Suns in the Military, Suns in Yuma, and Suns' Fans Down Under. Citizens of Planet Orange are both fun-loving and responsible — they even police one another's content and are quick to flag content if considered offensive or inappropriate. Planet Orange also extends fan experience beyond basketball through its connections with science, education, and community activities.

Planet Orange was not created as a result of a few marketing executives kicking ideas around the coffee machine. The idea was born by interacting with fans. When Sun's digital marketing team was observing and listening to basketball fan conversations in online social networks, they stumbled upon a video clip about the Suns on YouTube, which a fan had created. The video was fun to watch and had acquired a significant following. A large number of the Suns' fans had viewed the video and posted their comments and reactions to the content.

The big bang had occurred. The YouTube video led to a serious exploration of an online community for co-creating and enriching fan experience. Pros, cons, and risks were all discussed. The digital marketing team reached out to the creator of the YouTube video (and other fans who had interacted with the video) for inputs in refining their own thinking. Early versions of Planet Orange were tested among some of the Suns' most loyal fans: its employees. The involvement of the employees continues until today, and as citizens, they are just as prominent and active as the nonemployee citizens. Fully satisfied as to the merits and its features, Planet Orange was launched with due fanfare and a video contest. In less than one year, Planet Orange had over 10,000 active citizens and even a "king"; the creator of the original YouTube video appointed himself as the Planet Orange King!

Co-creating fan experience has produced enormous customer equity for the Suns, as evidenced by the continuing growth in fan support, and sold-out attendances (Box 2.1). As a core business practice in large companies, co-creation is still new, and best practices are still emerging. However, the Suns' fan experience

---

Box 2.1 Planet Orange Fan Experiences

Planet Orange is where the Suns and their fans co-create fun and unique fan experiences, and celebrate the bond that exists between the fans and the franchise. The invitation on the planet's website reads:

> The Planet is what you make it. So log in now and become a citizen.

Two standout examples of co-created experiences are:

All Night Sing Along

- Imagine famous basketball players like Grant Hill and Amare Stoudemire, riding in the team bus to the next city on their itinerary, after a grueling ball game. It's late, the players are tired, and all that they probably want is a comfortable bed to stretch their long legs, or an ice-bath to numb their aching muscles. But no bed or tub for these guys. Napping during the bus ride is an option; so is talking on the cell phone. But wait; there is an even better option to pass time. How about making a video of the players singing an old song and sharing it with their fans on Planet Orange and YouTube? That is exactly what Steve Nash and Leandro Barbossa did. The Phoenix Suns belted out Lionel Richie's 1983 hit "All Night Long," and shared their video creation with Suns' fans. Hundreds of Planet Orange citizens commented on the clip — *hilarious, so flipping funny, what a hoot.*[3]

Planet Orange Fan Video Challenge

- Most sports fans would agree that picking a favorite team happens at an early age. How early, you ask? How about two years! Yes, the winner of the Suns' Fan Video Challenge, and perhaps the Suns' youngest ardent fan is two years old. This toddler watches Suns' games at home on her large TV screen and celebrates each time the team scores by clapping and jumping with joy. Steve Nash is her favorite, and his baskets are celebrated with even more frenzy. The Suns organized a video challenge during the 2009–10 season, so fans could showcase the passion they typically exhibit in their living rooms. As a way of saying thanks, the franchise celebrated fan enthusiasm by airing their creations on giant screens at the US Airways Center, Sun's home court. The video featuring the two-year-old toddler — *The World's Biggest Little Suns' Fan* — received rave reviews, helping it to win the challenge.[4]

co-creation case presents several elements that can be labeled as best practice and are worthy of emulation. The case also shares qualities that have emerged from our own consulting work in this space. The rest of the chapter presents and discusses a framework of processes and competencies for designing and implementing co-creation programs. It also discusses an important prerequisite to embracing, effectively implementing, and reaping rewards from co-creation programs: a shift in management's mindset. Without that shift, the promise of collaboration and co-creation is likely to ring hollow, leaving customers unimpressed and disengaged.

Framework for Building a Co-creation Capability

Four interrelated components must work together to help a company build a core co-creation capability, as illustrated in Fig. 2.1. First, companies and organizations need to *listen* to their customers, as the Suns' managers did in monitoring online discussions among fans. Second, they need to meaningfully *engage* their customers, as the Suns did by creating Planet Orange. Third, they need to *respond externally* and create vehicles for co-creating value with customers: the Suns let the creative energy of its fans run the new planet, even to the extent of celebrating the coronation of a self-appointed "king." Finally, companies need to *respond internally*, by investing in co-creation structures and processes, as the Suns did in working with a core group of zealous fans and employees to build, test, and roll out the site to the broader fan community. These four elements working in concert create the capability of customer collaboration and co-creation in companies. Each of these components will be discussed in more detail below.

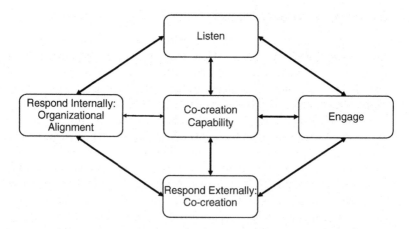

Fig. 2.1 Framework for Building a Co-creation Capability

Listen

Today's networked consumers are involved in interactions with one another, with media, and with companies in a variety of public forums. Many of these interactions take the form of wide-ranging conversations, rich in both content and sentiment. According to Technorati's 2008 survey, "The State of the Blogosphere," the leading reasons for creating and reading blogs are:[5]

- Sharing consumption experiences
- Obtaining information and providing opinion on brands, and
- Providing referrals.

Fifty percent of adults who use social networks like Facebook and MySpace regularly tell friends about the products they purchase. A 2007 survey from Hitwise observed that MySpace sends more traffic to retail websites than Yahoo and MSN search engines combined. More recently, a 2010 survey by the company Hitwise confirmed continuation of that trend. It revealed a 37 percent increase in traffic driven to Retail 500 stores by social networking sites and forums in 2009 compared to 2008, as depicted in Table 2.1.[6]

Buzzillions.com is an active platform for sharing and listening. Companies share information about their products and in turn get to listen to what thousands of consumers are saying about their products. Buzzillions.com collects thousands of consumer reviews a day from across 2,800 websites. This model is an effective way for companies like Toys "R" Us, Staples, and Zappos to stay in touch with customer conversations involving their products and services. Buzzillions.com is featured again in Chapter 3.

Table 2.1 Sources of Traffic to Retail 500

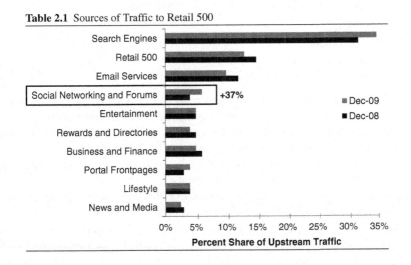

Buzzillions.com offers valuable benefits to all parties engaged in sharing and listening:

- Companies benefit, because they get unadulterated feedback on their products.
- Consumers benefit from peer-to-peer reviews and experiences, which they trust more than what the company says about its own products.
- Retailers' websites get more traffic and a higher proportion of qualified customers focused on making a purchase.

Listening takes on even greater importance in situations where it may not be immediately clear how consumers will vote with their consumption dollars. A good example is current conversations and purchase behaviors concerning innovative green products. In terms of sentiment, consumers may send one signal: namely that they have unequivocal commitment to engaging in pro-green behaviors. However, when it comes to future purchase behavior, they may send the opposite signal. A McKinsey survey of over 8,000 consumers in several developed countries reported that 87 percent of consumers worry about the impact of their purchases on the environment, but less than 33 percent of the consumers are currently buying, or intend to buy, green products.[7]

Engage

Companies engage customers to provoke conversations, to elicit responses and reactions, and to generate fresh insight by disturbing the current equilibrium. In all cases, engagement creates new patterns of interactions and relationships between a company and its customers. Operating through dialogue and conversations, engagement seeks to tap into ecosystems of relationships, such as:

- Self with self
- Self with others
- Self with causes, and
- Self with brand and/or company.

Timberland developed such an engagement ecosystem by tapping Facebook members in a viral campaign to help translate their concern for the environment into concrete action. Following a highly successful launch of their Earthkeeper boot brand — a boot for people to enjoy the outdoors made completely from recycled plastic bottles and rubber tires — Timberland decided to extend this concern for the environment through an Earthkeeper community.

According to Jeff Swartz, Timberland's CEO, the purpose of the Earthkeepers movement is to inspire 1 million consumers to take action to lighten their environmental footprint by planting trees. Through their own website and videos posted on YouTube, Timberland has been able to inspire and provoke the Earthkeepers community to create virtual forests and dedicate trees to loved ones. One hundred thousand community members sent 1,750,000 seeds in a four-month period for trees to be planted. By the end of 2008, the community, through its collective action, planted over 250 acres of trees in the Horquin Desert in Mongolia.[8]

Respond Externally: Co-creation

Co-creation rarely happens in one large spontaneous step. That's because it is driven by consumer needs and preferences, rather than rigid engineering specifications. Since consumer needs and preferences are fluid and malleable, several iterations of exploration and development are usually needed before companies and customers arrive at a finished value proposition. In order to shorten the development cycle and time to market, companies adopt a variety of tactics to empower customers and improve the productivity of the co-creation effort. Examples include selecting high-value customers to collaborate with, such as lead users, and experimenting with tool kits and prototypes to empower customers and involve them earlier in the innovation process.

The Search Division of Yahoo is a firm believer in experimenting to co-create. In a manner of speaking, the division is one big co-creation lab, since many of the employees who work there are among the heaviest users of the service. Their co-creation efforts revolve around engaging the user community (both employees and nonemployees) in a series of prototyping and experimentation exercises, in order to reduce development time and time to market. For example, Yahoo's search application development platform, *SearchMonkey*, allows developers and website owners to use a variety of embedded tools to build customized applications. Further, it offers developers a chance to collaborate, share, and build upon one another's suggestions. Both company and developers benefit from the co-creation effort. Yahoo benefits because it can now optimize its portfolio, offering only those tools and applications that are most relevant and valuable to its search customers. Developers benefit because now they have more effective tools to design applications that deliver optimal user experience, such as making search results more visually appealing and driving more relevant traffic to their sites.[9]

The South Beach line of products developed by Kraft, one of the largest food and beverage companies in the world, is a good example of how co-creation creates incremental value for both customers and the company. Before Kraft aligned itself with the South Beach Diet brand, it reached out to its community of consumers for their insights to avoid an expensive and lengthy national product rollout. Using insights provided by the community on product features, benefits, and emotional outcomes valued most, Kraft was able to co-create 48 product concepts that had the potential to meet consumers' needs. Through a series of quick experiments with the user community, Kraft zeroed in on a few winning concepts in categories such as cereal, meal replacement bars, refrigerated sandwich wraps, frozen entrees, and frozen pizzas. Within six months after the launch date, Kraft's new line of South Beach foods had generated more than $100 million in sales.[10]

Respond Internally: Organizational Alignment

Successful implementation of collaboration and co-creation programs requires more than just intentions, no matter how honest. It requires an accompanying investment in organizational culture, structure, and processes. Without these enabling factors, co-creating value with customers is likely to remain stuck in the starting blocks.

Whatever Dell's problems may have been with its computers and its old business model, they are in the past. The company has blown the competition away in collaborating with its customers and co-creating product and service experiences through its innovation site, *IdeaStorm*. The company was alerted to serious customer service problems indirectly, by media articles, such as Business Week's "Hanging Up on Dell," and directly, by a raging torrent of customer complaints. Wait times were horrendous; some customers would be on hold for as long as 45 minutes when trying to reach customer support. Even worse, after finally connecting with a customer service representative, it was not uncommon to be transferred among multiple customer service technicians because the first, second, and even third technician was unable to solve the problem.[11]

Rather than hiding from the market's anger, Dell used the negative energy directed against it to co-create a business transformation program. The company created IdeaStorm, an online community designed to co-create a better product and service experience. By responding and following through with implementation suggestions generated within IdeaStorm, Dell has redefined customer relationship management and set a new standard for responsiveness. The company did not just celebrate insights, suggestions, and ideas; it organized itself around these inputs and implemented concrete initiatives. It is difficult to say to what extent Michael Dell's personal involvement helped — he is reported to regularly read comments posted on the site — but the numbers speak for themselves. Based on data regularly published on the website, by early 2010, the community had submitted over 13,000 ideas, inspiring Dell to implement over 400 unique initiatives.[12] IdeaStorm will be discussed in greater detail in Chapter 6.

A Shift in Mindset

The framework described above and the resulting customer collaboration capability for co-creating value are at odds with existing value-creation beliefs in companies. The emerging platforms of customer collaboration and co-creation have an uneasy relationship with existing mental maps of managers that favor traditional company-centric methods of value-creation. Charlene Li and Josh Bernoff in *Groundswell* and C.K. Prahlad and V. Ramaswamy in *The Future of Competition* also discuss how organizations and management teams are threatened by customers' demands for co-creation.[13] Such teams perceive these demands to be a threat that can weaken and undermine a company's control of its transactions with consumers.

Three Prerequisites for a New Mindset

- Authenticity
- Flexibility
- Conviction

Fig. 2.2 Three Prerequisites for a New Mindset

Consequently, developing and implementing a customer collaboration capability is not merely a matter of implementing the framework recommended in Fig. 2.1; it also requires a shift in management's mindset. Fig. 2.2 and the discussion that follows present three prerequisites for a new mindset that can potentially facilitate migration from traditional models of value-creation, where customers are mere passive recipients of value created for them by the company, to newer models, where customers are active participants in the value-creation process.

Authenticity

Companies have agendas; customers have agendas, too. The difference is that customer agendas have, for the most part, been transparent and out in the open. For example, customers want safe toys, easy-to-use, plug-and-play products, and hassle-free customer service. Company agendas, on the other hand, are not always unambiguous or easy to understand. Several authors have stressed the importance of customer service in helping the company put its best face forward.[14] Yet, behind-the-scenes agendas related to cost cutting, reduction in training dollars, and a freeze on hiring new talent are not in sync with the company's stated intentions of providing hassle-free service. It is not always clear to customers where, on a continuum of affordable service to uncompromising service, companies reside on a regular basis.

Authenticity, as we conceptualize it, is part ethics, part transparency, and part trust. It is an orientation, or intent, that a company brings to its efforts to collaborate and co-create value with its customers. Over time, if reinforced by the right actions, it gets transformed into being a recognizable company trait. It is recognizable not through formal analysis, but through the right-brain emotional response of consumers. An authentic Patek Phillipe sitting out of reach in Tiffany & Co. on Fifth Avenue evokes a very different right-brain response than a knock-off version selling right outside its doors on the pavement.

Few companies wear the badge of authenticity as well as Johnson & Johnson. Its recent efforts in establishing relationships with customers through its award-winning global community *BabyCenter* reinforce that perception. Tina Sharkey, the Chairman and Global President for BabyCenter, points out that "Moms come to BabyCenter seeking trusted and personalized information."[15] They get that and more. The most prominent items on the site's landing page are consumer-centric tools such as due date calculators, videos allowing a peek inside the womb, and health-related content checked and previewed by a Medical Advisory Board. Most important is the connection moms make with a community of other parents. Through this community, parents share ideas, seek guidance on deeply personal issues, and discuss the joys and challenges of raising children.

Achieving authenticity is impossible if every interaction with the customer involves an element of commerce. Consequently, participation in this community is not conditional on purchase. Though the site links to a BabyCenter store, all moms visiting Babycenter.com are secure in the knowledge that no attempt will be made by Johnson & Johnson to unilaterally further its own sales agenda by using inputs from the site. By focusing on long-term connections with consumers, Johnson & Johnson has elevated its relationship from being just a brand of baby products to being a trusted advisor and a source of valuable information on how to raise healthy and happy children.

Flexibility

Today's customers have a definite point of view on a number of issues, ranging from T-shirt designs (Threadless), nutritional value of various foods (Acai fruit berry), and appropriateness of diets (South Beach Diet),[16] to issues related to child labor and living conditions of workers in Nike and Levi's factories in Asia. Today's customers also have a large number of opportunities to voice their opinions, making it easier for them to draw attention to conflicting issues and to companies resisting honest customer objections.

Flexibility implies a greater willingness on the part of the company to accommodate opposing points of view. There is no rule that says companies and customers must agree all the time. What is absolutely essential, though, is to demonstrate that the company is aware of opposing opinions, that it is listening, and having listened that it is willing to reconsider its own beliefs, values, and actions (Box 2.2).

Consumer activists first brought Nike's attention to child labor in its Asian shoe-producing factories. Nike admitted its blunder, acknowledging that it "blew it" by employing children in its Asian factories. Nike did not close down its Asian factories, but instituted significantly more stringent age monitoring and hiring controls, which it broadcast widely in its corporate responsibility reports. The activists have yet to give Nike a passing grade, but the market seems to have accepted Nike's accommodation and self-policing.

Starbucks, too, felt the heat from activists. Fair Trade International made strong demands for Starbucks to sell certified fair trade coffee. Initially, the company resisted, as it believed the coffee was below coffee roasters' quality standards. Following a series of protests attacking Starbucks of social irresponsibility, the

Box 2.2 Fish2Fork: Flexibility for Sustainability
_____

Imagine an ocean without fish! In less than 40 years, this will be the future if commercial fisheries do not change the way they catch fish, restaurants do not take endangered fish off their menu, and consumers do not change their eating habits. This is the message of *End of the Line*, the first major documentary revealing the impact of overfishing.

Based on Charles Clover's highly acclaimed book, *The End of the Line: How Overfishing Is Changing the World and What We Eat*, the documentary explores and examines firsthand the impact of current global fishing policies, and consumers' fish-eating preferences.[17] Filmed over two years across the world — from the Straits of Gibraltar to the coasts of Senegal, from Alaska to the Tokyo fish market — it features top scientists, indigenous fishermen, and fisheries enforcement officials. The film confronts critical issues, such as the imminent extinction of bluefin tuna brought on by increasing western demand for sushi, and the profound implications of a world with no fish.

This stark realization has spawned several major collaboration efforts.

- M & J Seafoods, the UK's largest independent seafood supplier to restaurants, hotels, pubs, schools, and wholesalers, actively campaigns to promote sustainable fishing. It will not buy or supply fish like orange roughy, shark, and bluefin tuna, European eel, and North Atlantic halibut.
- Food retailers like Whole Foods are altering their fish retailing policies. While they continue to sell farm-raised fish, they are aggressively pushing sustainable aquaculture policies on fish farms that supply them with their fish.

The most notable grassroots collaboration initiative to have emerged to involve everyday customers is the fish2fork rating system. It is designed to inform customers whether a restaurant is doing all it can to serve sustainable seafood and reduce its impact on the world's oceans at a time when overfishing is of serious concern. Restaurants are scored for the sustainability of the fish on their menu using a blue fish–red fish scale. A blue fish rating signifies environmentally responsible menus, and a red fish rating, the opposite (the highest rating is five blue fish, and the lowest is five red fish). The fish-2fork initiative also encourages everyday customers to download fish eating guides published online by objective watchdogs like Monterey Bay Aquarium's Seafood Watch in the United States, and Marine Conservation Society in the UK.

company relented. Starbucks collaborated with non-governmental organizations (NGOs) to co-create value for both the growers and its consumers by creating a line of "fair trade" products.

Conviction

Nothing sabotages customer collaboration and co-creation initiatives faster than lack of follow-through. Symbolism — mere talk not backed by sincere action — is likely to be penalized by today's customers, who value follow-through and transparency. Lack of conviction will show, no matter how hard a company tries to disguise it, and will weaken the market's willingness to engage in any meaningful way with the company.

Wal-Mart's attempt at engaging teens in their community, The Hub, lasted only 10 weeks.[18] For social networks to be successful, they need to provide users with freedom and space. Wal-Mart did neither. Rather than treating the community as a different way of doing business, they used it as another avenue for implementing traditional merchandising and promotion programs. Teens had to get parental approval before registering; community members were flooded with advertisements and subjected to promotional programs featuring fake models, instead of real people – all of which actually led to the teens disengaging with Wal-Mart. Critics conducting postmortems were in strong agreement that Wal-Mart seemed to have been driven more by the need to keep up with the Joneses, mimicking what other big corporations were doing, rather than out of a sense of conviction about the importance of listening to and interacting with customers.

Contrast this with the example of WePC.com, a joint venture between computer hardware manufacturer ASUS and chipmaker Intel. The goal of the project is to build a community-designed personal computer. The conviction and commitment of the sponsors is plainly visible to all potential collaborators. Visitors to the site are encouraged to dream — submit ideas for development on Notebook, Netbook, and Gamer PCs — vote on ideas submitted by others, and participate in ongoing discussions, or create their own discussion. The site tracks and broadcasts progress on ideas selected in a very objective and transparent way. It is clear that the sponsors are serious about generating ideas and following through by developing them. Rather than policing the community, the sponsors see their role as facilitators, igniting ideas and shaping conversations among leading online voices of designers, engineers, hardware geeks, and gamers.

This chapter opened with a case study, demonstrating how the Phoenix Suns use elements of the Listen-Engage-Respond framework to co-create unique fan experiences, both on and off the basketball court. Now that the framework has been formally presented, it would be beneficial to review another case study that demonstrates how the process of co-creation transforms marketing and innovation when implemented correctly. When all the elements of the Listen-Engage-Respond framework are implemented in a synchronized and systematic manner, the result is nothing short of a co-creation master class.

Marmite XO: A Co-creation Classic

Unilever's Marmite is a 100 percent vegetarian product made from yeast extract, which is a by product of brewing beer. A UK brand, it is most commonly consumed as a savory spread on toast. Over 100 years old, Marmite is a cult brand. People either love it or hate it. The brand embraces this fact unabashedly and places it at the heart of everything it does. In March 2010, Unilever launched an extra-mature variety of Marmite, called Marmite XO, for the brand's most ardent lovers. Marmite XO is made from yeast sourced from four specially selected breweries, and matured four times longer to give the consumer a rich, full-bodied, and intense flavor experience. From a co-creation perspective, more important than the physical characteristics of the new formulation is that XO was developed in partnership with Marmite lovers and launched through social media.

Let us drop in and learn how Marmite developed and launched XO.[19]

Act 1: Listening and Recruiting

In 2009, when the brand was planning the launch of XO, it decided against developing and marketing XO the traditional way. It wanted to implement a new form of development and marketing, one that was based on social media, and one that used social networks of Marmite lovers and made them part of the development journey. Along the way, the brand wanted to amplify interest and intrigue around the launch of XO to pre-build demand for the new formulation.

Experimenting with social media as an alternative platform for development and marketing was a natural extension of Marmite's ongoing involvement and interaction with the medium. It had been actively listening to fan conversations on social media sites like Facebook, blogs, and Twitter for a few years. The Marmite Facebook page, originally created by fans, has almost a quarter of a million members and has grown organically because of the passion the fans have for the brand. Marmite currently shares this site with its fans and routinely initiates and takes part in conversations with the brand's consumers. So when the time came to pick collaborators to help co-create XO, Marmite turned to its strongest asset, its fan base. Working with a social networking and communications agency, We Are Social (http://wearesocial.net/), the brand handpicked 30 "super fans," people who had created the most positive content around Marmite, for participation in the XO development journey.

Act 2: Engagement and Development

The development journey began with Marmite staging an extraordinary event full of intrigue and dash. First, a Victorian-style secret society, The Marmarati, was created. Legend has it that The Marmarati had been the guardians of the Marmite brand for a century, protecting it from all enemies at home and abroad (from marmalade in the UK, and from Vegemite in Australia and other countries). They were revealing themselves to the world again to celebrate their centenary with the launch of XO and recruit the next generation of the society's members. Exhibit 2.1 narrates the Marmarati history and legend.

Next, the 30 "super fans" were invited to a fabulous setting in a listed building in central London. Think red velvet drapes, sterling silver candelabras, low lighting, dark wood, and a luxuriously laid banquet table. The event was hosted by the Marmite marketing team, all dressed in period Victorian costumes. Matt Burgess and Tom Denyard, Managing Director and Marketing Manager of Marmite in the UK, respectively, who kindly provided all the details for this case study, played key roles at the event. As Lord Marmarati, Matt Burgess initiated the guests into the society with an oath of allegiance and personally signed their initiation certificates. Tom Denyard played host to the selected group, which was dubbed the "First Circle" of the Marmarati.

Following their induction to the society, the "First Circle" participated in a blind tasting of three versions of XO at the banqueting table. Based on their tastes and preferences, they provided feedback and suggestions to influence the further development of Marmite XO. They were also involved in a review and discussion of prototype designs and presentation of the new formulation. The rest of the evening was devoted to merry-making: drinking Marmite-infused cocktails and eating Marmite-inspired canapés.

Act 3: Creation and Launch

The "First Circle" left that evening with a lot to talk about and a very specific brief: to recruit people to the "Second Circle." To be admitted to the "Second Circle," consumers had to upload something creative to Marmite's website (www.marmite.org) to show their love for the brand. The brand received a range of materials from poems to films and everything in between — 750 total entries and 23,000 unique visitors to the website in five weeks. One hundred sixty winners were selected by a public vote from the total pool of entries.

The "First Circle" plus the 160 "Second Circle" winners each received a commemorative jar of Marmite XO — beautifully made, one of only 200 in the world, with a wax-dipped lid and a Marmarati crested wax seal on the front. They also received a special request from the brand: to try the brand and film their reactions. This time, incentives were offered through the Marmarati Ambassador program.

To achieve Junior Ambassador status, a Marmarati had to upload a video of his or her own reaction and that of at least five other Marmite lovers. For their submission, Junior Ambassadors received a first batch production jar of Marmite XO when it went on sale in March 2010. To achieve Senior Ambassador status, however,

MARMARATI
HISTORY

1902 Marmite comes into being. Peace arrives to the British Colonies with the end of the Boer War, happiness and trust is restored to the nation.

Things begin crumble by 1909. Social circles think it fashionable to expose closely guarded secrets to gain credibility amongst their peers. The more precious the secret uncovered, the more rungs climbed on the ladder to high society.

In that year alone Madame Eusapia Palladino, a famous spiritualist medium at the time, is branded Madame Fakerio by the media after being exposed as a fraud. Oudini, a Houdini impersonator releases a book exposing the tricks of the most famous escape artists. The foundation of MI6 marks the Government's intrusion into the public's personal lives, obtaining ever-increasing amounts of private information and inspiring Frances Hodgson Burnett to write 'The Secret Garden', an allegorical tale capturing the paranoia and hysteria felt by the public throughout this period. The only reprieve from living in this chaotic, terrifying year was the creation of one the most important inventions of the 20th century; the modern toaster.

It was against this cultural backdrop that the founders and close friends of the Marmite Food Company decided to go underground with Marmite's recipe. Burning all public documentation of Marmite's blending and production processes, and binding the group through the swearing of a solemn oath ensured the secret was kept and passed down to the carefully selected next generation throughout the ages.

From the day of its inception this clandestine society went under the name of the 'Marmarati'; Hand-picked guardians of the Marmite code, entrusted to pass on the knowledge only to those that are deemed worthy.

100 years have now passed since the Marmarati was formed and it is time to select the next line of Marmaratis. This momentous occasion will be marked by the launch of the most powerful Marmite ever made. Currently codenamed 'MXO', this new Marmite will be blended and made only by lovers; only for lovers.

TANTUM PRO DILIGO

Exhibit 2.1 Marmarati History

a Marmarati had to go above and beyond. They were required to host a "tasting party" and upload a video capturing the reactions of more than ten people. Depending on how heroic a Marmarati was willing to be, rewards could range anywhere from a year's supply of Marmite to a lifetime's supply, and even more: a money-can't-buy experience involving a trip to the Marmite factory and a brewery sourcing the raw ingredients for XO.

There is no doubt that the launching of Marmite XO is an extraordinary illustration of collaboration and co-creation. The splendor, creativity, and the manner in which it was staged sets it apart. But there is more. It is also an excellent illustration of the Listen-Engage-Respond framework in action. Consider the following:

- Marmite was *listening* to its fans and was engaging them in conversations before it decided to embark on the co-creation of XO journey.
- This ongoing conversation with its fans gave Marmite the platform to *amplify its engagement* with the Marmarti, which was made easier because of the *passion and attachment* consumers had for Marmite.
- Marmite *responded* both externally and internally.
- Externally, the company launched a *carefully managed set of activities* to help co-create XO's formulation and presentation.
- Internally, Marmite marketing and product development executives *worked closely* with one another and the Marmarati to help refine the XO formulation currently on sale to the general public.
- All through the development and marketing cycle, *consumers had a voice*; they were able to speak to the brand and the brand was able to speak to them, *making it unnecessary for the company to push and sell its product;* in short, collaboration was not just a platform for co-creating XO, it was also a platform for *rethinking marketing.*
- Marmite's *authenticity and commitment* to the Marmarati, or to the co-creation of XO, was never in doubt.

The role that the elements of the Listen-Engage-Respond framework play individually and collectively in shaping the design and implementation of collaborative innovation programs is explored in greater detail in the next several chapters.

Notes and References

1. Website: National Basketball Association. (2009). *2008–2009 NBA Community Report: NBA Cares.* Retrieved February 2, 2010, from http://www.nba.com/2009/allstar2009/01/18/nba.cares/index.html
2. Information for this section was gathered through conversations and conference calls with Amy Martin, Phoenix Suns, Former Digital Marketing Director.
3. Website: Planet Orange (19 Nov. 2009). *Suns Sing All Night Long.* Retrieved February 13, 2010, from http://suns.planetorange.net/_Suns-Sing-All-Night-Long/video/869234/9952.html
4. Website. Planet Orange. (2009, October). Press release. Retrieved February 13, 2010, from http://www.nba.com/suns/fans/planet_orange_promotion.html

5. Madasky, M. & Arenberg, P. (2008). State of the blogosphere. *Technocrati*. Retrieved November 19, 2010, from http://technorati.com/blogging/feature/state-of-the-blogosphere-2008/

6. Li, C. (2007). Consumers use social networks. *Forester Report*. 3–6. Retrieved December 12, 2008, from http://www.forrester.com/rb/Research/how_consumers_use_social_networks/q/id/41626/t/2; Hong, L. (2008).Top 10 things retailers should know about social networks and what to do. *Gartner, Inc.* 3. Retrieved December 13, 2008, from http://www.gartner.com/DisplayDocument?ref=g_search&id=633007; Dougherty, H. (2010). Social network impact for retailers. *Hitwise Intelligence*. Retrieved February 12, 2010, from http://weblogs.hitwise.com/heather-dougherty/2010/01/social_network_impact_for_reta.html

7. Bonini, S.M.J. & Oppenheim, J. (2008, October 7) Helping green products grow. *The McKinsey Quarterly*. Retrieved November 7, 2008, from http//www.mckinseyquarterly.com/Help_green_products_grow_2231>

8. Website: Youtube. (2008). About earthkeepers. Retrieved October 30, 2008, from http://www.youtube.com/earthkeepers

9. Website: Yahoo. (2008). Search Monkey — How does it work. *Yahoo Developer Network*. Retrieved February 13, 2010, from http://developer.yahoo.com/searchmonkey/; Perez, J.C. (2008, May 5). Yahoo Search Monkey opens to all developers. *PC World*. Retrieved November, 2008, from http://www.pcworld.com/article/145941/yahoo_search_monkey_opens_to_all_developers.html

10. Customers co-create 48 products THEY want to buy. (2008, October 21). In NewComm Collaborative. Retrieved November 7, 2008, from http://www.newcommreview.com/?tag=online-communities

11. Information Technology (2005, October 10). Hanging up on Dell? *Business Week*. 3954, 80–81. Retrieved November 2, 2008, from http://www.businessweek.com/magazine/content/05_41/b3954102.htm?chan=tc

12. Weiss, T.R. (2007). Dell to Offer Ubuntu in Linus on PCs, Laptops. In *Computer World*. Retrieved October 8, 2008, from http://www.pcworld.com/businesscenter/article/131447/dell_to_offer_ubuntu_linux_on_pcs_laptops.html

13. Li, C. & Bernoff, J. (2008). *Groundswell: Winning in a World Transformed by Social Technologies*. Boston: Harvard Business Press; Prahalad, C.K. & Ramaswamy, V. (2004). *The Future of Competition Co-creating Unique Value with Customers*. Boston: Harvard Business School Press.

14. Lucas, R. (2008). *Customer Service Skills for Success*. McGraw-Hill: New York; Rayport, J. & Jaworski, B. (2008). *Best Face Forward: Why Companies Must Improve Their Service Interfaces With Customers*. Boston: Harvard Business Press.

15. Quinton, B. (2008, July 15). BabyCenter delivers parenting social network. In *Pro Mom Magazine*. Retrieved October 5, 2008, from http://promomagazine.com/socialmedia/babycenter_delivers_parenting_social_network_0715/index.html

16. Williams, R., Spencer, J., & Rice-Evans, C. (2004, April 1). Flavonoids: Antioxidants or signaling molecules? *Free Radical Biology and Medicine,* pp 838–849; Agatston. A. (2003). *The South Beach Diet*. Emmanus: Rodale Books.

17. Clover, C. (2006). *The End of the Line: How Overfishing Is Changing the World and What We Eat*. New York, NY: New Press.

18. Crump, J.W. (2008, December 5). A look at failed social networks. *The Bivings Report*. Retrieved January 8, 2009, from http://www.bivingsreport.com/2008/a-look-at-failed-social-networks/

19. Details of the Marmite XO case study were obtained through conversations with Unilever marketing executives Matt Burgess and Tom Denyard, and from documents shared by them.

Chapter 3
Listen

Throughout history, politicians have sold themselves for power, position, and prestige. The selling of an American presidential candidate, though, is a post World War II phenomenon. With TV extending its reach to virtually all U.S. households, and a greater proportion of voters voting for the candidate than their party of affiliation, presidential hopefuls were able to show up in people's living rooms and advertise themselves like brands of detergents, peanut butter, and automobiles.

Political analysts consider the 1960 presidential race between John F. Kennedy and Richard Nixon as a watershed in this new style of campaigning. What started off as three rather mild-mannered, almost civil TV debates between Kennedy and Nixon has turned into a bloody contact sport over the years. Both the audience and the candidate's campaigners expect it to be an all-out marketing war, much like the ones we have become accustomed to witnessing between Pepsi and Coke, MacDonald's and Burger King, and GM and Ford trucks. The accepted formula is simple — more is better. Each successive presidential election has seen a more vigorous application of this bare-knuckled formula — more advertising, more campaigning, more in-your-face edgy rhetoric, more promotion of the candidate as an indispensable savior that America and the voting public can't do without (Box 3.1).

On the face of it, there was no reason to believe that the 2008 presidential election would be any different. Then Barack Obama threw his hat in the ring! Our interest in the Obama campaign and his subsequent election is not historical, social, or political. We are more interested in describing how the Obama election machinery used the dynamics of collaboration and co-creation to win an election. Rather than try and beat the voters senseless with endless and loud rhetoric, the Obama campaign flipped tradition and built their campaign around listening. Having a multitude of physical and digital conversations with voters was an important differentiating characteristic of the Obama campaign and a key contributing factor to his victory.

G. Bhalla, *Collaboration and Co-creation: New Platforms for Marketing and Innovation*, DOI 10.1007/978-1-4419-7082-4_3, © Springer Science+Business Media, LLC 2011

Box 3.1 Branding and the American Presidency

The branding of American presidential candidates has become increasingly important in recent years. Technological and political developments, like an increase in media channels and campaign funds, have significantly increased the amount of clutter and background noise through which the image of a presidential hopeful must cut through to make an impression. A strong brand helps.

- George W. Bush Jr's brand was built using quaint Bush English — "a uniter not a divider, who aimed to restore honesty and integrity to the White House."
- His father, George W. Bush Sr., aiming to distance himself from his predecessor Ronald Reagan, presented his brand essence as — "a pragmatist, not an ideologue, who promised America a kindler, gentler nation."

The brand of a presidential hopeful, or for that matter of the American president, is not just about claims and slogans; it also extends to dress, carriage, and persona.

- Remember the brouhaha when President Obama was photographed in the Oval Office on his first day of work without a jacket, reversing an official Bush branding dictum — jackets and ties at all times in the Oval Office? The Obama brand was more about "warmth, informality, and accessibility."
- The Mike Dukakis (Duke) brand had persona limitations — *he was perceived as impassive, undemonstrative, and impersonal* — limitations Dukakis was unable to shake off.

Frequently, negative branding also occurs when parties or candidates ascribe negative attributes, or lack of value, to their opposite numbers to put them down.

- Ronald Reagan was instrumental in re-branding the Democratic Party as "a party that was divided, lacked a coherent ideology, or a clear direction."
- By negatively branding Bill Clinton as *Slick Willie*, Republicans wanted to link the Clinton brand to negative attributes like *lack of morality, untrustworthiness, and unfit to be president*, to strengthen their Bill Clinton impeachment campaign.[1]

How Listening Shaped the Obama Campaign

It is customary for political analysts and pundits to dissect and analyze the outcomes of elections, especially if the results happen to be spectacular. Irrespective of one's political leanings, few will disagree that the outcome of the 2008 presidential elections was indeed stunning and spectacular. Also, regardless of how one slices and dices Obama's campaign strategy, there is little disagreement among experts on the reasons that made Obama's campaign so wildly successful. They unanimously attribute it to his willingness to start meaningful and intelligent conversations with multitudes of American voters. This desire to have meaningful and ongoing conversations with the population was not just another political ploy. It was a genuine effort to make the election a collaborative effort, to transform the election from one man's ambition to a collective ambition. If Obama won, all who supported him would win; if Obama lost, the loss would be as much theirs as his. What enabled and subsequently sustained this collaboration was not Obama's rhetoric, his youthful good looks, or his candid demeanor, though all that did help; it was the effort and investment his campaign made in actually *listening* to the American people.

The majority of American voters were a disenfranchised lot by the time the 2008 elections rolled around. To use an analogy, voters were in a similar state as the average consumers were in, before the emergence of the digital, interconnected, networked era. Chapter 1 described how most consumers felt alienated and disconnected from the companies whose products and services they consumed. American voters were no different; they felt estranged and disconnected from the government they had helped install, or that others had installed for them. Like consumers who felt that the only thing companies were interested in was their consumption dollars, voters felt that the only thing politicians were interested in was their vote.

Communication between politicians and voters was no different than communication between brands and consumers. It was a one-way street. Like consumers, a steady barrage of TV ads, polls, direct mail campaigns, telemarketing sales, and door-to-door campaigners confronted voters. Barak Obama had a tough job. In order to be elected, he needed to be heard, understood, and appreciated. But the election climate was loud and noisy, and the voters were largely unmoved. Traditional wisdom of pushing the Obama brand through mass media marketing would have backfired. Instead of shouting out his message to shape voter preference, Obama decided first to listen.

Listening as a means of building common purpose was not new for Barack Obama. He developed an appreciation for listening and honed his skills at it as a community organizer in Chicago. Rather than starting meetings with his own talking points, he would first take note of what people were saying.[2] He realized that allowing people to tell their stories first was a more effective way of starting conversations. He also realized that this simple courtesy did more than just help him understand people's backgrounds and needs. Listening helped him build relationships. Intersections between his audience's needs and his own agenda helped transform individual agendas into a co-created common agenda.

Obama used this background and experience to shape his campaign's listening strategy. Using an extensive mailing list that helped the campaign reach a wide swath of Americans, potential voters were invited to join the MyBarackObama (MyBO) online social network. Based on conversations and debates within the walls of this network, Obama was able to listen and learn a great deal about voters'

Table 3.1 Obama Campaign's Listening Platform

Channel	Benefit
Email	• Took pulse of likely supporters before announcing presidential intentions
MyBO (My Barack Obama)	• Gauged supporters' reactions to Obama's speeches and media coverage; fostering conversations and collaboration among supporters • Examined decision making process of ambivalent voters
Listening to America (Democratic platform for change)	• Supported Listening to America events; interaction and conversations with voters • Captured thoughts and concerns from voters to create the 2008 Democratic Party Platform called "Renewing America's Promise"
Social media networks	• Used Facebook as a conversation channel; gained insights into concerns of supporters and first-time voters • Reached out to younger audiences through MySpace
Video sharing sites (YouTube)	• Listening through observation; gained insights on lifestyles, concerns, and agendas of voters by viewing and analyzing voter/supporter-generated videos

concerns and perspectives on key issues, such as health care, education, the wars in Iraq and Afghanistan, and the economy. Table 3.1 summarizes the major components of the campaign's listening platform.

The listening strategies deployed within MyBO were reinforced and expanded following his nomination as the official Democratic presidential candidate. A party-wide listening platform, the 2008 Democratic Platform, was co-created with the help of interested and energized voters. The party invited ordinary citizens to host meetings on this platform that were attended by party leaders. It was the job of the party leaders to listen to voters' concerns and preferences, and produce a summary of their findings. The campaign staff, Obama, and the party were diligent in reviewing these summaries. Their response, *Renewing America's Promise*, was formulated based on what they heard.[3] As more supporters linked up with Obama on MySpace, YouTube, and Facebook, the campaign team extended its listening to these networks as well.

Listening Works

On November 5, 2008, Obama's supporters were ecstatic. History was made. There was the obvious reason; Obama was the first African-American to be elected to the office of the President of the United States of America. However, there was another equally palpable, but less obvious reason. The anthem of democracy — government for the people, by the people, of the people — was ringing truer that night than it had for some time. There was no doubt that the large majority of the people were not just celebrating a political election, they were celebrating an event they had co-created. In many ways they were celebrating the outcome of their collaboration, their own investment of time and effort. They were celebrating their co-ownership of Obama's victory.

By pursuing an aggressive listening strategy, the campaign liberated the voices of millions of silent voters. An average voter was transformed from a passive, sometimes cynical bystander, to an active, committed investor in co-creating a mutually valued outcome. Let's examine this transformation by stepping into Malcolm Critcher's shoes. A young man from Tucson, Arizona, Malcolm was not quite 16 years old when he became involved in Obama's campaign. He joined MyBO and became a volunteer. Within a few weeks, Malcolm was using Facebook and MySpace to connect with friends, relatives, and anyone he knew to urge them to register to vote. He organized a "get out the vote" event in Tucson to which more than 10,000 people showed up. He spoke of the importance of participating in government, of selecting government officials who heard the voices of the electorate, and of the privilege of voting. Listening gave Malcolm a voice, which he used not just to collaborate with Obama's election machinery and co-create Obama's Presidency, but also to co-create his own future.[4]

Stories like Malcolm's were repeated several thousand times across America.

- In Burlington, Vermont, Neil Jensen trained volunteers on how to set up Obama events and raise funds.[5]
- Marcia Carlyn from Loudoun County, Virginia, used MyBO to download materials that would help her reach out to her conservative fellow citizens. She grew her neighborhood support base from five members to more than 2500.[6]
- More than 1 million donors who had never contributed to a campaign in the past made a contribution to the Obama campaign. Each of them gave less than $200. This group funded 26 percent of Obama's campaign war chest.[7]

Companies marketing branded products and services can learn from the Obama campaign. They have a choice. They can either continue to pummel customers with endless one-way broadcasts proclaiming "why my brand is best for you," or they can begin to invest in meaningful customer conversations, with the goal of building a common purpose. Just as it did with voters, listening will liberate the voices of customers, which can only help brands win at innovation and customer value-creation.

Several times during our conversations with companies and executives interviewed for this book, we were told how customers' interactions with companies were transformed when they were convinced that the company was genuinely interested in their input. Customers were more willing to reward a company with their time, effort, and creative energy in response to the company's desire to listen. They felt recognized and rewarded. For many, the opportunity to be heard, influence, and co-create was fulfilling and satisfying in its own right; even more important than receiving a monetary rebate or a promotional coupon. As described in Chap. 1, an enviable relationship has developed between Hallmark and its Circles of Conversation community members as result of the company's listening efforts. Consumers are willing to walk several extra miles to support and promote Hallmark and its products.

The converse is also true. When companies are more interested in telling than listening, customers' attitudes and feelings toward the offending company usually harden. Offending companies are often punished through negative social media chatter. Take the example of electronic billing. Several companies are keen to transition their customers to paperless billing because it saves the company time and money, and because it is good for the environment. However, some customers, younger and older, prefer paper because they are not yet comfortable with e-billing and electronic payments. So when T-Mobile decided in August 2009 to ignore customer preferences, and arbitrarily charge its customers $1.50 per month for paper bills received in the mail, a large portion of its customers screamed angrily, "You are not listening!" Angry customers swarmed the forums at T-Mobile.com accusing the company of taking advantage of customers who prefer paper bills. They insinuated that it was all about money and had little to do with the planet.[8] Fortunately, T-Mobile caved in to the pressure and withdrew the proposed charge, stating that the company hopes to continue its drive to paperless billing, but also intends to remain mindful of the different options out there. Some consumers praised the company for "listening to its customers." Others were less charitable, and wanted to continue punishing the company through their negative comments in blogs and forums.[9]

Gateways to Listening

At its core, listening is a metaphor for how organizations sense and perceive the world in which they operate. All organizations, regardless of their business model or sector focus, operate in complex environments, comprising independent agents and institutions, such as consumers, competitors, technologies, and regulatory agencies. Since the organization is part of this environment and yet distinct from it — its boundaries, walls, and ego ensure that — it needs a mechanism to let the outside world in, to sense it, and make sense of it. Active listening can help organizations adapt more effectively to environmental change as the case of National Geographic attests (Box 3.2).

Organizations that take listening seriously generally use more than one method to listen to the multidimensional realties they are a part of, especially those related to the customer. Key ways in which organizations listen are:

- Traditional marketing research: To listen to the voice of the customer
- Observation: To record the ways in which customers behave and the contexts within which those behaviors occur.
- Digital Listening: To capture the sound of customer conversations that occur in a variety of sites: social media, dedicated company websites, support forums, and chat rooms.

Box 3.2 How Listening Contributes to National Geographic's Longevity

National Geographic has been inspiring people to care about the planet since 1888. At a time when the Internet is leaving traditional media and magazine powerhouses shaken and shattered, National Geographic's longevity and reader following deserves a sustained round of applause.

The magazine's survival and continued ability to grow can be attributed to a very fine-tuned ability to listen to its readers, understand how their lives are changing, and change with them. It is in lockstep with its readers, and doesn't seem to miss a beat, thanks to ongoing dialogues with a variety of audiences, such as women readers, outdoorsy men, conservationists, technology enthusiasts, and even armchair travelers. New magazines like *National Geographic Traveler* and *National Geographic Adventure*, and new sites like National Geographic Kids (http://kids.nationalgeographic.com/) were launched, largely due to the magazine's ability to sense, and make sense of, how its readers' lives and content preferences are constantly changing.

National Geographic was listening when it spotted the Web 2.0 trend early, and invested in several collaborative tools to engage its many audiences (engagement is discussed in-depth in Chap. 4). The magazine created a National Geographic Wiki for collaborating with librarians.[10] It also established a presence on social media sites like Facebook, Twitter, and YouTube. Additionally, its websites act like a magnet, attracting audiences to engage with the magazine and one another, by sharing conversations and information through a variety of applications like puzzles, games, maps, and photographs.

Traditional Marketing Research

There is a reason why organizations have a functional focus. Functions, or specialized divisions within organizations, are supposed to know more about the area they are in charge of than anybody else in the company. Most organizations wrongly believe that marketing owns the customer. So it is not surprising that Marketing Research (MR), a specialized department or function with a specialized set of skills within marketing, has historically been given responsibility for listening to the customer. The literature on MR, and its full repertoire of tools and techniques, are too vast to cover in one section of a single chapter. Readers who are interested in learning more about the techniques and their benefits are referred to specialized books written on the subject. Alternatively, if the reader is more inclined to read articles and essays on the subject, relevant and current reference material can be found in the Wiley Encyclopedia of MR.[11]

This section focuses mainly on how marketing researchers listen and why their efforts are not enough to help companies listen effectively. Typically, MR relies on open or exploratory listening techniques when it comes to developing a deeper understanding of the customer — current needs, unmet needs, anticipated future behavior, and the context within which the behavior is likely to occur. As one element in a portfolio of listening tools, this may be helpful, but not if it is the only element, or if it accounts for a disproportionately high share of listening resources. The issue is not whether the output of marketing research is right or wrong; the discipline has enough technical skills and resources to ensure that its output is both valid and reliable. The issue is one of fit and completeness.

- Marketing research is in the business of extracting information from respondents. The ask-a-question, get-an-answer approach is not consistent with listening. Marketing research is orderly, point-in-time information gathering, which ends when a project ends. What is known at that moment lives on as unchangeable fact until the next project is conducted. Listening, on the other hand, is relational and evolutionary. It places a premium on spontaneity, on zigzagging, and on taking deliberate detours. Not everything needs to make sense at all times. A modicum of chaos is healthy because meaning and intent evolve over time; they can't be captured all at once, in one cross-sectional swoop.
- Additionally, marketing research output is often only partially complete. Its obsession with being right filters out factors like imagination, personal meaning, and contradictions, which often play the role of catalysts in helping transform ideas to relevant consumer value. The preoccupation of MR with precision and efficiency is reductive in nature, narrowing the channel of probing. What is needed is exactly the opposite, a widening of the channel of probing, because it enables a richer, more complete understanding of the customer.
- A preoccupation with precision can be limiting, as Gerald Zaltman, pioneer of the Zaltman Metaphor Elicitation Technique (ZMET) has warned. ZMET uses metaphors and visual images to understand consumer needs and attitudes. Zaltman advocates expanding channels of listening by focusing on rich people-involving methods, not people-excluding methods. The former are more likely to retain the uniqueness and idiosyncratic aspects of customers. The latter are more likely to lose them, by reducing real people to averages and percentages.[12]

MR, as currently practiced, is stuck in a paradox of its own making. It is used to help a company get closer to the customer. But its dominant tools and logic actually erase all distinguishing features of the customer, thereby putting more distance between a company and its customers. This is the main reason why, even though MR budgets have increased significantly year over year, the total stock of a company's customer insights has remained stagnant, and in some cases involving rapid technological change, has actually decreased. It is not surprising therefore, that improving the quality of customer insights continues to be a top priority for CEOs and CMOs.[13]

In addition, by focusing on issues important to the company, marketing research can both consciously and unconsciously promote tunnel vision, since MR is often deployed to cater to the needs of a company's core businesses. This tendency is likely to result in a greater amount of attention being paid to customer signals within known areas of operations, while simultaneously creating large listening black holes: areas related to the customer's mind and heart, in adjacent and discontinuous areas of operations that remain unnoticed and therefore unheard.

Observation

"Walk the Talk" is an interesting contemporary expression referring to the discrepancy between what people say and how they behave. If people were to only walk the talk, an objective onlooker could listen to people merely by observing how they walked. Alfred Adler, founder of the school of individual psychology, had an interesting way of describing the same phenomenon. He was fond of saying that people have two tongues, one in their mouths and the other in the soles of their feet. He went so far as to say that if you wanted to understand people's true intent, you should only listen to the tongues in the soles of their feet.[14]

Despite its obvious power and appeal, observation is an underutilized form of listening in the business world. Whatever the reasons for its underutilization, when used intelligently, and with imagination, it can be an extremely powerful tool for listening and developing customer insights. Fidelity and P&G don't need convincing; observation plays a key role in how they develop an understanding of what the customer actually values.

Peter Lynch is legendary in the world of investing and fund management. During his 13 years at the helm, from 1977 until his retirement in 1990, Fidelity's flagship Magellan fund consistently beat the market, recording an annual average return of 29 percent. He was a strong proponent of observation as a method of listening. In his books, *One Up on Wall Street* and *Beating the Street*, he states that one of the most effective ways of researching great stock selection stories is by actively playing the role of a consumer.[15] He believed that great success stories could often be found by simply observing which stores or products are enjoying fantastic popularity. With that kind of a mindset, he would have spotted the lines forming outside a relatively unknown coffee chain called Starbucks, and iPhone buds plugged into teen and young adult ears earlier than any of his competitors.

In their book, *The Game Changer*, A.G. Lafley and Ram Charan state that the customer is boss. They clarify that it's not just a slogan, but the most essential component of game-changing innovation, because nothing is more important than understanding the customer at both rational and emotional levels. This understanding of the customer begins with close observation:

> by keenly watching consumers, face-to-face, knee-to-knee, by listening with ears, eyes, heart, brain, and your intuitive sixth sense

The development of Downy Single Rinse (DSR) detergent was the product of this kind of close observation of laundry habits and practices of Mexican consumers. In a water scarce environment, DSR's key customer benefit — making laundry easier and less water-intensive — is a huge draw; the product has been immensely successful since its market launch in 2004.[16]

Observation also plays a key role in helping marketers understand the shopping behavior of consumers. When asked direct questions on how they shop, most consumers will err on the side of providing rational answers, such as — "I never shop without a shopping list," "I know prices of products I buy regularly," or "I seldom indulge in impulse buying." However, a very different picture emerges when shopping trips are videotaped or observed by a human observer, silently shopping along with the consumer.

In his book, *Why We Buy*, Paco Underhill uses observation to derive insights on shopping behavior, ranging from sizing up a shop for its selling potential, to understanding gender differences; how males and females approach shopping very differently, and have very different shopping styles.[17]

- Women do have a greater affinity for what we think of as shopping — walking at a relaxed pace through stores, examining merchandise, comparing products and values, interacting with sales staff, asking questions, trying things on and ultimately making purchases.
- In general, men, in comparison, seem like loose cannons. We've timed enough shoppers to know that men always move faster than women through a store's aisles.
- 86 percent of women look at price tags when they shop. Only 72 percent of men do. For a man, ignoring the price tag is almost a measure of his virility.

Digital Listening

The web is alive with chatter — questions, experiences, preferences, announcements, recommendations, and even condemnation. Table 3.2 presents a sampling of web conversations from a few select product categories.

Table 3.2 A Sampling of Web Conversations

Mountain biking	• Wanting to upgrade to formula k24s, any input? i currently am running hayes trail strokers.
Consumer electronics	• ...called Mitsubishi Customer Relations, was told wait time is 24 (twenty four) minutes. Was told someone from tech support will call me on Monday. The phone call never came.
Prescription drugs	• I'm taking this medication to alter my hormone levels in order to increase my fertility level. Has anyone else been prescribed this drug for this reason?
Cosmetics	• Stila Stay All Day Waterproof Liquid Eye Liner: "Love this product. It is very very easy to apply for a liquid liner. Can definitely make this a day or night look. Got a great deal on it too..Love STILA!" ...
Credit card	• I opened a Capital One account with a $500 credit limit as most people usually get, after a year and a half of using and paying on time they increased my limit to $2,500 and I have been more than happy ever since.
Business school/ MBA programs	• Prof. X[a] was by far the worst teacher I have had at University Y[a]. Make that my entire life.

[a] Names disguised to protect identity

So what are the options if a company wants to listen to web conversations? Using digital technologies, a company essentially has two options for listening to customer conversations on the web: open listening on the web or listening in walled proprietary communities.

Open Listening on the Web

Every day, interesting and relevant conversations occur in hundreds of sites on the web. A few examples of these sites are blogs, discussion forums, reviews, social networking, video sharing, and news media sites. The nature and content of the conversation varies, depending on where the conversation is occurring. Some sites offer a broad listening canvas as they host conversations on a wide variety of topics. For example, a bank or financial institution in the United States interested in listening to a wide range of financial conversations would find a site like moneycentral.com insightful. Customers routinely visit http://www.moneycentral.com to share thoughts and perspectives on a number of personally relevant issues, such as credit cards, educational loans, mortgages, security of online banking, and retirement. Similarly, U.S. colleges or universities wishing to listen to conversations of both prospective and current students would find a site like http://www.collegeconfidential.com very useful, as it carries a large number of conversations on issues pertinent to students — such as admissions, social life, campus facilities, extra-curricular activities, and job prospects.

Other sites offer more focused listening opportunities as they are designed to host conversations on specific issues. Consider a review site like Buzzillions.com, discussed briefly in Chap. 2. It is a very popular review site carrying over 7 million product reviews from everyday customers on product categories ranging from electronics to clothing to dishwashers. It is a treasure trove for customers seeking advice and for companies wishing to learn about customer's experiences and recommendations, on their own and their competitors' brands. A screenshot of the Buzzillions. com website for video game reviews, including reviews by brands and consoles, is shown in Table 3.3. Manufacturers of video games and consoles, their advertising agencies, and their market information providers can all benefit by listening to customers in review sites such as Buzzillions.com.

Examples of sites offering focused listening opportunities abound in the Information Communications and Technology (ICT) world. Support forums feature

Table 3.3 Listening To Video Game Reviews @ Buzzillions.com

Video Games by Game Console	Video Games by Brand	Video Games by Pros	Video Games by Other Criteria
Wii (1189)	Electronic arts (882)	Graphics (882)	Use
Playstation 3 (571)	Activision	Easy to learn (874)	Lifestyle
Xbox 360 (770)	THQ (517)	Good audio (753)	Price
Playstation 2 (1437)	Ubisoft (462)	Challenging (726)	Greenness
Xbox (436)	Nintendo (448)	Multiplayer (538)	

Numbers in parentheses indicate total number of reviews

ICT problem and solution oriented conversations on specific application and usage needs of IT departments, small businesses, and end-users. A few examples follow:

- BlackBerry community forums (http://supportforums.blackberry.com/) provide a rich listening environment for conversations on specific applications, such as media and sales force automation.
- EggHeadCafe (http://www.eggheadcafe.com/) bills itself as the .Net developers' portal of choice; it carries questions, solutions, and support related conversations on a number of different topics, brands, and providers, such as web programming, data bases, graphics design, Microsoft, Java, Adobe, Mac, and Linux.

Listening in such information-dense environments offers companies an excellent chance to understand the world as experienced by the customer. These forums provide rich insights for a variety of business agendas, like product improvement (fixing bugs), product refinement and development (adding features and benefits in future releases), improving customer service and support, innovation, and market expansion (new uses, applications, and segments).

Given the volume of conversations, and the large number of sites where these conversations take place, it is impossible for a single individual to listen and make sense of all the conversations occurring at one time. Fortunately, there are companies who help their clients listen to the full range of conversations taking place on the web — blogs, discussion forums, rating and review sites, Twitter, YouTube, and more. A representative list of large and small companies offering listening services is provided in Appendix 3.1.

Listening in Proprietary Communities

Open web listening offers companies both broad and focused listening opportunities, as the preceding examples demonstrate. However, there are times when a company may want to listen to just a portion of the market — a specific segment, or a subsegment of special interest. In such cases, the ideal solution is to build walled communities that allow companies to have targeted conversations with specific customer groups. Mini case studies demonstrating how two companies — CDW (technology solutions provider) and Mercedes-Benz (automobiles) — use customer communities for collaborating with and listening to their customers follow.

- CDW is one of USA's largest providers of technology products to businesses, government organizations, and education institutions. The company's position as a market leader is largely due to its unwavering focus on customer needs. Since 2004, CDW has used three private online communities of approximately 300 members each, to listen and collaborate with its customers. The company's innovative use of consumer communities to engage business customers has helped it earn Forrester's 2009 Groundswell Listening award. The company continuously taps community members to listen to ideas, suggestions, and advice concerning products and services, marketing, and innovation. Community members have had a strong impact on CDW's sales process; the new approach of listening to the community is now an integral part of sales training at CDW's Sales Academy. Calvin Vass, senior manager of research, states that the company's online communities have "revolutionized the way CDW interacts with customers." The dialogue between the company and its customers has yielded bold initiatives to co-create new customer experiences.[18]

- Mercedes-Benz (MB) has also invested in a walled community to listen to a new generation of car buyers. This new group of potential Mercedes buyers is drawn from a larger cohort of Generation Y customers (a label used to refer to people born during the 1980s and the early 1990s), a group the company is not as familiar with as its mainstream customers. In order to learn more about this group's attitudes toward cars, specific automotive brands, urban transportation, and the environment, MB launched an online community — Generation Benz — with the help of Passenger, a leading platform provider and developer of online communities. The company hopes that listening to the voice of emerging new Generation Y customers in Generation Benz will help it keep in touch with significant market changes and contribute to preserving its iconic status in the luxury car segment. Achieving this listening objective through open web listening alone would have been difficult for Mercedes Benz.[19]

Characteristics of Effective Listening Programs

Effective listening programs usually have the following characteristics:

- Formality: Involve a formal commitment of resources (time, money, and people) to the listening process
- Framing: Rely on multiple frames and perspectives, to listen, understand, and cultivate insights
- Diversity: Employ a diverse set of listening tools to match the complexity of the listening task
- Dynamism: Move listening efforts to where the action is, or where consumer conversations are taking place.

Formality

Formality is essential because it fosters commitment, and commitment focuses listening. A formal commitment of resources (time, money, and people) is likely to produce two important benefits. First, as the school of cognitive dissonance suggests, that if a company spends time, money, and effort on an activity it will pay more attention to the outcomes of the effort and take the activity more seriously.[20] Second, formalization of the listening effort is more likely to generate valid and actionable insights. People in organizations are generally more willing to line up behind formal programs that have the blessing of a formal budget, a formal organization (people), with formally acknowledged responsibilities.

Hallmark's Circles of Conversation, described in Chap. 1, is an excellent example of formal listening. Hallmark has a long-standing tradition of listening within its customer communities. The effort is formally funded and led by a specific group within the customer insights division. Output of the listening program is not just bound and shelved, but is shared regularly with senior executives and key decision makers within the company, and is used as a key input in shaping Hallmark's customer-led innovation initiatives. This, in turn, reinforces and fuels the company's ongoing commitment to listening.

Framing

Framing is a word that was introduced to the world by psychologists like Erving Goffman and Gregory Bateson.[21] Frames are like schemas that guide the way we interpret what we see or hear. In the context of this book, framing refers to the filters, the system of rules and assumptions, that companies employ to make sense of what they are hearing. If companies persist in using the same frame to interpret the output of listening, the conclusions and insights they draw will be skewed toward the logic of the frame being used. This will result in partial and incomplete listening. For complete and effective listening to occur, it is important that listeners experiment with different frames to interpret what they are hearing and not get overly attached to any one frame. In simpler terms, companies should change their own position relative to what they are listening, and experiment with a variety of filters. Fixed, intransigent positions are incompatible with effective listening.

Consider an example from the world of prescription medications. Patients' conversations on medications like Coumadin, prescribed for life threatening conditions such as stroke and blood clots, often mention side effects. Verbatim portions from real patient conversations are shared below:[22]

> Chills, fatigue, sweat easily, tire easily
> sensitive to heat which also affects my INR (international normalized ratio) big time
> blotchy skin, weight gain of 15 lbs, headache, hypersensitivity, and itching scalp

There is no doubt that side effects like bleeding, weight, gain, and nausea are extremely undesirable. But Coumadin has also saved lives, and patients also talk about how grateful they are to Coumadin for having given them a second chance. A few verbatim posts follow:

> The medicine seems to be doing what its intensions are
> This drug is a lifesaver. I have had no problems keeping my INR. stable
> I am so thankful for this medication even though it can be a pain in the butt

If one listens using a side-effect frame only, Coumadin's value proposition will be heavily skewed toward its costs, namely side effects. The listener is bound to walk away with a very negative perception of the drug. However, if one also listens with the frame of benefits, the listener is now better placed to assess the true value proposition of Coumadin: namely, a drug that has a problematic side-effect profile, but also one that has delivered significant value to a large number of patients, either by alleviating their condition or by saving their lives. Shifting frames allows the listener to develop a more balanced understanding of the cost-benefit profile of the drug (Coumadin), especially its benefits (positive outcomes experienced by patients taking blood thinners to treat thrombosis).

Diversity

The listening environment is complex and diverse. There are a variety of digital forums within which conversations occur and there is a great deal of variety in terms of the conversations taking place — complaints, recommendations, suggestions, advice, questions, and sharing of personal experiences. Conversations are also taking place offline, in naturally occurring environments, in the brick and mortar world of sights, sounds, and smells. Given this complexity, it is unlikely that simple, one-dimensional approaches to listening will provide sufficient breadth or depth of customer insights.

There is actually a law to help us; it is the law of requisite variety.[23] The law states that the complexity of what is being investigated should be matched by appropriate diversity in the person or organization doing the investigating, so that more sense can be made of the subject of inquiry. In the context of our discussion, the main idea translates to the following assertion: a single listening tool, no matter how sophisticated, will not be able to help a company do justice to the diversity of customer conversations taking place. This is why even before we arrived at the discussion of diversity, we have consistently emphasized using a portfolio of listening tools.

A number of companies, such as P&G, Coke, Schwab, Wells Fargo, Nike, and Unilever, use a portfolio of listening tools. This enables them to listen to the customer comprehensively, and on several different dimensions. Most companies, however, still rely heavily on marketing research (MR) as a listening tool. Reservations about the ability of MR to truly listen to the customer have been expressed earlier in this chapter. Industry leaders and domain experts routinely call for rectifying this situation, urging companies to transform their MR efforts and venture into new areas for listening. Books like *Groundswell* have addressed this issue, as have presenters from different companies and consulting firms in The Advertising Research Foundation's (ARF) industry leader forums on "Transform Your Research by Listening."[24]

Dynamism

The challenge with listening is that customer conversations are constantly shifting — in terms of where they are taking place and the topics that are being discussed.

Two cases best illustrate this. In April 2010, Apple launched iPad; in November 2009, Google released Android, its mobile operating system. Both launches were a virtual listening nirvana experience with conversations ranging from and rapidly shifting between unbridled enthusiasm (best thing since sliced bread) and vitriolic criticism (total waste of money).

- The buzz around the iPad was intense, with conversations zipping at light speed around the web (news media, blogs, Twitter and other social media sites) and between topics (sharing experience, making usage recommendations, downloading apps, providing product and software information).
- Android conversations also appeared in a multitude of sources, including its own site and blog. Conversations touched on a number of themes, such as frustration (applications may not work), excitement (multiple products at multiple price-points), anticipation (customer response and its implications for Christmas 2009 sales), and expert commentary (Google's Android is already getting confusing!).

Customer conversations will surge and shift in unpredictable ways without much warning. That is their nature. In order to cope with this surging and shifting, companies are advised to deploy listening tactics that are flexible and dynamic, so as to have the best chance of capturing changes in the location and content of customer conversations.

Companies like Citi and Mercedes-Benz build in a dynamic component to their listening efforts by following two simple strategies:

- First, they listen to a wide cross-section of topics that have varying degrees of relationship to their business interests, some directly and strongly linked to their core business, others in spaces adjacent to their core business. In the case of Mercedes-Benz, this means listening to conversations on issues related to cars, commuting, and auto financing (core business), as well as listening to issues related to the environment, urban congestion, and alternatives to car ownership (Zipcar), and public transportation (adjacent spaces).
- Second, while these companies take their listening effort to locations where the bulk of customer conversations are taking place, they also regularly scan fringe locations to ensure that they remain sensitive to conversations on emerging trends. In Citi's case, they can listen to conversations on credit cards, mortgages, and loans (their bread-and-butter businesses) in locations such as moneycentral.com, in their own customer community, through focus groups, and in natural environments, such as cafes, and bank lobbies. However, it is unlikely that they will pick up on conversations related to peer-to-peer lending or mobile money, some of the fastest growing threats to conventional banking, by staying within the confines of their bread-and-butter listening locations. This will require augmenting their core listening efforts with listening for peripheral conversations that have yet to become mainstream.

It is impossible to have a meaningful and authentic conversation with customers about value-creation without listening. But listening alone is not sufficient in sustaining that conversation. Ongoing interaction on issues related to value-creation requires that customers be engaged with the company in ways that are relevant and meaningful to them. That is the domain of customer engagement, the focus of the next chapter.

Appendix 3.1 Sample List of Companies Providing Digital Listening Services

Biz360 — http://www.biz360.com/
Cymfony — http://www.cymfony.com/
Dow Jones Insight — http://www.dowjones.com/product-djinsight.asp
Knowledge Kinetics — http://www.knowledgekinetics.com/
Nielsen BuzzMetrics — http://en-us.nielsen.com/tab/product_families/nielsen_buzzmetrics
Omniture — http://www.omniture.com/en/
Radian 6 — http://www.radian6.com/
Ripple 6 — http://www.ripple6.com/
Scout Labs — http://www.scoutlabs.com/
Sysomos — http://www.sysomos.com/
Techrigy — http://www.techrigy.com/
Visible Technologies — http://www.visibletechnologies.com/

Notes and References

1. Cosgrove, K. (2003, August 27). "The Branding of the President." Paper Presented at the annual meeting of the American Political Science Association. Retrieved February 28, 2010, from http://www.allacademic.com/meta/p_mla_apa_research_citation/0/6/4/7/7/p64777_index.html
2. Moberg, D. (2007, April 3). Obama's community roots. *The Nation.* 284 (15) 16–18. Retrieved November 11, 2008, from http://www.thenation.com/doc/20070416/moberg
3. Democratic National Convention Committee. (2008, August 25). *The Democratic National Platform: Renewing America's Promise.* The 2008 Democratic platform was created thanks to the input of thousands of volunteers who hosted "listening events." The notes taken during these events were given to their party representatives. The platform reflected the concerns expressed by voters during the "listening events."
4. Author conversations with Malcolm Critcher Tucson, Arizona 2009 and 2010.
5. McGirt, E. (2009, April 1). How Chris Hughes helped launch Facebook and the Barack Obama campaign. *Fast Company.* Retrieved February 28, 2010, from http://www.fastcompany.com/magazine/134/boy-wonder.html
6. Website: MyBO. (2008). Leesburg Halloween Parade — Community service. Retrieved February 14, 2010, from http://my.barackobama.com/page/event/detail/4v587

7. Website: MSNBC. Obama raised $104 million as campaign ended. Retrieved December 4, 2008, from http://www.msnbc.msn.com/id/28060983/#storyContinued

8. Stross, R. (2009, September 19). What if people don't take the bait to go paperless? *The New York Times*. Retrieved on February 14, 2009, from http://www.nytimes.com/2009/09/20/business/20digi.html?_r=1&scp=22&sq=T-Mobile&st=nyt

9. Mies, G. (2009, September 28). Skeptical shopper: Pushing consumers for paper billing. *PCWorld*. Retrieved on February 14, 2010, from http://www.pcworld.com/article/172771/skeptical_shopper_punishing_consumers_for_paper_billing.html

10. Huffman, K. & Jourdan, M. (2007, February 28). National Geographic 2.0. Wikis @ Work. Libraries Information Services – National Geographic Society. Website: National Geographic Wiki. (2008). Retrieved February 28, 2010, from http://www.ngslis.org/about/history.html20. Festinger, L. (1957). *A Theory of Cognitive Dissonance*. Stanford: Stanford University Press.

11. Bhalla, G. (2010 — in press). Marketing research proposal and marketing research process. The Wiley International Encyclopedia of Marketing, edited by Naresh Malhotra and Jagdish Sheth. Hoboken, NJ: John Wiley & Sons Ltd. Chichester.

12. Zaltman, G. (2003). *How Customers Think: Essential Insights into the Mind of the Market*. Boston: Harvard Business Press; Zaltman, G. & Zaltman, L. (2008). *Marketing Metaphoria: What Deep Metaphors Reveal About the Minds of Consumers*. Boston: Harvard Business Press.

13. CMO Council. (2009). Marketing outlook survey. Marketing Outlook 2009. Retrieved February 19, 2010, from http://www.cmocouncil.org/resources/form_marketing-outlook-2009.asp

14. Beecher, W. & Beecher, M. (1971). *Beyond Success and Failure*. New York: Pocket Books Adler, A. (1998). *Understanding Life*. Dear Field, Beach FL: Hazelden.

15. Lynch, P. & Rothchild, J. (2000). *One Up on Wall Street: How to Use What You Already Know to Make Money in the Market*. New York, NY: Simon & Schuster; Lynch, P. & Rothchild, J. (1994). *Beating the Street*. New York, NY: Simon & Schuster

16. Lafley, A.G. & Charan, R. (2008). *The Game Changer: How You Can Drive Revenue and Profit Growth with Innovation*. New York, NY: Crown Business.

17. Underhill, P. (2008). *Why We Buy: The Science of Shopping — Updated and Revised for the Internet, the Global Consumer, and Beyond*. New York, NY: Simon & Schuster.

18. Wooster, M. (2007, April 17). Acting on the Voice of the Customer: CDW's Community-Based Approach. *Marketing Insight — Business Results*. Retrieved February 16, 2010, from http://www.itsma.org/NL/article.asp?ID=286; Customer-Centric Approach Earns CDW Corporation a Prestigious Social Media Award. (2009, October 28). *Business Wire*. Retrieved February 16, 2010, from http://www.businesswire.com/portal/site/home/permalink/?ndmViewId=news_view&newsId=20091028006388&newsLang=en

19. Mercedes USA and Passenger Launch Generation Benz: On Line Consumer Community for Generation Y. (2008, November 7). *Business Wire*. Retrieved March 3, 2009, from http://www.businesswire.com/portal/site/home/permalink/?ndmViewId=news_view&newsId=20081117005524&newsLang=en; Greenberg, K. (2008, November 17). Mercedes Intro's "Generation-Benz." *Social Network*. Retrieved February 13, 2010, from http://www.mediapost.com/publications/index.cfm?fa=Articles.showArticle&art_aid=94888

20. Festinger, L. (1957). A Theory of Cognitive Dissonance. Stanford, CA: Stanford University Press. Weick, K. (1979). *The Social Psychology of Organizing*. Columbus, OH: McGraw-Hill.

21. Goffman, E. & Berger, B. (1986). *Frame Analysis: An Essay on the Organization of Experience*. Holliston, MA: Northeastern; Bateson, G. (1973). *Steps to an Ecology of Mind*. London, ENG: Paladin.

22. Website: The World Health Organization. (2004). *List of NGOs in Official Relations with WHO*. Retrieved February 15, 2010, from http://www.who.int/civilsociety/relations/official_relations/en/

23. Conant, R.C. & Ashby, R.W. (1970). Every good regulator of a system must be a model of that system. *International Journal of Systems Science,* 1(2): 89–97.
24. Advertising Research Foundation. (2009, January 27). One day workshop 2009 ARF industry leader forum — San Francisco. *Transform Your Research by Listening.... West Coast Edition.*

Chapter 4
Engage

Customer Engagement: Nike's Joga.Com

International sporting events like the Olympics are not just about countries and athletes competing against one another. They are also about brands competing against one another. Few contests are as fierce as the one between Nike and Adidas. Both companies are global giants. Until a few years ago, the images of the two companies were mainly tied to markets they dominated; the core of Nike's image was built around running shoes in the U.S. market, and the core of Adidas' image was built around the soccer-crazy culture of Europe and Latin America. However, that turned topsy-turvy by the time the 2006 FIFA (Fédération Internationale de Football Association) World Cup rolled around.

When Germany hosted the 2006 FIFA World Cup, Adidas was the global powerhouse in the soccer world. It was also the market leader in soccer shoes and soccer apparel.[1] The World Cup was a dazzling spectator experience, drawing packed stadiums and record-breaking global TV audiences. Italy won its fourth world crown, beating France in a thrilling penalty shoot out. Given its pre-eminent position, it was not surprising that Adidas was highly visible during the tournament. For instance, the entire tournament was played with Adidas soccer balls and two of the most coveted awards during the Cup carried the Adidas brand name: the Adidas Golden Ball award, won by Zidane of France, and the Adidas Golden Shoe award, won by Kloss of Germany.

Curiously enough, the 2006 FIFA World Cup was also Nike's coming-out party in the football world, as the company mounted a serious challenge to Adidas' market domination. Through a variety of customer-based initiatives coinciding with the World Cup, Nike was able to establish a significant handshake with both professional football stars and passionate football enthusiasts. Nike enjoyed record-breaking growth in sales and profits that year. In discussing the company's performance with shareholders, Mark Parker, Nike's CEO, attributed the growth to innovation and, more importantly, to Nike's success in reaching, engaging, and appealing to football fans across the world.[2]

How did Nike create serious space for itself in a market where Adidas had been the unrivalled leader for several decades? The simple answer is: through customer engagement! The underlying dynamics, though, are more complex and infinitely more interesting. Nike reached out to football fans across the globe by creating Joga.com, its first online community specifically devoted to football, open to anyone who wished to join (*Joga* is the Portuguese word for *run*). The choice of name was a deliberate attempt to link the site with Brazil, a country boasting an opulent football heritage and a track record of having fielded some of the most charismatic and revered teams in World Cup football history. The site's name, Joga.com, invokes images of the well-known Brazilian phrase — *joga bonito* — means play beautifully. It also resurrects images of Brazil's legendary football stars like Pele, Ronaldo, Romario, Zico, and Rivelino.

Through Joga.com, Nike invited football fans to share and celebrate their love for football with one another, with Nike, and with professional football players.[3] The company's football brand ambassadors and staff were the first ones to join the community. They personalized their profiles and started chats and conversations that soon attracted hordes of football fans. In a few short months, the site was buzzing with activity. Community members were uploading personalized content, forming dream teams, discussing memorable football matches, and sharing mash-up videos that immortalized their favorite football players. It was only a matter of time that mash-up video contests started taking place, with members ranking and voting on favorites and winners on a monthly basis. Joga.com members also connected with World Cup football players through exclusive web-hosted events. Initially started within the walls of the digital community, this engagement soon spilled out into the brick and mortar world. Nike invited Joga.com community members, most of them serious amateur football players, to participate in real street football matches, and they showed up!

The 2006 World Cup was a significant milestone in Nike's attempt to engage amateur athletes beyond the world of runners and joggers. Fueled mainly by digital engagement initiatives, the two-pronged strategy of appealing to both professional football stars and to their star-crazed enthusiasts paid handsome dividends. More than half the World Cup's football players wore Nike boots. Through Joga.com, Nike created a closer relationship with 1 million football fans who became part of the Nike brand community.[4] This digital, viral strategy also gave Nike a significant competitive advantage in grabbing the attention of football enthusiasts and gaining market share in the only category in which it trailed Adidas. Nike discontinued the Joga.com community after the 2006 World Cup, but not its engagement or conversations with football enthusiasts. The company continues to use social media initiatives like Facebook and Twitter to engage football enthusiasts and continue the multi-way conversations started in Joga.com.

Characteristics of Successful Customer Engagement

Joga.com is an excellent example of how a company can successfully engage its customers. Later, this chapter will present a detailed discussion of factors that enable the successful execution of engagement initiatives. However, it is important to pause and reflect on three key characteristics of successful customer engagement programs.

- Customer interest and passion: Effective customer engagement is possible only if customers share a common passion and interest and are willing to act on that passion. Without the willing investment of time and energy, customer engagement is a non-starter. The game of football, and the passion viewers and players of all levels have for it, provided Joga.com the essential ingredients for engaging football enthusiasts from all parts of the world.
- Authentic intent: For shared passion to express itself in spontaneous and unique ways, people need to experience authentic environments for engagement, not be baited into false fronts for selling or promoting brands. Nike provided that by building a unique digital community devoted exclusively to football. Chap. 2 presented a similar dynamic at work in the Planet Orange and Marmite XO case studies. In the case of Planet Orange, the primary goal was to enrich overall fan experience in ways that basketball games alone could not do. Yes, merchandise and memorabilia are always available for sale on Planet Orange, but they are never pushed on unsuspecting visitors. Fans visiting the sites are seldom bothered by in-your-face promotions and selling campaigns.
- Multi-way interaction: Lastly, customer engagement truly bubbles up to its full potential when customers are able to interact with one another on their own terms, and the company sponsoring the engagement chooses to facilitate, not control the proceedings. It was the sharing of fantasy teams, photos, and personal stories of their favorite football stars that kept the engagement fires burning in Joga.com. On its own, Nike could never have achieved this level of spontaneous, highly fulfilling interactions.

Once these features are in locked in place, customer engagement has the potential of evolving and growing in new and unpredictable ways.

Arenas and Domains

In order to effectively engage customers, companies need to make two key decisions:

- Engagement arenas: Where will companies engage their customers?
- Engagement domains: What aspects or themes will provide the glue for engagement initiatives?

Engagement Arenas

Customer engagement can occur in physical spaces, in digital arenas, or in both. In the case of Joga.com, engagement began in digital arenas, but spilled over into physical spaces. More decisions await a company once the basic physical space or digital arena decision is made. These decisions are summarized in Fig. 4.1. To amplify, if a company decides to engage customers in physical spaces, then it must decide whether to engage customers individually, or in groups. Alternately, if a company decides to engage customers in digital arenas, it must choose whether to engage them in company-sponsored sites, in social media sites, or in both. Lastly, if a company decides in favor of engagement in company-sponsored sites, it must decide whether to engage all-comers, or restrict the engagement to a specific number of pre-invited customers from specific market segments.

Engagement in Physical Spaces

Car and motorbike enthusiasts are a breed apart. In fact, enthusiasts may be too mild a word; fanatics may be a more appropriate descriptor. Vintage car rallies have been a staple forum for collectors and classicists to share their passion and show off their possessions for several decades now. These rallies are annual events held in a variety of cities across the globe, from the princely cities of Jaipur and Jodhpur in India, to the highlands of Scotland. Rallies and outdoor driving events also offer manufacturers of cult brands like the Land Rover, Harley Davidson, and the Mini Cooper an exciting and visible forum for engaging brand owners. HOG (Harley Owners Group) events are legendary among both Harley owners and non-owners (Box 4.1).

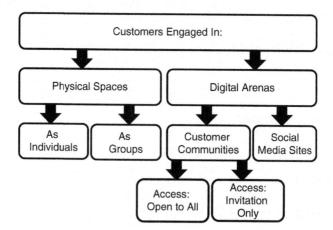

Fig. 4.1 Engagement Arenas and Options

Box 4.1 Que Vivan Los Harlistas (Long Live the Harlistas)

Once a Harley owner, always a Harley owner; you are never going to go near another bike. Harley owners — or Harlistas, as they are called in Latin America — are for life, not just for a few seasons.[5] Being a Harlista is more than just owning a bike. It's about community; a brand subculture rich in personal meaning, in folklore, symbols, mythology, and sometimes even legend. Harley owners come from all walks of life — lawyers, corporate executives, doctors, and mechanics, bar tenders, men, women, grandmas, and grandpas.

The Harley Owners Group (HOG), a company-sponsored community, or marketing club, is the Big Daddy of all brand communities. If there is any community that has the right to claim — *been there, done that* — it's HOG! The devotion of owners to their bikes and to other riders, and the commitment of the company to brand owners, has been written about and celebrated on numerous occasions. It is safe to say that discussing brand communities and engagement without paying homage to Harley and HOG borders on blasphemy.

Harley riders are fiercely loyal to their bikes, and are united with other riders by a shared ethos. The brand and HOG sites invite riders to express themselves in the company of others. Or as the Harlista website reminds its Latin riders:

Being a Harlista is about living without fear, overcoming obstacles, and experiencing the camaraderie of the *open road*.

You can find the *brotherhood of riders* expressing themselves in the company of others, experiencing the camaraderie of the open road from Chile to Canada, from United States to Japan, and from Finland to Australia. Few engagement examples can match Harley and HOG for sheer devotion and loyalty.

Mini Cooper celebrates 50 Years: Mini Cooper is one of the fastest growing cult brands in the automotive world. News that the iconic small carmaker is preparing to launch a special edition, outfitted by its ultra-luxury cousin Rolls Royce, only serves to add to the Mini's élan. Like Land Rover and Harley, Mini too has discovered the power of physical arenas to engage its owners. 2009 marked the fiftieth anniversary of the Mini Cooper. To celebrate its golden jubilee, Mini organized several outdoor birthday parties. The attendance and celebrations were both lively and enthusiastic, as the following example demonstrates.

- Russ Swift, one of the world's best-known stunt drivers, thrilled and awed fans with spectacular maneuvers to showcase the Mini's handling during the car's fiftieth birthday celebrations. More than 25,000 enthusiasts and loyalists from all over the world took part in this epic celebration at the Silverstone, Oregon party held on May 22, 2009. It was a celebration of all things Mini:

what the car stands for and the lifestyles lived by the people who drive them. Additionally, partygoers feasted on a variety of past and future models. On view were original Mini Cooper classics, limited edition models, and prototypes of new models. Among the jewels of the event was the very first Mini Cooper to have rolled off the Oxford production line in 1959.[6]

UK Army changes recruiting strategy: Facing a recruiting challenge, the UK Army decided it was time to change its traditional recruiting practices from the push strategy they had been using for years to a pull strategy. The time-honored method of recruiting was to invite potential recruits to the nearest recruiting office for one-on-one conversations with enlisted soldiers. However, this method was not working as well as it had in the past; potential recruits needed something more than just enlisted soldiers talking up the Army by describing their personal experiences. What the UK Army needed was a way for potential recruits to feel and experience a connection with the army for themselves. The UK Army needed to show rather than tell!

The UK Army created the "Start Thinking Soldier Campaign" to achieve this transformation. The campaign involved a series of simulations and virtual reality challenges, carefully designed to test an individual's leadership, teamwork, decision-making, and fitness abilities. Six bespoke customized pods were specifically designed for the campaign. Easy to transport, these pods traveled to different events, such as the Wakestock Festival in Wales, and the Fast & Modified Car Show in Edinburgh, where large numbers of individuals could be meaningfully engaged.

Response to the "Start Thinking Soldier Campaign" has been very encouraging. Driven partly by curiosity and partly by the thrill of the challenge, the pods attracted over 12,500 visitors between June and December 2009. Once people entered the pods, they were presented with a host of challenges and special missions, such as storming an enemy compound or diffusing an explosive. By stepping into the shoes of a UK Army soldier, participants got an opportunity to determine if they have what it takes to "Think Soldier." More than half the visitors to these events continue to have a connection with the UK Army.[7] The virtual reality challenges gave potential recruits an opportunity to sample the exciting and challenging nature of army life. Rather than having to be persuaded, potential recruits exposed to the campaign now walk into recruitment offices, of their own volition, for face-to-face conversations with enlisted soldiers.

Engagement in Digital Arenas: Communities and Websites

Companies have a choice if they wish to engage customers in digital arenas. They can either build exclusive digital arenas like Joga.com on their own or with the help of specialized agencies. Or they can leverage existing social media sites like Facebook and Twitter. Or they can do both. Appendix 4.1 provides a listing of companies that provide solutions and services for building digital engagement arenas.

Exclusive engagement arenas usually provide greater focus and mutuality of expectations. Joga.com had a singular focus — football. Customers visiting the site expected their passion for the sport to be fulfilled in a variety of ways, and Nike expected only football enthusiasts to show up. As a result of this focus, sponsoring companies and brands can be more effective in meeting their engagement objectives. This dynamic is well illustrated in the NASA and Meredith Corporation examples that follow.

NASA inspires the next generation of explorers: There was a time when NASA was a fenced-in organization. The average person on the street knew NASA mainly through its space missions, news reels of space shuttles blasting off or landing, awe inspiring photographs, and of course its ubiquitous sound bites:

- Counting down space shuttle launches (10,9,8,7 – liftoff), or
- Announcing mission accomplishments (Houston, we have touch down).

The twenty-first century NASA views its mission and mandate to be broader than safely and effectively organizing space missions. Its formal mission and vision statement acknowledge the role and responsibility that NASA has in bringing the wonders of space and earth science to millions across the globe and to inspiring the next generation of explorers. The official NASA website is a virtual treasure trove of interactive explorations for engaging students and non-students: people of all ages who want to be space explorers without taking science classes or leaving the comforts of their living room couch.[8] For example:

- PlanetQuest Historic Timeline: This link allows visitors to explore the history of planet Earth, and invites hunting and search for another Earth.
- NASA TV: Broadcasts details of missions, such as "cargo ship" arrival at Space Station, in addition to shuttle launches.
- Space Communications and Navigation (SCaN): Responsible for providing communications services for all NASA missions; the interactive demonstration shows how SCaN's ground and space-based facilities interact with NASA assets in space.

The story of the naming of NASA's Mars Rover to be launched in 2011 best exemplifies the new NASA and its ability to engage the next generation of explorers. The Mars Science Laboratory Rover will be larger and more capable than any craft previously sent to land on the Red Planet. NASA partnered with Disney-Pixar's WALL-E to organize a naming contest, inviting ideas from U.S. school students 5–18 years old. The contest started in late 2008 and ended in April 2009; the winning name was revealed in May 2009. Students were engaged not only at the idea generation stage, but also in the selection of the winning entry. Approximately 10,000 entries were received, six finalists were chosen by a panel of experts, and over 60,000 students worldwide voted for their favorite name from among the six. The winning name was — Curiosity (Box 4.2)!

Box 4.2 Naming the Mars Rover

There is something about asking children to name a space vehicle that liberates their creativity. Ask NASA. The first set of Mars Rovers were named *Spirit* and *Opportunity*, by nine-year-old Sofi Collis in 2003. In her entry essay, Sofi described the orphanage in Eastern Europe where she lived as cold, dark, and lonely, and how looking up at the sky made her feel better. For Sofi, the sky held a promise of a better life; looking up at the sky gave her hope. This hope materialized when a U.S. couple adopted her and brought her to live in Scottsdale, Arizona. Sofi's feelings of gratitude, the thankfulness she felt toward the sky for giving her *Spirit* and *Opportunity,* and toward America for making her dreams come true inspired her choice of names for the twin Rovers.

Twelve-year-old Clara Ma, a sixth grade student from Sunflower Elementary school in Lenexa, Kansas, is this time's winner. NASA's Mars Science Laboratory Rover, scheduled for launch in 2011, will be called *Curiosity*, based on an essay written by Clara.[9]

Clara's Essay

> Curiosity is an everlasting flame that burns in everyone's mind. It makes me get out of bed in the morning and wonder what surprises life will throw at me that day. Curiosity is such a powerful force. Without it, we wouldn't be who we are today. When I was younger, I wondered, 'Why is the sky blue?', 'Why do the stars twinkle?', 'Why am I me?', and I still do. I had so many questions, and America is the place where I want to find my answers. Curiosity is the passion that drives us through our everyday lives. We have become explorers and scientists with our need to ask questions and to wonder. Sure, there are many risks and dangers, but despite that, we still continue to wonder and dream and create and hope. We have discovered so much about the world, but still so little. We will never know everything there is to know, but with our burning curiosity, we have learned so much.

Any person with an interest in space and exploration, regardless of age, ethnicity, or social background can visit NASA's digital engagement sites. They are open to all. However, there are times when companies or organizations may want to limit the participation to selected customers, such as customers who meet a specific demographic or lifestyle profile, or those who belong to specific market segments. In these cases, engagement is limited and participation is by invitation only, as in Meredith's online customer community.

Meredith engages women readers: Meredith is one of the leading media and marketing companies in the United States. Its diverse business interests include publishing, TV broadcasting, integrated marketing, and interactive media. In 2009, the company created its own private online community — *Real Women Talking*. The goal of the community is to engage readers of publications like *Ladies' Home*

Journal and *Better Homes and Gardens* to better understand their needs for information and entertainment in an era of rapidly shifting tastes and preferences. The approximately 300 selected and pre-invited members of the Real Women Talking community also serve as an advisory board for Meredith Corporation, interacting with the company to help shape its future editorial, advertising, feature, and web site strategies.[10] Engagement with the community has also helped Meredith rethink its brand image as communicated by its magazines' redesigned cover pages and websites.

Hallmark's Circles of Conversation community discussed in Chap. 1, and Mercedes Benz' Generation Benz community discussed in Chap. 3, are also examples of community participation by invitation only. Hallmark restricts its listening and engagement to a select group of moms (under 45 with kids, and over 45 with no kids), while Mercedes Benz restricts its interaction to car enthusiasts belonging to the Gen Y demographic group.

Engagement in Digital Arenas: Social Media

Companies can also engage customers in social media sites, like Facebook. There is increasing evidence to suggest that people access social media sites, not just to meet their personal and social needs, like making new friends, sharing information, and staying abreast with the activities of current friends, but also to interact and engage with companies and their brands. Companies, organizations, and media celebrities understand and are in sync with this dynamic and routinely engage their customers, patrons, or fans in social media sites.

We have selected three environments — Facebook, Twitter, and Ning — to illustrate how social media can be used to foster engagement. All three social media sites meet our criteria of genuine engagement since they permit multi-way conversations on customer and company agendas. This is also the reason why we have not included social media sites like YouTube and Flickr, even though several companies and organizations, like Pepsi and National Geographic, routinely post content on these sites in the hope of engaging visitors. At their core, YouTube and Flickr, still operate in episodic and broadcast mode. The transmission of videos and photos takes place from one to many. Since the many essentially consume the content as individuals, there is little room for multi-way conversations or spontaneous shaping of collective agendas.

Facebook (www.facebook.com): Coca Cola has one of the most popular pages on Facebook. Its fan following at the end of 2009 was more than 4 million and growing. That Coca Cola is on Facebook is not surprising. The company has a strong need to be laser-focused in targeting and engaging the right consumers through a variety of media and channels. What is surprising is that Coke's Facebook page was started in August 2008 not by the company, but by two fans called Dusty Sorg and Michael Jedzejewski.[11]

Coke had missed a social-media engagement opportunity earlier, in 2005, when it objected and disapproved of the monster wave created by Steve Spangler and the Mentos-Diet Coke geyser experiment (interested readers can find more details on this experiment in Appendix 4.2). They were in no mood to make the same mistake twice. This time they were quick to seize the viral engagement opportunity provided by Dusty and Michael. They applauded and embraced the duo's effort and passion for Coke, invited them to Atlanta, and offered them the company's full support to help run the Facebook site as official brand ambassadors.

Working with them, and other fans, Coke has been very successful in engaging Facebook visitors with initiatives such as:

- Coca-Cola's Expedition 206: The company is sending a team of Happiness Ambassadors around the world to visit 206 countries in 365 days to help answer the question what makes people happy around the world.[12] Fans are being engaged ahead of the findings being shared publicly with provocative questions like "Is there more happiness in the Sahara desert or the Pacific Ocean?" Fans all over the world, like Toño and Kelly, will find out in 2010 at http://CokeURL.com/uxtr
- Coca-Cola has a favor to ask you: Coke enlisted fan support to help turn Copenhagen into Hopenhagen, and make the world a happier place: an engagement theme consistent with its vision to *refresh the world and inspire moments of optimism and happiness.* Over 2,000 fans responded to the request, helped spread the word, and got their friends involved as well through sites like http://CokeURL.com/342x
- Torch Relay: As the Olympic torch crisscrossed Canada on its way to the 2010 Winter Olympics in Vancouver, Coke's Facebook page allowed Canadian fans and supporters to track the progress of the Olympic torch, become aware of its route, and participate in local torch relay related events, such as the Temiskaming Shores Community Celebration.[13]

Twitter (www.twitter.com): Zappos, the idiosyncratic and fast growing online shoes, clothing, and bags retailer proudly declares that it is "powered by service." For Zappos, fast free shipping, 24×7 customer service, and 365-day return are not just slogans — they are its operating DNA. Their enthusiastic, difficult to emulate, service is why millions of consumers love to do business with them.

Not only is the company's service performance and track record cutting edge, so is its understanding and usage of web 2.0 technologies to engage its customers. Zappos' customer service department uses Twitter (http://twitter.com/Zappos_Service). Customers engage and are engaged by Zappos' customer service on several dimensions, such as customer appreciation and gratitude, help with merchandise selection, return procedures, and customer education.[14]

Rather than describe the interaction between customers and Zappos in our own words, we will let the tweets do the talking! All tweets, shared verbatim below, were generated by Zappos's customer service independently, or in response to customer actions, comments, and questions.

- Customer appreciation and thanks

  Thank you so much for being our customer!
  You're welcome. Let us know if we can help you out with anything more in the future!

- Help with merchandise

  Let us know if we can help you out with the shoes at all. You can always call 1-800-927-7671, too. :-)

- Return policy

  Their original packaging. You will just need to use one label.
  Just disregard the weight. UPS will bill us for the additional weight.

- No coupons

  Here is some information about "Zappos Coupons" http://www.zappos.com/truth-about-zappos-coupons
  Offer free shipping, 365-day return policy, our 24/7 customer service, etc. "All of these mean so much more than a Zappos coupon would."

Ning (www.ning.com): Ellen DeGeneres, popular talk show host, gadfly, and TV and film star, has iconic status among celebrities. She is a brand in her own right, much like scores of other music, sports, TV, and film personalities. Celebrity brands, just like their packaged and labeled counterparts, are also becoming increasingly adept at engaging their fans and followers in social media environments. Ellen's Ning-based community, "The Ellen DeGeneres Show Community," is a front-runner in illustrating fan engagement by a celebrity.[15]

With over 280,000 members, The Ellen DeGeneres Show Community oozes engagement. The *Ellen Show* and Ellen herself are the vital alchemists, mobilizing support for the members, as they face and cope with personal challenges, such as divorce and breast cancer. Members use the community to share information, participate in fund-raising events, and lend one another a helping hand. The engagement is about strength, personal empowerment, and about staying strong and hopeful. Most importantly, members can personalize this engagement to suit their own particular needs.

The bond community members experience with Ellen is intense and strong. In virtually all instances, directly or indirectly, she is part of the solution, or in the case of breast cancer patients, a vital part of their therapy. Breast cancer patients often watch the *Ellen Show* during their chemotherapy treatments. It helps them laugh, which helps them and other patients cope a lot better with their ordeal. Even the medical establishment approves! The nurses, for example, find it easier to deal with happier patients.

Engagement Domains

For engagement to be meaningful and mutually satisfying, the company needs a basis for focusing and channeling customer interest and passions. Our research and experience suggests that three domains are particularly effective catalysts in igniting and nurturing customer engagement.

- Relationships: Engagement that revolves around customers' relationships with themselves, their family, friends, and the communities they live in
- Causes and values: Causes and values that reflect customers' human, ethical, moral, religious, political, and social concerns provide a powerful focus for engagement
- Brand: Symbolic and/or material consumption of branded products and services that meet consumers' needs, wants, and desires; this could involve relationships with brands and/or companies

Case studies illustrating engagement in each of the domains follow.

Self as the basis of engagement: *Men's Health Magazine* (MHM) has an unambiguous value proposition — to feed its readers content on topics important to their self-image. The magazine offers its readers, mainly males, relevant content on issues like fitness, nutrition, sexual behavior, weight loss, grooming, and self-presentation. To engage its readers and create a closer relationship with them, the magazine publishes a weekly roundup of information and delivers it via mobile devices. Through mobile.mh.co.za, readers can download the application and receive a weekly short message service (SMS) text message. They can access quick tips on grooming, style, health, and fitness.[16] Readers can also customize the content of their weekly SMS. For example, they can add a section on healthy eating and healthy lifestyles. MHM fulfills readers' requests and often goes beyond. For instance, in addition to providing tips on healthy eating and lifestyles, it will augment the reader's experience by attaching a shopping list of healthy foods. The monthly print magazine and weekly SMS feeds provide virtually continuous engagement, enabling the magazine's readers to meet their personal goals, and elevating MHM's market position to that of a personal advisor.

Family as the basis of engagement: Moms have a long-standing relationship with Kraft Foods. The company and its products help moms meet one of their most important goals: providing healthy and nutritious meals — breakfast, lunch, and dinner — for the family, especially children. The Kraft community (http://www. kraftrecipes.com/community/main) caters to this need by making the family the focal point of consumer engagement, with discussions and activities related to children's meals, family dinners, holiday entertaining, and programs like *Restaurant Inspired Recipes Priced Right*, which is a collection of recipes that can be easily and affordably replicated at home.[17] Community members not only share recipe ideas and connect with other Moms that have similar needs and preferences, but they also become budget *wi$e*, courtesy all the advice offered by the website.

Causes and values as the basis of engagement: The loss of a loved one to life-threatening diseases like cancer and HIV/AIDS leaves permanent scars. Moved by their own grief and suffering, survivors and caregivers are often moved to do more than just make peace with their own pain. This is especially true in today's world, where collaborative technologies make it infinitely easier for people to reach out and provide support.

Susan G. Komen for the Cure® is the global leader of the cure for breast cancer movement. An outcome of a promise made by Nancy G. Brinker to her sister, Susan G. Komen, who fought a valiant battle against breast cancer, the organization has invested nearly $1.5 billion to find a cure for breast cancer since it began in 1982. It is the world's largest grassroots network of breast cancer survivors and activists working together to save lives, empower people, ensure quality care, and energize science to find a cure for breast cancer.

Fighting for a cause — a cure for breast cancer — offers the organization a strong platform for engagement. The organization engages its many thousand members and volunteers through annual events like the Susan G. Komen Race for the Cure® and through social interactions with other people, such as family members, spiritual advisors, and health care providers in its social networking community called *myKomen*.[18] In the words of Hala Moddelmog, former President and CEO of Susan G. Komen for the Cure®:

> myKomen allows users to share their knowledge, their support, their victories — even virtual hugs — 24 hours a day!

Brand as the basis of engagement: Few material things are less romantic than duct tape! It does not have any of the machismo, romanticism, or show-off appeal of a Harley or a Mini Cooper. The product is not parked proudly outside people's houses, but sits out of sight in garages, toolboxes, and forgotten closets until a need arises, like sealing a pipe, taping a shipping box, or patching a tear in a vinyl surface of a sofa or a suitcase.

That is until Duck, a leading duct tape brand, decided to broaden its appeal by injecting some romance into the product. The big idea was to build an annual contest around prom dresses, to expand the brand's appeal to nontraditional market segments, such as teenagers, by engaging their creativity and imagination. The company developed "Stuck at Prom® Scholarship Contest" challenging contestants to design prom dresses entirely out of duct tape. The company also created a dedicated digital site, where high school kids from all across the United States could submit designs and share video clips of their creations.[19]

For thousands of high school kids participating in the contest, it meant that duct tape effectively graduated from being an invisible forgotten item to becoming a permanent and prominent accessory in their sewing kits. Though only a handful of contest winners earn prize money — winners receive a college scholarship worth \$3,000 — everyone who participates wins at some level. Contest participants feel fulfilled by engaging in a truly out-of-the-box creative task. They also acquire first hand experience and valuable insights into important life skills like teamwork, constructively resolving conflicting ideas, and managing a project — like designing and making a dress entirely out of duct tape! Duck's Stuck at Prom® Scholarship Contest has been resoundingly successful, engaging thousands of high school contestants every year. The creative use of duct tape is a veritable cottage industry. Just Google — *uses of duct tape* — and entertain yourself!

Factors Enabling Engagement

A significant volume of customer engagement takes place in social media, or in company-controlled digital environments. In the foreseeable future, as social technologies and collaborative tools become even more entrenched in customers' daily lives, these environments are likely to account for even a higher proportion of customer engagement. A natural and important question follows. Are there best practices for more effectively fostering, nurturing, and sustaining customer engagement in these environments?

Companies can improve the performance of their customer engagement initiatives in digital environments by paying attention to four factors:

- Intent: Why does the company want to engage its customers?
- Control: Who controls the interaction agenda?
- Participation base: Do all participants have a role?
- Incentives for participation: How is participation rewarded?

Intent: Engagement, Not Sales

Consumers are human beings. So it should not be surprising to discover that they volunteer to interact with companies to meet a variety of personal needs, like social interaction, personal recognition, a chance to try new products, and to exercise their creativity. They don't show up with the intent of helping companies and brands meet their sales or promotion goals.

As discussed in Chap. 2, Wal-Mart learned this lesson the hard way. Their social networking experiment — *The HUB: SCHOOL YOUR WAY* — a networking site for teens, failed within 10 weeks.[20] Among other things, Wal-Mart made the mistake of putting their business interests ahead of the engagement needs of the teens. The company used The Hub to promote its products and stir up enthusiasm for shopping at Wal-Mart. To this end, the company used fake member profiles, a barrage of promotions and advertisements, and older models posing as teens to promote the merchandise. These tactics betrayed Wal-Mart's intent. The emphasis on sales and promotions ran counter to the expectations and interaction needs of the teen audience they were trying to engage.

Controlling Interactions and Agendas: Less Is More

For engagement to be effective, interactions between customers, and between customers and the company, need to be channeled, not controlled. Customers are not corporate assets. Consequently, attempts to fully control the nature, pace, and agenda of customer engagement are likely to backfire. Procter & Gamble's (P&G) successful engagement of teen girls through *Beinggirl.com* provides a sharp contrast to Wal-Mart's unsuccessful attempt at engaging teens through The Hub. The success of P&G's Beinggirl.com, a teen community by girls for girls, can be attributed largely to the company facilitating, but not wanting to control, the engagement. The company recognizes that teenage girls have a lot to contend with — body changes, friendships, family, boys — and that they would rather talk to one another, or someone they trust. So the company wisely stays in the background, encouraging its teen members instead to *Ask Iris's Experts:*[21]

> Our team of super smart medical experts are here to answer all your questions — no matter how embarrassing. They know what you're going through, and chances are, a lot of other girls have your exact same question. So ask Iris' Experts anything. They really know their girl stuff.

Participation: Make Room for Everybody

For meaningful and healthy engagement to occur, everyone participating, or invited to participate, should have a role. Based on researching several different communities, marketing experts Fournier and Lee identify 18 different roles that members can play in a community, such as Storyteller, Supporter, Greeter, and Guide.[22] While members of the Susan G. Komen for the Cure® community, may not play all 18 roles, every member of the community, depending on the situation, the stage-of-life they are at, and their own personal experience, does play different roles, such as advisor, supporter, virtual caregiver, and perhaps most importantly, virtual hugger! Members have the freedom to retain their individuality and the autonomy to choose which role they would like to play on which occasion, a potent formula for brewing vigorous engagement in any environment.

Incentives: Recognition Matters, Money Matters

Despite the passion and interest that customers bring to communities, sustaining engagement over a period of time is not easy. Also, just as in the workplace, where monetary rewards are necessary but not sufficient in sustaining employee motivation, a variety of rewards and incentives that create personal recognition and psychological value for the customer are needed to sustain engagement.[23] Issues related to recognition, rewards, and incentives, for securing customers' participation in collaborative innovation activities will be discussed in greater detail in Chap. 5.

Appendix 4.1 Sample List of Companies Providing Digital Customer Engagement Services

- Blue Kiwi — http://www.bluekiwi-software.com
- BzzAgent — www.bzzagent.com
- Communispace — http://www.communispace.com
- Hyve — http://www.hyve.de
- Jive Software — http://www.jivesoftware.com
- KickApps — http://www.kickapps.com
- Lithium (Salesforce) — http://www.lithium.com
- Ning — http://www.ning.com
- Passenger — http://www.thinkpassenger.com
- Telligent — http://telligent.com/
- Vision Critical — http://www.visioncritical.com

Appendix 4.2 The Mentos-Diet Coke Geyser Experiment

Who would have ever guessed that dropping MENTOS® chewy mints into a bottle of soda would produce an immense viral reaction? Steve Spangler, the pioneer of the experiment, describes the reaction as — "this generation's reaction to vinegar and baking soda".[24]

The reaction, a giant eruption of soda, is both mysterious and sensational. Although kids and teenagers have been having fun dropping candy and mints into soda to release the carbonation for years, it was Steve Spangler's Mentos geyser video from 2005 that started the chain reaction of flying soda. This video can be found on Steve Spangler's website (http://www.stevespanglerscience.com/experiment/00000109). Other sites owned by Fritz Grobe, Stephen Voltz, and EepyBird.com (www.eepybird.com) also carry the video.

The two companies responded very differently when the Mentos-Diet Coke experiment exploded on the Internet in 2006, and the media began requesting interviews.

- Mentos was thrilled. In 2006, when the experiment became news, the brand was spending less than $20 million on advertising. The company estimated that the attention it was getting alone due to viral media effects alone was worth $10 million; what's more they were getting it for free, and wanted the viral wave to continue.
- Coca Cola, on the other hand, was not thrilled at the prospect of their brand being used for entertainment purposes. The company didn't think it was right; and the company objected, for which they were roundly criticized on the web. Consumers were having fun creating their own geysers and running contests. They weren't going to let Coke ruin their party; regardless of what the company felt was the right usage for Diet Coke.

Notes and References

1. (2006, April 3). Adidas' World Cup Shutout. *BusinessWeek.com*. 3978, 106–107. Retrieved October 12, 2009, from http://www.businessweek.com/magazine/content/06_14/b3978079. htm>
2. Parker, M. (2006). Mark Parker's 2006 annual report's letter to the Nike Shareholders. Website: Nikebiz.com. Retrieved December 18, 2009, from http://media.corporate-ir.net/ media_files/irol/10/100529/Areports/ar_06/docs/Mark_Parker_Letter.pdf
3. (2006, March 20). Nike and Google create global online community for people who share a passion for football *Nike News Release*. Website: Nikebiz.com Retrieved February 19, 2010, from http://invest.nike.com/phoenix.zhtml?c=100529&p=irol-newsArticle&ID=1072121& highlight
4. Holmes, S. (2006, July 24). Nike: It's not a shoe, It's a community. In BusinessWeek.com, 3994, 50–50. Retrieved September 25, 2009 from http://www.businessweek.com/magazine/ content/06_30/b3994068.htm
5. Harlistas Latino Rider Journeys. (2010). Website: Harley Davidson.com Retrieved February 28, 2010 from http://www.harley-davidson.com/wcm/Content/Pages/harlistas/harlistas_UGC. jsp?locale=en_US&bmLocale=en_US; Fournier, S. & Lee, L. (2009). Getting brand communities right. *Harvard Business Review*, 87 (4), 1-5-111; Tony LaMonica Story. (2010). Website: Harley Davidson.com Retrieved February 28, 2010, from http://www.harley-davidson.com/wcm/Content/Pages/harlistas/harlistas_UGC.jsp?locale=en_US&bmLocale=en_US#loc=detail/video/894131
6. (2009). Mini Films Mini United at Silverstone. Website: Minifilms.com. Retrieved December 23, 2009, from http://www.minifilms.co.uk/minidvds.html; Dobie, S. (2009, May 22). Mini United at Silverstone. *EVO blogging*. Retrieved December 23, 2009, from http://www.evo. co.uk/news/evonews/235882/mini_united_at_silverstone.html
7. Milligan, P. (2009, December 1). Jack Morton attracts 12,000 visitors to Army recruitment campaign. Website: avinteractive.co.uk. Retrieved December 23, 2009, from http://www. avinteractive.co.uk/News/MostEmailed/970942/Experiential-agency-Jack-Morton-attracts-12000-visitors-Army-recruitment-campaign/; Hepburn, Aden. (2009, April 8). Start Thinking Soldier Campaign. *Digital Buzz Blog*. Retrieved February 19, 2010, from http://www.digitalbuzzblog.com/start-thinking-soldier-campaign-by-the-british-army

8. Timeline. (n.d.). Website: planetquest.com. Retrieved March 4, 2010, from http://planetquest. jpl.nasa.gov/timeline/timeline.html; Website: spacecomm.nasa.gov. About. Retrieved March 4, 2010, from https://www.spacecomm.nasa.gov/spacecomm/

9. Mars Rovers Named "Spirit" and "Opportunity. (2003, June 8). Website: space.com. Retrieved February 19, 2010, from http://www.space.com/missionlaunches/mer_names_030608.html; Be a Part of History. (2003). Website: Lego.com. Retrieved February 19, 2010, from http:// www.lego.com/rovers/

10. Research Meredith Media. (2009). Website: meredithdirectmedia.com. Retrieved December 27, 2009, from http://meredithdirectmedia.com/research; Meredith's Silver Bullet. (n.d.). Communispace. Website: Communispace.com. Retrieved December 23, 2009, from http:// www.communispace.com/assets/pdf/C_Cli_ExecSummary_Meredith_final.pdf

11. (2006–2009). History 2006–2009 the Coca Cola Company. Website: Thecocacolacompany. com. Retrieved February 20, 2010, from http://www.thecocacolacompany.com/ourcompany/ mission_vision_values.html; Robles, P. (2009, 16 March). Coca-Cola: The social media side of life. Blog. Website: eConsultancy.com. Retrieved February 27, 2010, from http://econsultancy.com/blog/3484-coca-cola-the-social-media-sideof-life

12. Expedition 206. (2009, November 16). Website: Thecocacolacompany.com. Retrieved March 5, 2010, from http://www.thecoca-colacompany.com/presscenter/presskit_expedition_206_ press_release2.html

13. Kenora|Torch Relay — Relais de la flame. (2009, June 25). In Facebook. Retrieved February 20, 2010, from http://www.facebook.com/pages/Kenora-Torch-Relay-Relais-de-la-flamme/ 103262297941

14. Chafkin, M. (2009, May 1). Zappos Way of Managing. Inc. 31 (4), 66–73. Retrieved March 5, 2010, from http://www.inc.com/magazine/20090501/the-zappos-way-of-managing.html>

15. Ellen Degeneres Show. (2010). Website: Ellen.warnerbros.com. Retrieved March 5, 2010, from http://community.ellentv.com/; Wagner, L. (2009, December 20). Forum Comment. Website: community.ellentv.com. Retrieved January 3, 2010, from http://community.ellentv. com/profile/LaurieWagner492

16. Butcher, D. (2009, August 29). General Mills uses mobile to reinvigorate Wheaties Brand. In Mobile Marketer. Retrieved December 22, 2009, from http://www.mobilemarketer.com/cms/ news/advertising/3967.html; Mobile Applications. (2009). Website: Menshealth.com. Retrieved December 22, 2009, from http://mobile.mh.co.za/

17. Budget. (2009). In Kraftfoods. Retrieved December 22, 2009, from http://www.kraftfoods. com/kf/Budget/BudgetLandingPage.aspx

18. About Us. (2009). Website: Komen.org. Retrieved February 22, 2010, from http://ww5. komen.org/AboutUs/AboutUs.html; Welcome to myKomen. (2010). Retrieved March 5, 2010, from http://apps.komen.org/mykomen/

19. Daring Duct-Tape Dress Design Finalist. (2008, June 18). In Ducktape Channel on YouTube. Website: YouTube.com. Retrieved December 27, 2009, from http://www.youtube.com/ watch?v=LHIq8LWFjO0

20. Rosmarin, R. (2006, October 3). Wal-Mart's My Space Experiment Ends. Forbes.com. Retrieved February 20, 2010, from http://www.forbes.com/2006/10/02/myspace-walmart-youtube-tech-media-cx_rr_1003walmart.html; Crump, J.W. (2008, December 5). A Look at Failed Social Networks. Bivingsreport. Website: Bivingsreport.com. Retrieved February 20, 2010, from http://www.bivingsreport.com/2008/a-look-at-failed-social-networks/

21. The Scoop. (2010). Website: Beinggirl.com. Retrieved March 5, 2010, from http://www. beinggirl.com/en_US/articleslibrary.jsp; Ask Iris' Experts. (2010). Website: Beinggirl.com. Retrieved March 5, 2010, from http://www.beinggirl.com/en_US/askiris.jsp – Dr. Iris Prager has a Ph.D. in Health Education and is the past President of American Association of Health Education. She answered over 1,000 questions each week on beinggirl.com. At the time of writing, Dr. Prager was preparing to retire, and BeingGirl created a special link for members to "wish Dr. Iris happy goodbyes."

22. Fournier, S. & Lee, L. (2009). Getting brand communities right. *Harvard Business Review*, 87(4), 1–5–111.
23. Schau, J.H., Muniz, A., & Arnould, E. (2009). How brand community practices create value. *Journal of Consumer Research*, 73(5), 30–51.
24. Spangler, S. (2005, September 5). Mentos Diet Coke Geyser. Website: Stevespanglerscience. com. Retrieved February 20, 2010, http://www.stevespanglerscience.com/experiment/00000109; Who is EepyBird? (2005–2009). Website: EepyBird.com. Retrieved March 5, 2010, from http://www.eepybird.com/about.html; Vranica, S. & Terhune, C. (2006, June 12). Mixing Diet Coke and Mentos Makes a Gusher or Publicity. *The Wall Street Journal*, Page B1.

Chapter 5
Respond Externally: Co-creation

"There is a tide in the affairs of men, which, taken at the flood..." The famous lines of Shakespeare are just as relevant here as they were in his play "Julius Caesar". Listening and engagement provide the momentum. But that momentum still needs to be converted to value that will benefit both the customer and the company. The mere desire to collaborate with customers does not guarantee co-creation of value. How do companies harness the creativity and energy of customers? How do they marry this creativity with their own knowledge and resources? Are there specific processes, tools, and technologies that enable and expedite value co-creation?

Collaboration and co-creation are relatively new business practices. Like all new business practices, they are weaving their way through the various stages of diffusion and adoption. While it would be difficult to pinpoint exactly where they are in this cycle, the number of companies using co-creation for new product development, marketing, and innovation has grown steadily over the past 10 years.[1] Answers to the questions posed at the end of the previous paragraph can be found by examining how two companies, Audi and Blizzard Entertainment, convert the momentum they generate through their listening and engagement to innovate and create new value with their customers.

Co-creation Praxis

Audi

Audis are like potato chips with a twist — once you've owned one, you want to own them again, and again. It's not unusual for people in their thirties to be on their second or third Audi. This attachment to the brand has given the company an excellent platform for engaging its drivers, and for its owners to connect and bond with one another. Examples include sponsorships of sports preferred by its customer base, like soccer, alpine skiing, regattas, and golf. The brand has also been very responsive in catering to

G. Bhalla, *Collaboration and Co-creation: New Platforms for Marketing and Innovation*, DOI 10.1007/978-1-4419-7082-4_5, © Springer Science+Business Media, LLC 2011

the driving passions of its owners by sponsoring motor clubs in several countries, like Audi Club – Taiwan, Audi Club of North America, and Audi Club of South Africa.[2]

The opportunity for co-creation presented itself in the form of an important Innovation by a competitor that required a response. In 2001, BMW introduced the driving world to an innovative computer-aided vehicle control system, called the iDrive, in its seven-series model. The market was not impressed, and the response to the iDrive was extremely disappointing.[3] Drivers complained of being over-whelmed; there were too many features, it was difficult to learn, and complicated to operate. The iDrive did not make driving more fun, which was the original goal. Instead, it introduced an unnecessary source of frustration, reducing the overall quality of the driving experience.

Audi needed to respond. But it needed to do something different if it was to avoid repeating the same errors made by BMW. One thing was immediately clear to Audi: designing a competitive console driven solely by its technological prowess was not the way to go. That's what BMW had done, and they had gotten burned. The iDrive may have been an engineering marvel, but was not user-friendly. Audi reasoned that a customer-driven approach would work much better. It would allow the company to address two issues simultaneously:

- What features should be built in to the intelligent drive console?
- How could the console best be designed so that it was perceived to be user-friendly and easy to operate?

Audi created *Virtual Lab*, a walled digital arena, to spark and facilitate the collaboration with a select community of passionate car drivers. The goal was to design and develop a multi-media console that would debut in Audi's new A8 series. The company used several channels, including its website, chat rooms, and social net-working sites (autospiegel.com and audiworld.com) to invite collaborators. For passionate Audi owners, the invitation to collaborate with Audi to co-create a new infotainment console was a dream come true. Over 1,600 drivers from Germany, Japan, and the United States volunteered to sit in the proverbial driver's seat, and work with Audi employees to help design the new console.[4]

The company assembled a team of engineers and marketing professionals to work with the community of customer collaborators. The initial design prototype was developed by the Audi team and was presented as a stimulus to the customers to ignite their creativity. Using virtual technologies, customers could introduce their own feature requirements, and modify the initial suggestions of the Audi team. To make the experience as realistic as possible, Audi used visual and auditory aids such as high caliber graphics and sound sequences. These tools gave sensory feed-back to the collaborators. Through this sensory feedback loop, customers could see and hear the consequences of their design choices. Simultaneously, thanks to the technologies available in the Virtual Lab, customers could also observe and experi-ence the evolution of the console's design. Based on features selected or rejected by individual collaborators, Audi was able to constantly update its understanding of the needs and preference of its collaborators, and reflect this understanding in new designs of the infotainment console.

The new A8 debuted on November 15, 2002. A key feature of the new car was the brand new Multi-Media Interface (MMI), an infotainment console to rival BMW's iDrive. The MMI innovation offered incremental value to Audi owners, allowing them to select several options previously not available, such as customizing suspension setting, checking tire pressure, determining if the car needed to be serviced, tailoring the internal climate of the car for both front and rear passengers, and customizing audio entertainment settings. Unlike the iDrive, drivers felt more in sync with the MMI. They perceived it to be instinctive in its operation and design. Most Audi drivers were able to achieve a high degree of operating familiarity and proficiency with the interface in no more than 10 to 15 minutes, leading critics and experts alike to hail the MMI as an industry leader.

Blizzard Entertainment

There is nothing more damaging to the reputation of a video game manufacturer than glitches, especially if gamers discover them first. Gamers are a tough bunch. They are passionate about their games, intolerant of defects, no matter how small, and have no qualms shouting out their approval or disapproval of a game to the rest of the world. A nod of confidence from marquee gamers can give a significant boost to the sales of new video games. Conversely, thanks to the Internet, chatter about "lame" games, and complaints about slow response on the part of the company to fix problems, can spread like proverbial bush fire in chat rooms, blogs, and rating sites, killing potential interest in the game.

Blizzard Entertainment, makers of World of Warcraft (WoW), the best-selling "massively multiplayer online role-playing game" (MMORPG), is no stranger to the tough, unforgiving world of gamers. Since the early 2000s the company has actively engaged with its brand community to protect the image of its brand and improve the value of its games. Though the company started developing and marketing video games in the early 1990s, it was not until gaming chat rooms and review forums mushroomed on the Internet that Blizzard Entertainment began to actively listen to gamers' conversations.

Blizzard was quick to catch on that for the heavy gamers, MMORPG games are like religion. Players are deeply involved in both the life and the after-life of the game. They actively debate and discuss their likes, dislikes, and preferences for features and characteristics that are cool and awesome. They have ideas, and are vocal in discussing what the next incarnation of the game should look like. To appease the passion of its die-hard gamers, Blizzard organizes annual gatherings called "BlizzCon." Gamers from all over the world flock to the Anaheim Convention Center in Anaheim, California, where BlizzCon has been held since 2005.

At first glance, it may appear that BlizzCon is nothing more than an over-attended jamboree. The 2009 conference attracted more than 20,000 people. But BlizzCon is no jamboree; it's serious business. The attendees come fully armed to take on the establishment on serious issues, such as the status of the gaming industry, emerging technologies, and the future direction of the game, its plot, and characters. Full of vim and vigor, they are a fascinating source of ideas and creativity. Most importantly, they are a failsafe sanity check and a fertile source for co-creation of value for the gamer world and for Blizzard.

At events like BlizzCon and through broadcast invitations on its website, Blizzard Entertainment recruits *heavy hitters* who form the core of the company's co-creation effort. Heavy hitters are expert gamers, who are walking-talking encyclopedias on the game, its history, WoW's worlds, and winning tactics. They are blessed with fatigue-free derrières and can play for hours on end with intense concentration. Blizzard calls its army of collaborators "Beta Testers." This group has one overriding objective — to find glitches and shortcomings in the game's design and the gaming experience, so that the company can fix them before new versions of the game are released. The Beta Testers are provided with video game "keys" with which they access the Beta Testing portal — a specially constructed secure site for playing the game, observing gamers reactions, listening to their feedback, fixing glitches, and refining features of the game. At various times, over 300 players may be interacting with one another in this MMORPG environment. Meanwhile, Blizzard's development team is all eyes and ears as they observe the Beta Testers' many complex moves and listen to the gamers' reactions, comments, and wish lists.[5]

Co-creation helps Blizzard optimize the overall value and gaming experience. Without help from the Beta Testers, delivering on the game's overall promise and gaming experience would be very difficult, if not impossible, for Blizzard's internal development team. Solutions to questions that follow can be found only through collaboration with gamers.

- Is it challenging enough, or can it be made more challenging?
- Is it complex enough to get the adrenalin flowing or too complex for all but the expert gamers?
- Are the winning strategies too plain and obvious, or do they keep the gamer scrambling and hustling?
- Is the diversity and balance of characters, races, and worlds appropriate, or does the game need more diversity?
- What about possible extensions and augmentations: which direction to go, what next, what to add, what to leave out?

Structure of Co-creation

Audi and Blizzard operate in distinctly different market environments. The value and experiences they offer their customers are poles apart. However, despite these obvious differences, the co-creation case studies presented above share common characteristics. For instance, both companies had a concrete co-creation objective. Both deliberately recruited certain types of collaborators to work with. In both cases, collaborators worked with the company's representatives in environments specifically created for the purpose of co-creation. Together, the company and its

Fig. 5.1 Structure of Co-creation

collaborators followed a systematic co-creation process. Finally, in both cases, the contract between the collaborators and the company was clear — all rights to the outcome of co-creation would belong to the company, and collaborators would not receive any monetary payment for their efforts. Being selected to participate in the co-creation exercise was reward enough for the customers.

This section discusses these characteristics of collaboration and co-creation more formally. Collectively, these elements will be referred to as the structure of co-creation. They are presented in Fig. 5.1.

Objectives

Unlike engagement, which can revolve around either general issues (financial security) or specific ones (purity of drinking water), co-creation is always focused and specific. Companies engage in co-creation projects because they want to co-create value with their customers, or other stakeholders.

Most co-creation goals can be classified into one of three categories:

- Generation: Here the company's objective is to solicit ideas, suggestions, and/ or designs, from customers, through contests or open-ended appeals, for later use in the design and development of products and services. Selection, or the short-listing of ideas to develop further, is subsumed under this objective.
- Refinement: In this case, collaborators work with company representatives to refine one or more features or aspects of a target product or service to help enhance the customer's overall experience.
- Creation: Collaborators and the company's professionals work together to develop a prototype of an entirely new product or service. In almost all cases, the prototype needs additional refinement and improvement before it is ready for commercialization.

Case studies illustrating the three categories of co-creation objectives follow.

Generation

Electrolux is a global leader in household gadgets and appliances, selling more than 40 million products to customers in more than 150 markets every year. According to its corporate website, the company bases its innovations on extensive consumer insight, and designs them thoughtfully to meet the real needs of consumers and professionals.

One of these innovations is the Electrolux Design Lab (www.electroluxdesign-lab.com), a forum for generating ideas for new products and services.[6] Established in 2003, Electrolux Design Lab is an annual global design competition open to undergraduate and graduate industrial design students, who are invited to present innovative ideas for household appliances of the future. Over the years, the competition has featured different themes. The contests always culminate with an international press event held in a major city. Previous themes and venues have included:

- Designs for the next 90 years, London, 2009 (to coincide with the company's ninetieth anniversary)
- Designs for the Internet generation, Zurich, 2008
- Green designs, Paris, 2007
- Designs for healthy eating, Barcelona, 2006.

The theme for the 2010 competition, which closed on May 1, and was once again scheduled to culminate in London, was *The 2nd Space Age*. The official brief reached out to potential collaborators with the following appeal:[7]

> Your ideas will shape how people prepare and store food, wash clothes, and do dishes in the homes of 2050 when, according to the UN, 74% of the world's population are predicted to live in an urban environment. Growing populations living in concentrated areas dictate a need for greater space efficiency. This year, special consideration will be given to designers that submit a design within the context of a range or suite of solutions/appliances. Your design ideas should address key consumer requirements; being green, adaptive to time and space, and allowing for individualization.

Refinement

In the Blizzard Entertainment case study, Beta Testers were confronted with a single co-creation objective — to suggest improvements and refinements that would produce a game that, in gamer parlance, would evoke the reaction — "awesome, mind blowing, dude!"

Refinement is also the goal at Nokia's Beta Labs (www.betalabs.nokia.com). Nokia is in the business of connecting people; the company views itself as much more than just a cell phone company.[8] Its website welcomes visitors to a world of mobile music, games, maps, photos, email, and conversations. Nokia built the Beta Labs for shaping the future. It uses the site for two-way sharing with its multitudes of collaborators. The first leg of the sharing takes place when Nokia shares exciting new ideas that the company has been working on with its customers. The second leg of sharing occurs when Nokia invites customers to suggest refinements and improvements to make Nokia's products better.

> We welcome you to suggest ideas that would make existing products better. So if you have an idea of a killer feature that is missing from an application, do share that with us.

To illustrate how refinement is implemented, consider Nokia's Ovi, its main desktop application for synchronizing content between an individual's cell phone and PC, such as downloading maps, backing up data, and updating software. Collaborators can download the Ovi suite, test run its many features, and then provide feedback by taking part in a discussion, writing a review, reporting a bug, or making a suggestion in the space reserved for Ovi on the Beta Labs website. The site is refreshed periodically to provide the latest feedback, updates, and information on key new features to Ovi's community of collaborators. For example, an update posted on the Ovi site on January 21, 2010, for the Nokia Ovi Suite 2.1 version shared the following refinements, new features, and performance improvements with the community:[9]

- Contacts sync with Ovi.com: Keep your contacts safe online
- Video support: Transfer, play, and share your videos
- Get new device applications (Independent Application Delivery, IAD): Keep your device applications up-to-date
- Windows 7 support: Extended support for new operating system versions
- Download Ovi Share library: Get a copy of your Ovi Share content to your computer
- Contacts sync with Mozilla Thunderbird: Support for new, popular desktop PIM applications
- Error fixes and performance improvements
- New languages (Hindi, American English, and Ukrainian).

Creation

In the Audi case discussed at the beginning of the chapter, the co-creation efforts focused on developing physical and tangible value, namely the MMI. But what about the development of services and other intangibles like advertising and customer education materials? Can similar co-creation approaches be used effectively in those cases as well? Let's examine how Frito-Lay used co-creation to develop a ratings-topping, award-winning commercial to crash the Super Bowl ad party.

The season-ending championship game of America's National Football League (NFL), the Super Bowl, is not just a sporting event; it is a pilgrimage. Broadcast live to millions of people in the United States and around the globe, it's a time for partying and rooting for one's favorite team. Without exaggeration, the Super Bowl is really two contests. The first contest takes place between the two football teams in the stadium. The second contest occurs between a multitude of advertisers and their advertising agencies on the TV screen, and on the Internet. Each year advertisers showcase louder, more spectacular ads than the previous years.

So much so, that it is not uncommon for viewers to remember the commercial, but not the brand or advertising company, or to ask in a slightly apologetic confused way, "What was that ad trying to say?" While every company wants to win the jackpot on Super Bowl Sunday, the table stakes are high, and requires deep pockets. *Advertising Age* reports that in 2009 a thirty-second TV spot sold for $3 million! In all 67 spots were sold, netting a grand total of $206.5 million for National Broadcasting Corporation (NBC), which aired Super Bowl XLIII.

In this ferociously aggressive, big spending world of Super Bowl advertising, Anheuser-Busch (Busch), the largest brewing company in the United States, stands like a colossus. For 10 consecutive years, from 1999 to 2008, the self-proclaimed king of beers was the publicly acclaimed king of Super Bowl advertising.[10] It kept topping the ratings charts with memorable hits featuring the famously funny "Frogs," its one-of-a-kind stable of "Clydesdale Horses," and "Hitch Hiker." During these years, USA Today's AdMeter #1 prize, for the best Super Bowl ad was a fixture in the trophy case at Busch's corporate headquarters. The question was not who would win; it was more like who would come second, third, and fourth.

Then Frito-Lay appeared and crashed Busch's Super Bowl party. Everybody knew Busch's winning formula: do all the right things — research the market to death, work with only the best advertising agencies, throw in dollops of humor, and back it with a deep cavernous budget. It was no secret, just very difficult to emulate. Frito-Lay didn't want to emulate Busch – much like Audi didn't want to emulate BMW. The company wanted to do something different. An early adopter of social media, Frito-Lay was very impressed by the talent and creativity of everyday consumers. It decided that the best way to crash the Super Bowl party was by engaging its consumers, and collaborating with them to co-create advertising.

Frito-Lay debuted in the Super Bowl advertising bullring in 2007. The company invited participation by promoting the event on both traditional and social media, like MySpace. Appropriately, it called this initiative, "Crash the Super Bowl." Consumers who wanted to participate and create a "Crash the Super Bowl" video could download a variety of tools from the "Crash the Super Bowl's" toolbox, like Doritos's logos, stock photos of the brand, animations, and even music clips. With these tools, participants could create more polished, professional-looking videos. The company gave "Crash the Super Bowl" some serious legs by making company personnel available for ongoing conversations and ad development assistance. The outcome of the experiment exceeded the brand's expectations. Expecting no more than a few hundred entries, the brand received more than 1,000 thirty-second videos. The company honored its end of the bargain, and aired the winning ad during the Super Bowl XLI.[11]

The contest was repeated in 2008, for Super Bowl XLII, with equally impressive results. Frito-Lay entry generated a great deal of brand buzz. All this momentum generated by Frito-Lay would culminate in the brand achieving the unthinkable in 2009, winning the Super Bowl ad contest. For Super Bowl XLIII in 2010, Frito-Lay upped the ante. The company announced that the contest winner would take home $25,000, and an additional $1 million if the ad won USA Today's Admeter #1 prize. Frito-Lay received more than 2,000 entries. Among them was an entry from two unemployed brothers, Joe and Dave Herbert. They called their commercial, "Free Doritos." Using peer voting, "Free Doritos" was ranked among the top five entries. From this pool of finalists, Frito-Lay selected "Free Doritos" and one other commercial, "Power of the Crunch," as its two official entries to Super Bowl XLIII.[12]

The rest, as they say, is history. "Free Doritos" made viewers laugh, it created a palpable buzz in the e-world, and a huge explosion in the ad world when the next morning it received the first prize based on USA Today's Super Bowl AdMeter ratings. Not only did Frito-Lay soar above every other advertiser, most notably Busch, on Super Bowl XLIII Sunday, it legitimized user-generated content (UGC) as a valued source of advertising material (Box 5.1).

Box 5.1 User-Generated Content Crosses the Chasm with MOFILM

Robert Redford is more than an actor. He is what the business world calls an out-of-the-box thinker, an innovator and entrepreneur, committed to artistic experimentation. Best known for his role in *Butch Cassidy and the Sundance Kid*, he is also the founder of the Sundance Institute, a non profit organization dedicated to the discovery and development of independent artists and audiences, which he helped create in 1981.

What he is not as well known for is MOFILM (www.mofilm.com). Started in early 2007 as an artistic project, MOFILM has grown into a global community of filmmakers working with world's leading iconic brands to create and distribute made-for-mobile content. The organization's mission is to allow creative people from anywhere in the world, with any background, to *get creative, get noticed, and get famous*! Currently, MOFILM works with mobile operators in over 50 countries around the world to distribute content to mobile devices from within the MOFILM community, sharing revenues 50–50 with filmmakers.

MOFILM also runs the world's largest annual mobile film festival in Barcelona, Spain in conjunction with the GSM Association (Groupe Speciale Mobile, a confederation of European Posts and Telecommunications agencies). So in 2009, when the Cannes Lions International Advertising Festival welcomed MOFILM with open arms, it signaled the crossing of the chasm for user-generated content, and its increasing impact on the world of mainstream marketing.

With Frito-Lay's user-generated ad displacing ten-time winner Anheuser-Busch as the king of Super Bowl ads, other members of the M50 (an exclusive fraternity of Chief Marketing Officers — www.w50.com) banded together to tap into the power of UGC. They launched a competition that was chaired by acclaimed director/producer Spike Lee, and culminated at Cannes, the Oscars of the advertising world. Participating brands included AT&T, Best Buy, Doritos, HP, Kodak, Nokia, Unilever's Omo, Philips, Marriott's Renaissance,

---

(continued)

Box 5.1 (Continued)

Telstra, Visa, and Vodafone. The competition gave interested individuals an opportunity to gain exposure to 10 million video, Internet, and mobile viewers worldwide and win more than $120,000 in prizes, and a chance to be on the set of Spike Lee's next production.

The MOFILM website runs user-generated video ad contests to coincide with major film and advertising festivals like The Tribeca Film Festival and the Cannes Lions International Advertising Festival.[13]

Arenas

Just as with engagement, co-creation can also occur in physical or in digital arenas. Several examples shared in this chapter depict co-creation in digital arenas. Audi invited collaborators to Virtual Lab, a digital arena specifically created to help co-create the multi-media interface (MMI). Similarly, Blizzard's Beta Testing portal, the Electrolux Design Lab, and Nokia's Beta Labs are all examples of co-creation occurring in digital spaces. Given the ubiquitous reach of the Internet, and the ever-increasing use of digital technologies ranging from bedside alarm clock radios to the dashboard displays in automobiles, it would be tempting to conclude that all co-creation takes place in digital arenas. However, the world of brick and mortar also offers excellent opportunities for shaping co-creation, as the following example from Pitney Bowes illustrates.

Pitney Bowes: Co-creation in Physical Work Environments

Some companies are so successful in dominating the category in which they operate that they become synonymous with it. For example, when people think of aspirin, they think Bayer, when burger lovers think of ketchup, they think Heinz, and when companies think of postage meters, they think of the industry leader, Pitney Bowes (PB). Founded in 1920, PB is more than just postage meters. Today it is a global leader in mailstream technology, operating in 130 countries, with a portfolio that comprises a wide range of mail and document management solutions and services.

Innovation is one of PB's core competencies and has contributed significantly to the company's growth. The company's approach to innovation is customer-centered, meaning that customer needs and solutions lead the way, not technology. The bulk of PB's collaboration and shared value-creation with customers occurs in real work environments. In 2001, Advanced Concepts & Technologies (AC&T), a division of PB, was reorganized and charged with leading customer-centered innovation. Its mission was to help PB benefit from emerging business opportunities by peering into the future.

Collaboration and co-creation projects at PB always begin with a strategic question.[14] The strategic question that launched *Project Mail Creation*, the case under discussion, was phrased as follows: "How can PB provide value to untapped segments in the low volume batch mailer market, companies mailing less than 50,000 pieces of promotional and informational material per year?"

A two-person team from AC&T, comprising an anthropologist and a software engineer, with assistance pulled in from across the organization as needed, initiated the innovation process by observing customers in their natural work environments. Working with over a dozen companies, both customers and non-customers, PB organized the observation sessions to coincide with mailing activities. During these sessions, PB observers paid special attention to people, processes, tasks, and the flow of the mailing materials to better understand customers' needs.

Following the listening phase, AC&T was able to generate over a dozen different solutions, a mix of products and services. PB approached the customers again, this time to engage them with prototypes of the potential solutions. The prototypes were rough and rudimentary. The main goal at this stage was not to converge on a single solution but to ensure that PB had accurately identified and understood the customer's problems related to batch mailing, and to give the customers an opportunity to suggest refinements to both PB's understanding of the customers' problems and the solutions being offered. The focus was on imagining and estimating the potential effectiveness of the proposed solutions in the actual work environment. Several iterations later, AC&T was ready to take the next step: collaboration with PB's engineering team and its customers. The project was ready to move from imagining to using and testing, to experiencing and refining the proposed solutions in real work environments.

But innovation is messy, and projects rarely move from ideas to finished solutions in straight unbroken lines. PB knows that. For several months while the company worked to refine the customer value proposition, the solutions that had percolated to the top were put on hold while PB waited for its options to mature. A few months later the project was resurrected under a new name: Mail Master. Ideas and prototypes generated by the previous engagement and refinement stages were extensively use-tested with real mail, in real mailing environments. Positive results and learning from the use-testing stage played a significant role in influencing and shaping a new addition to PB's portfolio of solutions and services named AddressRightNow™. The new offering adds value to low volume batch mailing operations through features such as address verification, which results in less returned mail and lower overall mailing costs.

This section has presented examples of co-creation in both digital and physical arenas because both are viable options that can be used depending on the nature of the co-creation task. While it is true that physical environments can't compete with digital spaces on dimensions such as reach, interactivity, connectivity, and scale, there are times when the ability to actually witness customers in action is not a luxury, but a non-negotiable necessity. Consider the following cases:

- Customer teams trying to solving nagging work flow problems
- Managers trying to simplify customer facing tasks to minimize the incidence of service failures
- Parents or teachers interacting with young children to help them learn how to draw.

In instances like this, where the ability to watch context-bound behavior is especially important, the opportunity to be present as an immersive participant is vital, making physical spaces more relevant for collaboration and co-creation.

Collaborators

To say that all customers are not equal in terms of their needs or their consumption potential is to be boringly obvious. But in the context of collaboration and co-creation, the inequality of customers takes on a different meaning. All customers are not equally creative, nor do they have the same desire to collaborate with companies, which raises an interesting question: With whom should a company collaborate? Which customers, or types of customers, should a company recruit for its collaboration and co-creation programs? A discussion on the choices and options available to companies follows.

Companies essentially have two options. The first option is to collaborate with end-users, or customers (hereafter referred to as customers for convenience), who are creative, who have ideas, passion, and energy, but who are not formally trained in the co-creation task. Audi's drivers who collaborated with them in developing the MMI would fall in this category. They were not professionally trained in automotive electronics. The second option is to collaborate with professionals and specialists, people who are formally trained, like scientists, engineers, and computer specialists. TopCoder, a company that will be discussed later in this chapter, falls into this category. Its army of professional software programmers, engineers, and developers collaborate with its clients to help co-create software, systems, and design solutions.

Collaborating with Customers

How does a company or brand decide which customers to select for participation in its co-creation programs?

Brand passion: Most companies prefer to collaborate with customers who have extraordinary passion for their brands. Marmite co-created XO by collaborating with a small group of ardent Marmite lovers (Chap. 2). Harley owners and HOG are more than just motorcycle enthusiasts, they have obsessive love for their bikes and for the life-style that owning a Harley represents (Chap. 4). Earlier in this chapter, we described how Audi collaborated with passionate Audi drivers to co-create the MMI and how Blizzard's WoW aims to deliver an *awesome* gaming experience by collaborating with fanatical gamers.

Customer/segment demographics: Companies also use target audience demographics of attractive or untapped market segments to select participants for collaborative innovation projects. In the Hallmark and Kraft cases, the preferred demographic group is moms, with and without kids (Chaps. 1 and 3). For Mercedes Benz, it is Gen Y customers (Chap. 3). For Electrolux, discussed earlier in the chapter, it is undergraduate and graduate industrial design students. Choosing collaborators based on market segment affiliation is a frequent occurrence in business to business (B2B) settings. Project Mail Creation, described earlier in the chapter, was launched by Pitney Bowes to determine how it could provide value to untapped segments in the low volume batch mailer market.

Lately, experts have recommended that companies also consider the innovation behavior of customers and select only those customers that exhibit a high co-creation potential. In all product categories, there exist a group of individuals who are far ahead of the rest of the rest of the population in terms of their aggressive and early adoption of innovations and their obsessive desire to develop and create solutions where none exist. These individuals are perceived to have high co-creation potential. The general thesis is that by collaborating with high co-creation potential customers companies can improve the overall effectiveness and productivity of their collaborative innovation activities.

Two different, but related, approaches are recommended to determine the co-creation potential of collaborators. Both are based on The Diffusion of Innovation literature, popularized by Everett Rogers, who classified customers into five non-overlapping categories based on their speed of adoption of an innovation.[15] Figure 5.2 depicts these categories, their relative relationship with one another, and their approximate proportion in a population to which an innovation is targeted.

Innovators and early adopters: Innovators and early adopters, as the labels suggest, are most aggressive in seeking out new products and services. They exert a disproportionate influence on an innovation's subsequent diffusion in the rest of the population. To illustrate, consumers who buy new products like Apple's iPad or Google's Android phone within the first few days of their market launch are most likely to be innovators and early adopters. By relying more heavily on their inputs in the value-creation stage, companies hope to pre-build an adoption edge in their innovations, thereby aiming to accelerate post-launch performance in terms of sales and market share. Blizzard was extremely selective in handing keys to its Beta Testing portal to heavy hitters, or Beta Testers for this reason. As described previously, not only are the heavy hitters among the first to buy and try a new game, they are also the most influential in determining the response of the rest of the gamer market. Positive reviews from heavy hitters can lead to an exponential surge in sales; negative recommendations, on the other hand, generally cause sales to limp along.

Lead users: Eric von Hippel is credited with pioneering the concept of lead users.[16] Just like innovators and early adopters, lead users are also ahead of the majority,

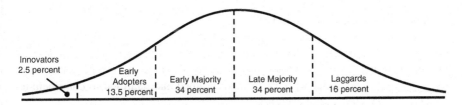

Fig. 5.2 Diffusion of Innovation Categories

Fig. 5.3 Lead Users and Early Adopters

but there's a twist. The two key differences between lead users and early adopters are that lead users are ahead of the majority with respect to an important trend and they have a vested interest in finding a solution to their need because no solution yet exists! Despite the elegance of the preceding explanation, identifying and recruiting lead users for collaborative innovation projects continues to be a challenging proposition. Figure 5.3 depicts the position of lead users relative to early adopters on the diffusion of innovation continuum.

Lead users are a highly attractive co-creation resource because they are always looking to develop solutions to solve their own needs. Viewed from the perspective of innovation adoption, this behavior is invaluable, as it lowers the probability of market failure. The mountain biking case study discussed in Chap. 1 is an excellent example of lead users at the leading edge of a yet-to-be formed mass market. Nokia Beta Labs, discussed earlier in the chapter, also wishes to collaborate with lead-users. Here's how it announces its intentions on its website:

> Nokia Beta Labs is a lead-user community. While this site is open for all, it is not intended for everyone. Let us do a quick quiz:
>
> Which of the following applies to you?
>
> - I own a relatively new and advanced Nokia device
> - I'm willing to tolerate rough edges, – to get my hands on bleeding edge cool stuff
> - I often get ideas on how to improve the gizmos I'm using
> - I want to make a difference — and I am not afraid to share my opinions
>
> We do not turn anyone away, but if most of the list items didn't fit you, this community might not suit you particularly well. Don't get us wrong, we're happy to see you here — we are just not sure you would enjoy it.[17]

Collaborating with Professionals

As mentioned earlier in this section, an alternative to collaborating with end-users or customers is collaborating with professionals — who may or may not be end-users or customers — but who are formally trained and qualified to contribute to the goals of the co-creation exercise.

Recaro: When aircraft manufacturers and airline operators like Boeing and Lufthansa embark on co-creation programs to develop aircraft cabin interiors, they work with companies like Recaro and its team of professionals. Recaro is a top-notch aircraft-seating manufacturer that has won several awards for its quality and innovative designs.[18] The company and its staff of engineers and designers are formally trained in disciplines that drive effective and aesthetic design, such as material selection, structural integrity, and ergonomics.

Topcoder: The website of Topcoder, the world's largest community of competitive software developers, proudly proclaims, "We've been *crowdsourcing* since before there was a name for it." And they are right. Topcoder's clients – companies like AOL, ESPN, Ferguson, Geico, and LendingTree – collaborate with the company's worldwide freelance software development community to co-create software ranging from something as simple as a webpage to full-blown complex enterprise resource planning (ERP) systems.[19]

When companies engage with TopCoder, they engage with a global community of thousands of programmers, developers, software architects, graphic artists, and other talented individuals who are formally trained in their disciplines. Depending on the task, different groups of TopCoder professionals collaborate with the company's clients to co-create unique solutions and experiences. For example:

- If a client has a programming need, it collaborates with professional coders.
- If its need is component design and development, TopCoder's best developers battle it out.
- If a company or an individual wants to create logos, webpages, banner ads, flash animations, and application UI's, then they collaborate with Topcoder's army of professional graphic designers.

Tools and Processes

Co-creation doesn't just happen. It must be organized, managed, and facilitated. A group of customers or professionals — their passions, interests, and energy notwithstanding — are at best mere potential for value-creation. In order for this potential to materialize, collaborators need tools and processes to convert their creativity to tangible value. While both tools and processes are necessary, the relative emphasis between them will vary depending on the co-creation challenge.

In certain cases, tools may be easily available, resulting in processes taking center stage. To illustrate, members of TopCoder's global development community are professionals, and as such have easy and open access to tools for building software or applications, such as Linux, Java, Visual C++, VM Ware, PHP, and Dreamweaver. Consequently, TopCoder spends its energies on managing the process of co-creation, rather than worrying about providing tools to its collaborators.

In other instances, providing collaborative tools may take priority because without them the co-creation event would remain grounded. In the Audi example, it was the right mix of tools, such as visual and auditory aids, high-resolution graphics, and realistic sound sequences, that enabled the collaborators to become more effective co-creators. Frito-Lay's "Crash the Super Bowl" contest drew a large number of contestants and entries, mainly because the company made it easy for customers to submit an entry, even if they had no previous video-making experience. Customers wishing to participate in the "Crash the Super Bowl" contest were provided with a full range of video-making tools, such as brand logos, stock photos, and sound clips.

Co-creation Processes

A sample of co-creation processes inherent in the various cases presented in the book until now is presented in Table 5.1. Despite the different names used to describe them, these processes often overlap and share the same conceptual and methodological foundations. Some of them, like the lead-user process, have been discussed explicitly. Others, like empathic design, have been presented implicitly through the value-creation dynamics of select case studies.

One specific process not yet discussed is Innovation Jams.[20] Pioneered and made popular by IBM, Innovation Jams are large-scale Internet-enabled brainstorming events that focus the creative energy of participants on complex issues, such as:

- Identifying business opportunities for placing future strategic bets
- Building businesses around customer solutions rather than technologies
- Transforming an organization's culture.

Table 5.1 A Sample of Co-creation Processes

Process description	Case study
Lead-user design: Collaboration and co-creation fueled and driven primarily by lead users	• Mountain biking • Nokia Beta Labs
Contextual/user design: Co-creation relies on processes that incorporate deep ethnography, contextual observation, and the use of prototypes	• Pitney Bowes • Audi's MMI console
Participatory design: Similar to user design; co-creation emphasizes involving all relevant stakeholders to ensure the end result meets their needs and is usable	• Recaro, Boeing, and Lufthansa: Aircraft cabin interior design
Empathic design: Similar to user and participant design; co-creation emphasizes observation of the emotional aspects of user-product relationships	• Blizzard Entertainment, World of Warcraft
Crowdsourcing: The crowd or the market is the main contributor to co-creation	• Top-coder; Frito-Lay, "Crash the Super Bowl" contest

The concept of jamming, whether at IBM or at other organizations is not new; John Kao's book on business creativity and innovation is called *Jamming*.[21] What is new is the magnified scale on which effective collaboration can occur, due to the Internet. Taking inspiration from jazz jams, which value listening, improvising, and pushing boundaries as much as they do raw skill with an instrument, innovation jams attempt to push the boundaries of current solutions by unleashing the collaborative imagination and creativity of jam participants. An example of a jam conducted in early 2010 follows.

- Global eco-efficiency: From January 27 to 29, 2010, IBM conducted a by-invitation-only jam to generate a dialogue on energy, the environment, and sustainability. The web-based event provided an unrivaled opportunity for thousands of public and private sector sustainability leaders from around the world, to pool their knowledge and experiences through a series of focused discussions and exchanges of best practices with one another, and with acknowledged subject matter experts. The jam focused on topics like Green IT, Smarter Industries-Smart Cities, and the New Work Place.

Naming conventions for jams tend to be quite simplistic; their names often broadcast their mission. For example, culture jams brainstorm on issues related to organizational culture, and green jams brainstorm on issues related to the environment. Of late though, several organizations have started to use the word "jams" quite loosely. So we feel a friendly warning is in order. For example, when the U.S. state of Vermont organized Vermont 3.0 Innovation Jam on October 26, 2009, what it was really referring to was a one-day event featuring exhibitions, technology demos, learning workshops, and career advice. Collaboration and co-creation, in the way we discuss it in this book, was not on the menu![22]

Co-creation Tools

The Audi and Blizzard Entertainment case studies discussed at the beginning of this chapter illustrate the value of tools in enabling effective implementation of co-creation programs: Virtual Lab in the case of Audi, and the special portal for Blizzard's Beta Testers. The relevance and applicability of different tools will vary depending on the co-creation objective being pursued. Co-creation tools help a company play three key roles; connect with customers' ideas, select which ideas to pursue, and then convert the selected ideas into tangible customer value.

At the front end of the co-creation continuum, the emphasis is on generation and selection of ideas. Consequently, tools like listening (Blizzard, Pitney and Bowes), dedicated websites (Nokia Beta Labs), and contests (Frito-Lay, Electrolux) are frequently used to help companies connect with customers' ideas.

Once ideas are generated, the task of selecting which ones to pursue for development remains. Companies will usually rely on a mix of collaborator input, like voting, and their own judgment to determine which ideas to take to development. An interesting forum for jointly addressing the generation and selection of ideas is prediction or idea markets. In these markets, collaborators bid up or down the value of ideas based on their attractiveness, very much like traders bid up or down the prices of stocks on a stock market. These markets have existed outside the corporate world for more than two decades. For example, since 1988, the Iowa Electronic Markets has predicted presidential election results more accurately than many high profile pollsters.[23] Hollywood Stock Exchange (HSX) is another prediction market that operates like a stock exchange, bidding up or down the value of a picture or an actor. HSX traders (collaborators) were virtually flawless in picking Oscar winners in March 2010 (Box 5.2). In recent years, several companies like HP, Motorola, IBM, GE, and Nokia have experimented with these markets to improve the quality of their internal forecasts and decision-making. However, the full potential of these markets in co-creating value with customers has yet to be realized.

Once ideas are selected, the focus shifts on development, refinement, and commercialization. The focus, therefore, is on tools like simulation, experimentation, toolkits, and prototypes that allow the company to move speedily from idea to the development of the final value proposition. A brief discussion on each of these tools follows.

Simulation: These technologies have been instrumental in transforming innovation from a *show and tell* world, to a *show, ask, and suggest* world.[24] Imagine the reaction of collaborators if Audi would have merely described its MMI console, rather than let its collaborators experience it in the Virtual Lab. The majority of customer responses would probably have been: "great, cool, hmm, stinks, or nothing here that really wows me." Not enough for Audi to build a winning MMI. Simulation technologies allowed Audi drivers to experience the MMI in a virtual environment and make productive suggestions on how it could be refined and improved.

Play and experiment: Approved collaborators can download Beta applications like Ovi, from the Nokia Beta Labs website, and play with it. It is only after they have had sufficient time to experience the software and its features through play that the collaborators can help Nokia refine, improve, and re-create specific aspects of the software. How effective would Blizzard's heavy hitters be if the ability to play were omitted from the co-creation agenda? Without the ability to play and experiment with the actual game in the Beta Testing portal, Blizzard's Beta Testers would be seriously handicapped in helping improve the gaming experience of World of Warcaft; their contributions would hardly be game changing!

Toolkits: These uniquely featured technologies and design kits allow companies to effectively share the responsibility of value-creation with customers. International Flavors and Fragrances (IFF) is an accomplished user of tool kits. The company has developed a Consumer Fragrance Thesaurus (CFT), which is an easy-to-use, interactive perfumer tool for refining and creating new fragrance ideas. The CFT is a database of fragrances that allows the company's creative staff and its clients to collaboratively determine which fragrances to develop further, based on the product's ability to create a specific mood experience for the customer. Following this, IFF's creative staff can focus on refining the fragrance

---

Box 5.2 HSX Traders Sizzle at Predicting the Oscar Winners

The 82nd Academy Awards, better known as the Oscars, was not just a big night for Katherine Bigelow; she became the first woman ever to win the Oscar for the Best Director. It was also a big night for traders in the Hollywood Stock Exchange (HSX). They picked six of the eight winners correctly, demonstrating yet again the wisdom of crowds and the power of collaboration.[25]

Best Picture
Winner — *Hurt Locker*. HSX traders picked correctly; initial trading favored James Cameron's *Avatar*, but late trading put *Hurt Locker* over the top.

Best Director
Winner — Katherine Bigelow. HSX traders picked correctly; traders were betting on history being made.

Best Actress
Winner — Sandra Bullock for *The Blind Side*. HSX traders picked correctly; the race between Meryl Streep and Sandra Bullock was close.

Best Actor
Winner — Jeff Bridges for *Crazy Heart*. HSX traders picked correctly; no contest.

Best Supporting Actress
Winner — Mo'Nique for *Precious*. HSX traders picked correctly.

Best Supporting Actor
Winner — Christoph Waltz for *Inglourious Basterds*. HSX traders picked correctly.

Best Original Screenplay
Winner — Hurt Locker. HSX traders picked Inglourious Basterds.

Best Adapted Screenplay
Winner — *Precious*. HSX traders picked *Up in the Air.*

---

for market launch, and suggesting additional commercial applications. The result of using this toolkit is increased speed to market, and a better, more interesting fragrance that can be used by clients and their customers to co-create a variety of fragrance experiences, such as perfumes, bath gels, room and air fresheners, and laundry detergents.

Prototypes: These are the lingua franca of development and innovation. They do for innovation what horns (saxophones, trumpets) do for music; they give innovation a voice. Since people always react better to things that evoke their senses, prototypes, no matter how crude or one-dimensional, help make the migration from ideas to solutions more tangible. Prototypes played a key role in helping the Pitney Bowes team respond to a very general strategic question: "How do we add value to low volume batch mailers of information and promotional materials?" Prototypes also enabled Marmite's ardent lovers to converge on the final formulation for XO, its packaging, presentation, and labeling.

Contracts

There are very few situations in life where the "what's in it for me" rule does not apply. Collaborative innovation is no exception — What's in it for the collaborators? Why should they part with their effort and time? The picture painted by popular books, blogs, and media depicting customers stampeding to participate in collaboration and co-creation programs doesn't help. True, sometimes there is a stampede. In certain parts of the world, like China, electronic queues begin at least two weeks before Blizzard starts awarding Beta Testing keys to heavy hitters. But this should not mislead us into believing that customer collaboration operates independent of incentives.

Customer passion notwithstanding, collaboration and co-creation is a formal business process that requires contracts if it is to function effectively. As Charles Leadbeater emphasizes in his book *We-Think*, hippie communes is not an apt metaphor for collaboration and co-creation.[26] Collaborators need incentives and promises to part with their effort and time. Clay Shirky makes the same point when he declares that the promise is the essential piece that convinces a customer to become an active collaborator.

> Everyone already has enough to do, every day, and no matter what you may think of those choices ("I would never watch that much TV," "Why are they at work at ten p.m.?") those choices are theirs to make. Any new claim on someone's time must offer some value, but more important, it must offer some value higher than something she already does, or she won't free up the time.[27]

Consequently, the naïve belief that collaborators are driven by altruistic motives needs serious refinement. Jumping to the other end of the spectrum and boldly declaring that collaborators are only in it for the money is also not correct. Reality lies somewhere in between, and is more nuanced than either altruism or financial gain. A variety of contracts, some explicit and some implicit, some benefiting the individual, others benefiting an organization or cause they support, have proved to be strong incentives for customers to part with their time, effort, and creativity, as illustrated by the examples that follow.

Self-image: Moms don't participate in Hallmark's Circles of Conversation communities for monetary or material gains. In fact, they sign a legal document giving away any and all rights to ideas and monetary gains that materialize as a result of their interaction with Hallmark. Moms participate in Hallmark's communities because of how it makes them feel about themselves. Being asked for advice and opinions, being heard and taken seriously, and seeing their ideas implemented fills them with a sense of pride and accomplishment.

Belonging: Sometimes the mere ability to belong to a group and be affiliated with its activities is reward enough. Certain groups, like the Harley Owner's Group (HOG), Audi drivers, and Blizzard gamers wear their group identity as a badge of honor. The act of being invited to collaborate and co-create is incentive enough to participate.

Consumption: The reward of being the first to try new products and emerging technologies should not be underestimated. It is this desire to be the first to try, and subsequently own, new products, that drives customers to websites like Nokia Beta Labs and to co-creation clinics for the Mini Electric. The reward of early trial, adoption, and ownership is a powerful incentive for innovators to offer their effort and time.

Need for a Solution: The need for a solution is a potent motivator for collaborating. Lead users are attractive resources for innovation precisely for this reason. They are looking for solutions before actual markets come into existence. It was the need for a solution that led bikers speeding downhill on fat-tire bikes to pool their resources and develop a specialized mountain bike. It was also the need for a solution that led users and developers to collaborate with Sun to refine and improve the Java platform, which ultimately led to the co-creation of Java 5.

Supporting Causes: Supporting a cause, whether it is finding a cure for breast cancer, or fighting global warming by buying green products, is a powerful incentive to offer time and effort. In the Susan G. Komen for the Cure® case study discussed in Chap. 4, individuals experienced multiple rewards, like increased self-worth, the reward of affiliation, and the knowledge that they were offering time and effort for a noble cause, namely finding a cure for breast cancer.

Monetary Rewards: Money has been and continues to be an important motivator for participating in collaboration and co-creation activities. TopCoder winners receive prize money, as do winners in the Electrolux design lab contest. Even companies like Hallmark, where the rewards for collaboration are mainly psychological, offer some form of monetary rewards in the form of coupons and sweepstakes prizes. Dr. Peter H. Diamandis, a key figure in the development of the personal spaceflight industry, is a staunch believer in prize-based competitions. His X Prize Foundation is built entirely around prize money. According to the organization's philosophy, radical breakthroughs for the benefit of humanity are best brought about by contests driven by prize money. McKinsey & Company agrees with Dr. Diamandis.

In a special report dedicated to the subject, McKinsey recommends that prize-based competitions be part of the toolkit of many of today's philanthropists. They believe that prize-based competitions are unique and powerful in producing global change because of the way in which they simultaneously mobilize talent and capital.[28]

Notes and References

1. Schau Jensen, H., Muñiz, A., & Arnould, E. (2009, September). How brand community practices create value. *Journal of Marketing Research.* 73, 30–51.
2. Holt, Doug. (2004). *How Brands Become Icons: The Principles of Cultural Branding.* Boston: Harvard Business Press; In Audi Club Taiwan. (n.d.). About page. Retrieved November 12, 2009, from http://forum.audiclub.com.tw/; In Audi Club of North America. (n.d.). About page. Retrieved November 13, 2010, from http://www.audiclubna.org
3. Brauer, K. (2004, July 8). Why iDrive Won't Fly. *Edmunds.com.* Retrieved February 21, 2010, from http://www.edmunds.com/news/column/carmudgeon/102470/article.html
4. Fuller, J., Hienerth, C. (2004 Autumn). Online consumer groups as co-innovators: Virtual integration of community members into new product development. *European Business Forum.*
5. Website: Blizzard Entertainment. (2009, February 17). Blizzcon®2009 Tickets on Sale May 16. Retrieved May 5, 2009, from http://www.blizzard.com/us/press/090217.html; In Slashdot. (2008, October 15). Blizzard Answers Your Questions – From BlizzCon. Retrieved January 1, 2010, from http://interviews.slashdot.org/story/08/10/15/1639237/Blizzard-Answers-Your-Questions-From-Blizzcon>
6. Website: Electrolux. (n.d.). Design Lab Page. Retrieved December 12, 2009, from http://www.electroluxdesignlab.com
7. Website: Electrolux. (2010, February 17). Design in Central and Easter Europe. Retrieved February 24, 2010, from http://designeast.eu/2010/02/17/electrolux-design-lab-2010-the-2nd-space-age/
8. Website: Nokia. (n.d.) Open Labs Page. Retrieved December 14, 2009, from http://events.nokia.com/openlab/
9. Website: Nokia. (n.d.) Ovi Page. Retrieved January 21, 2010, from http: //http://betalabs.nokia.com/apps/nokia-ovi-suite-20
10. Horovitz, B. (2009, February 4). Two Nobodies from Nowhere' Craft Winning Super Bowl Ad. *USA Today.* Retrieved November 14, 2009, from http://www.usatoday.com/money/advertising/admeter/2009admeter.htm
11. In Associated Content. Huber, JA. (2007, February 4). Review of Doritos "Live the Flavor" Super Bowl XLI Commercial." *Associated Content.* Retrieved January 3, 2009, from http://www.associatedcontent.com/article/141438/review_of_doritos_live_the_flavor_super.html?cat=9
12. Website: Frito-Lay's Corporate Homepage. (2008, September 24). Dorito's Puts Up $1M for Consumer Created Doritos Commercial that Beats Seasoned Ad Pros During Super Bowl XLIII. Retrieved October 11, 2009, from http://www.fritolay.com/about-us/press-release-20080924.html; Petrecca, L. (2007, June 21). Madison Avenue Wants You! (or at least your videos). *USA Today.* Retrieved January 3, 2009, from http://www.usatoday.com/printedition/money/20070621/cannes_cover.art.htm; In Associated Content. Huber, JA. (2007, February 4). Review of Doritos "Live the Flavor" Super Bowl XLI Commercial." *Associated Content.* Retrieved January 3, 2009, from http://www.associatedcontent.com/article/141438/review_of_doritos_live_the_flavor_super.html?cat=9
13. Sachs, M. (2009, June 5). UGC Debuts at Cannes. Ampersand. Retrieved March 29, 2010, from .http://blogs.hillandknowlton.com/ampersand/ugc-debuts-at-cannes/; (2009, June 21–27). Cannes U12 Competition. *MOFILM.* Retrieved March 28, 2010, from http://www.mofilm.com/competitions/cannes2009

14. All information for the Pitney Bowes case study was obtained through telephone conversations with Alexandra Mack and Austin Henderson and from documents shared by them.

15. Rogers, E. (1967). *Diffusion of Innovations*. Charlottesville: Free Press.

16. Website: Eric Von Hippel Homepage. Lead User Project Videos. Retrieved August 23, 2009, from http://web.mit.edu/evhippel/www/tutorials.htm; Von Hippel, E. (2006). *Democratizing Innovation*. Cambridge: The MIT Press; Figure 5.3 is also adapted from materials available on the above referenced website.

17. Website: Nokia Beta Labs. (2009, February 16). Kudos for a Clean Description of the Problem. Retrieved March 28, 2010, from http://betalabs.nokia.com/apps/ovi-maps-30-beta-for-mobile/bugreport/not-enough-memory-to-start-application

18. Website: PR Hub. (2009, March 31). Crystal Cabin Award 2009 Hamburg: Boeing, Lufthansa — Technik, B/E Aerospace and Recaro are Winners. Retrieved February 24, 2009, from http://blog.taragana.com/pr/crystal-cabin-award-2009-hamburg-boeing-lufthansa-technik-be-aerospace-and-recaro-are-winners-783/

19. Website: TopCoder. (n.d.). About. Retrieved January 13, 2010, from http://topcoder.com/home/

20. All materials on the IBM Jams were obtained through telephone conversations with Liam Cleaver and from documents shared by him.

21. Kao, J. (1997). *Jamming: The Art and Discipline of Business Creativity*. New York, NY: Harper Paperbacks.

22. Website: Vermont 3.0. (2009, August 18). Save the date: Innovation Jam, October 26. Retrieved January 14, 2010, from http://www.vermont3.com/2009/08/save-the-date-innovation-jam-october-26.html

23. What is the IEM? (n.d.) *In Iowa Electronic Markets*. Retrieved May 2, 2010, from http://www.biz.uiowa.edu/iem/index.cfm

24. Schrage, M. (1999). *Serious Play: How the World's Best Companies Simulate to Innovate*. Boston: Harvard Business Press.

25. Website: Hollywood Stock Exchange. (2010, March 8).Traders Predicted the 82nd Academy Awards. Retrieved March 28, 2010, from http://www.hsx.com/blog/view.php?id=401

26. Leadbeater, C. (2009). *We Think: Mass Innovation, Not Mass Produced*. London, ENG: Profile Books

27. Shirky, C. (2008). *Here Comes Everybody: The Power of Organizing Without Organizations*. New York, NY: Penguin Press.

28. Website: XPRIZE Foundation. (n.d.). Overview. Retrieved February 19, 2010, from http://www.xprize.org/x-prizes/overview; 2009, March 3). And the winner is.... *The McKinsey Report*. http://www.mckinsey.com/App_Media/Reports/SSO/And_the_winner_is.pdf

Chapter 6
Respond Internally: Organizational Alignment

There is no such thing as a free lunch, especially when it comes to designing and implementing collaboration and co-creation programs. Call it what you may — crowdsourcing, wikinomics, wisdom of crowds, or we-think — it is fanciful to believe that collaborative innovation projects happen spontaneously, with a minimum amount of effort or organization. Penguin Publishing discovered this the hard way when it tried producing a book relying exclusively on the ability of volunteer authors to self-organize and synchronize their contributions. As Box 6.1 illustrates, a million penguins enthusiastically thrashing away on computer keyboards, on their own are unlikely to produce literature to rival Shakespeare, let alone best him.[1]

Skeptics may point to the August 2008 Business Week special double issue on workplace challenges, which relied on user-generated content (UGC), with readers contributing ideas and content. However, a team of editors and experts worked diligently behind the scenes to organize the diverse and sometimes conflicting contributions into a cohesive, easy-to-read informative magazine. The special issue didn't just materialize spontaneously, without organization and without effort.[2]

Let's revisit Dr. James Murray and the Oxford English Dictionary (OED) co-creation project discussed in Chap. 1. Thousands of English-speaking volunteers collaborated to create the great dictionary. This time, however, let's examine the project from a different perspective. It took 70 years to print the original ten volumes. Had it not been for Dr. Murray's personal contributions as a philologist, editor, and indefatigable organizer, perhaps it would have taken longer. Consider Dr. Murray's investments in time and effort alone:

- Finding a base from which to launch this effort; before Oxford University agreed, both Macmillan and Cambridge Press had rebuffed Dr. Murray
- Identifying the 200+ books to be read; organizing them by the century in which they were written; procuring copies of rare books to make them available to volunteer readers; and having a follow-up system to make sure that readers returned the books on completing their task
- Formulating a precise submission format for entries: every word should be written at the top left, with the date just below it; followed by name of the

G. Bhalla, *Collaboration and Co-creation: New Platforms for Marketing and Innovation*, DOI 10.1007/978-1-4419-7082-4_6, © Springer Science+Business Media, LLC 2011

Box 6.1 A Million Penguins Go to Sleep

On March 7, 2007, a million penguins were asked to stop writing and put their pencils down. The Penguin wikinovel experiment had come to a close.

The project was an experiment to determine whether crowdsourcing or wisdom of the crowds worked in artistic fields, such as writing a novel, without a central organizing and editing body. There was evidence that it had enjoyed some success in a few artistic fields. For example, TV programs are often written by a team of programmers and film endings are often edited and revised based on audience reaction. But it had never been tried to co-create a novel. The project posed some probing questions:

- Can a group of people develop a believable fictional voice?
- How would the plot evolve? What sort of coherent trajectory would it develop if different people had different ideas about how the story should end, or even begin?
- Would it be possible for writers to leave their egos at the door?

Sponsored jointly by Penguin UK and De Montfort University, Leicester, UK, the novel was organized into sections, like "The Half Lotus Begins to Flower" and "Murderers and Millionaires," for ease of editing. Potential collaborators were also provided with technical and ethical guidelines.[3]

Did it work? Can a collective really write a novel? Here's an excerpt from the novel itself:

> The man was clearly mad! No rules? It would never work! You may as well get penguins to write a novel. (from the wikinovel)

In the words of Jeremy Ettinghausen, Digital Publisher at Penguin:

> I guess the answer has to be a qualified maybe — clearly opening this experiment up to 'the whole world' caused problems — we had vandals, pornographers, spammers and any number of people who had such differing ideas about what would make a good novel that a real sense of cohesiveness was always going to be hard to achieve.

---

author and title of the cited book, the page number, and the full text of the sentence being quoted

- Having large numbers of assistants to sort incoming entries, and pigeon holes to store them
- Above all, having unlimited patience to deal with volunteers' questions like "Does every single use of the word *the* within any one book require an illustrative quote?"

The purpose of citing the Penguin, Business Week, and OED examples is not to criticize one or praise the other. It is to reaffirm that while it is possible for several thousand volunteers to collaborate and co-create value, it does need the guiding hand of organization. A formal authority — like an editor, in the case of Business Week and OED, or a facilitating group of people in the case of companies — is needed to select contributions that are valid and valuable and reject those of questionable quality. With this understanding in mind, this chapter will focus on investments organizations need to make in culture, structure, and processes to implement the Listen-Engage-Respond framework.

The discussion opens by studying two companies: Dell and Threadless. They provide an interesting contrast. Dell is a recent adopter, having embraced collaboration and co-creation to solve its vexing product and customer service problems. It's now a way of life at Dell. For Threadless, on the other hand, co-creation is part of its DNA. The company has lived and breathed collaboration from the day it came into existence.

Dell Embraces Customer Collaboration and Co-creation

Chap. 2 described briefly how Dell used the Listen-Engage-Respond framework to first understand the service problems its customers were experiencing, next to engage its customers to invite and explore solutions, and finally to work with them to develop and implement a sub set of the proposed solutions. Let's go behind the scenes for a more detailed look at how Dell achieved this transformation, from "Dell Sucks," to being a *best-in-class example* of co-creating value with customers.

Dell's service problems bubbled over in the summer of 2005, with Jeff Jarvis venting his frustrations over his encounters with Dell's technical support. In his blog entitled "Dell Sucks," Jarvis recounts the numerous emails and calls he made just to try to get some help.[4] Unfortunately for Dell, Jarvis was no ordinary blogger; he was a *Business Week* correspondent, whose blog, BuzzMachine, attracts thousands of readers. Spurred on by his blog, readers began posting comments sharing their own frustrations with Dell's technical support. Customers even resorted to activism, complaining against Dell with the Better Business Bureau, and using personal blogs like *IhateDell, DellHell, DellLies* to voice their irritation.

To compound problems, Dell's service inadequacies were written up in a series of magazine and newspaper articles.[5] Media reports highlighted problems like customers being switched between customer service agents and difficulty in understanding the English accents of service agents. With customer discontent reaching a crescendo by early 2007, Dell began implementing significant initiatives to improve product quality, resolve customer support issues, and address negative publicity. However, the computer manufacturer was acutely aware that merely reducing wait times and transfer rates between service agents and customers was not going to be enough to win back disgruntled customers, and regain lost market share. Customers were not going to reward Dell for getting the basics right. Dell had to do something extra to regain lost ground.

Dell's first step in going the proverbial extra mile was to create the official Dell Blog, "Direct2Dell." Through this official blog, Dell was able to demonstrate that it was listening to customer complaints. The company was also able to use the blog to answer questions, address thorny issues, and connect customer problems with solutions in an efficient way. However, this official blog did not offer Dell the opportunity to engage customers in any significant and meaningful way. Nor did it allow the company to demonstrate that it was serious about implementing customers' ideas and suggestions.

In order to overcome these limitations, Dell created a customer community, IdeaStorm, in February 2007. This community offered Dell the opportunity to listen, engage, and respond to its customers. It had the full support of senior management. Dell assigned full-time staffers to manage the community, listen to and participate in customer conversations, engage customers on their ideas and suggestions, explore potential solutions, share insights with the rest of the company, and follow through with implementation to resolve customer complaints and service problems.[6]

In the IdeaStorm community, customers have a voice at all stages of the value-creation continuum. Registered community members can:

- Voice their opinions and share ideas on how Dell can improve its customer service and refine its product features
- Read the ideas of other community members and engage them and the company on the pros and cons of these ideas
- Vote up an idea, if they like it, or vote down an idea, if they don't like it.

Dell's goal is to be totally transparent in how it deals with the community. It provides community members with a biweekly update that presents the status of ideas and actions it intends to take, including details on which ideas will not be implemented, along with a rationale for the decision.

A note, *IdeaStorm Recap — 1/22/2010,* posted on the IdeaStorm site by Dell staffer Vida K provides an excellent ringside view of the effort and organization required to implement co-creation initiatives. Relevant contents of the note are reproduced in Fig. 6.1.

Threadless: Built on Collaboration and Co-creation

Let's switch now to Threadless, a company built on collaboration and co-creation. Founded in 2000 by Jake Nikell and Jacob De Hart, the company is headquartered in Chicago, Illinois, and is a division of SkinnyCorp. Threadless is both a company and a community. Threadless, the company, offers a collaboration and co-creation platform through its website (www.threadless.com) that enables its online community of over 1 million members to design, sell, and purchase T-shirts. With the exception of certain decisions related to actual T-shirt production, community members are involved in every aspect of the design to sales process, as depicted in Fig. 6.2.[7]

However, as noted earlier in the chapter, and in the case of Dell, merely because the community is involved at every stage from design to sales does not mean that it works on autopilot. Threadless still has to manage the community and invest in

DELL-Vida K
Austin, TX

on 03/25/2008
Posts: 77
Points: 1980

Bronze

IdeaStorm Recap - 1/22/2010
22 January . 02:27 PM

Happy 2010 everyone! I know I'm a little late with the holiday greetings, but there is a lot to share on IdeaStorm with an exciting year ahead planned.

First, I would like to share that I will be moving on to new opportunities and IdeaStorm leadership will be transitioned to the very capable hands of Jeanette, who will also continue to work with Jackie. Jeanette has been quietly working in the background over the last few months and was very involved with our recent redesign and the launch of Storm Sessions. She is actively working with teams across Dell on ideas and has a full roadmap of Storm Sessions planned. Stay tuned and see what specific questions our business teams would like to know and get ideas on from the community!

We also have a few updates on requests for new functionality on IdeaStorm. We upgraded phubert's idea from a partial to a fully implemented for Sort comments in DESCENDING order - add NEXT/PREV page buttons when we added the ability to select on each idea how you would like to view the comments - ascending or descending. This week we also implemented phubert's idea In the Recent Replies list, link DIRECTLY to the UNREAD comment! Lastly on IdeaStorm ideas, we implemented jervis961's idea to Pick up the pace on the status tags. Each idea will be posted as Acknowledged when reviewed by Dell.

In addition to all of these, the following ideas for Dell have been implemented recently:

- Become a Discover Card reward member - jervis961
- 8GB and up for Laptop - cperng
- Add a link for Cloud computing - sugarbear
- No more plastic wrap, please - falbert
- Touchscreen Monitors - aDwh

Your next update will be coming from Jeanette. Thank you for letting me be part of this community for the last year and a half. I have thoroughly enjoyed it! And as always, keep the ideas coming!

Fig. 6.1 Dell Communicates with IdeaStorm Members

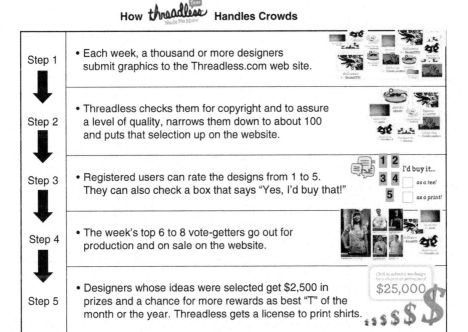

Fig. 6.2 How Threadless Handles Crowds

organizational capabilities that can enable customers to design, vote on best designs, and buy T-shirts, as explained below:

- Design selection and production: The process of design selection and T-shirt production needs to be actively managed. Deciding on which designs to produce is a little more complicated than merely picking the designs that get the highest score on the 0–5 evaluation scale. Some judgment needs to be exercised, since community members also provide a purchase-intent indicator called "I'd buy it."
- Taking risks and experimenting: Making the right decisions involves risk taking and experimentation. For example, the company has observed that passionate disagreement may actually represent a market opportunity rather than a choice problem. Markets exist on both ends of the scoring spectrum, for designs that score a 0 as well as those that score a perfect 5. Often, Threadless will take an informed risk and produce both types of designs.
- Analytics and business intelligence: Insights concerning preferences of customer segments, like boys vs. girls, those who buy a lot of T-shirts vs. those who buy a few, and frequent buyers vs. infrequent buyers, must be generated, as they play an important role in deciding what gets printed.
- Portfolio challenges: Balancing community preferences with the needs of the portfolio (depth of assortment, size, and variety) requires work, as does taking care of everyday business concerns, like the possibility of designs being plagiarized, or infringing copyrights.
- Reviews and insights: Community members invest a significant amount of energy and time writing reviews and commenting on designs. Someone at Threadless needs to read them, develop insights and implications based on what is read, share them with others within Threadless, and finally use that understanding to make informed design selection and production decisions.

Dell and Threadless: More Similarities Than Differences

Dell and Threadless may be two very different companies, but their investments in culture, structure, and processes to enable implementation of co-creation initiatives have a lot in common.

- In both cases, a dedicated organization manages collaboration with customers. In Dell's case, it is IdeaStorm staffers like Vida, Jeanette, and Jackie (discussed in Fig. 6.1); in the case of Threadless, it's the entire company.
- Both companies have a very crisp focus. Threadless is focused on designing and producing T-shirts; Dell is focused on creating value for customers by refining and innovating product features and customer service.
- The community is where both companies connect with ideas. In the case of Threadless, the company is the community; in Dell's case, it's the IdeaStorm customer community.

- The community is also where both companies decide which ideas to pursue and which to abandon. Both companies use a mixture of customer inputs (voting, commentary, and reviews) and managerial judgment to select winning ideas for implementation.
- The operations of both communities are completely transparent. Both companies provide regular updates to community members on ideas submitted, selected, and implemented, including those not implemented.
- Organizational culture is a key driver of co-creation in both companies. Threadless is built on collaboration and co-creation; in Dell's case, significant effort has been directed from the top at changing the company's culture. Michael Dell, by his own admission, is a regular visitor and participant in IdeaStorm sessions.[8] We will revisit Michael Dell's involvement in IdeaStorm toward the end of this chapter.

The track record of both companies suggests that they have been very successful in creating value for themselves and their customers. Toward the end of March 2010, the IdeaStorm website carried the following statistics:

The Dell community has contributed 13,776 ideas and Dell has Implemented 410 ideas.

According to information released by Threadless on its own operations:

Threadless selects and prints hundreds of awesome new T-shirt designs every year. Last year (2009), Threadless awarded over one million dollars to artists around the world.

Levels of Implementation

Will every company approach collaboration and co-creation like Dell and Threadless? Unlikely. This chapter opened by stating that co-creation requires effort and requires the organization to align itself with that effort through an investment of resources, both money and people. It also requires that companies buy in to the business model of collaborative innovation as an alternative to the traditional, hierarchical, firm-centric way of creating customer value. Readers will recall that in the Marmite case study (Chap. 2), the marketing team made a conscious decision not to develop and launch XO the traditional way.

This buy-in may not always be forthcoming, and even when it is, may only be partial. Just as no two snowflakes are the same, no two companies are identical in their desire and/or ability to disturb their current way of working. Corporate departments and functional silos have strong inertia that favors the status quo and are reluctant to cede control, especially to customers. Migrating to a more collaborative way of creating value with customers may also meet with resistance if the primary value-creators within the company, like R&D, suffer from a not-invented-here (NIH) syndrome and treat all ideas from external sources as second-class citizens.[9]

Consequently, the adoption, and subsequent implementation, of collaboration and co-creation is more likely to be a matter of degree, rather than an all-or-nothing proposition.

- At one end of the continuum will be non-adopters: companies that are content with sticking to their hierarchical, closed models of value-creation.
- At the other end will be companies that have fully and completely embraced collaborative innovation, like Dell and Threadless. We label this level of implementation high.
- In between the two extremes will be companies that have embraced parts of collaborative innovation, but not fully. We propose two levels of implementation here: light and moderate.

We use the descriptors light, moderate, and high in a relative sense, not as categories, but to draw attention to variations in the degree of collaboration and co-creation likely to be occurring between a company and its customers. There is no intention to judge any company or its efforts, merely to describe the range of implementation. Figure 6.3 presents a visual depiction of the differences between the various levels of implementation on two key dimensions: customer control and interaction, and co-creation focus.

Light-level Implementation

By definition, not much collaboration and co-creation takes place in this category. Companies are likely to connect to customer ideas by investing mainly in activities

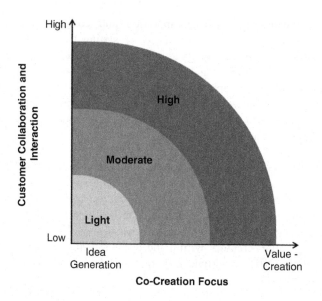

Fig. 6.3 Levels of Implementation

that enable them to listen to the voice of the customer. The listening agenda is likely to be company-centric rather than customer-centric. Listening initiatives are more likely to involve obtaining customer inputs to address specific information needs of the company, rather than starting meaningful, ongoing customer conversations. For example, companies may invest in ethnography to observe (a form of listening) shoppers in supermarkets, workers in office settings, or families entertaining themselves at home.

Companies may also invite customer suggestions and ideas through special appeals or links on their corporate websites. Customers have the ability to respond, but they don't have the ability to interact with the company or with one another. Additionally, customers don't usually participate in the actual value-creation process. Companies rely on their own resources and functional departments, such as marketing and new product development, to implement these activities.

Campbell Soup's desire to connect to consumer ideas through its website, http://www.campbellsoupcompany.com/ideas/, reproduced in Fig. 6.4, is an example of light-level implementation.[10] The company invites customers to submit ideas. Customers can do so if they choose, but they can't collaborate with other customers submitting ideas or with the company. Campbell Soup can of course move to a moderate, or even a high level of implementation, through a greater investment in

Fig. 6.4 Ideas for Innovation

structure and processes that permit multi-way interactions between consumers and the company across the entire value-creation spectrum, from submission of ideas, to selection, to value-creation.

Occasionally, companies at this level of implementation may also invest in customer communities. The purpose, though, is not to seek true engagement as described in Chap. 4, but to use the community as a marketing research substitute or as an additional channel for listening to the voice of the customer.

The Starbucks' community, *My Starbucks Visit* (www.aboutus.org/MyStarbucks Visit.com), is a platform for obtaining customer feedback. The community's website invites customers to fill out surveys, win cash prizes by doing so, and get coupons for free coffee or tea. As explained in the "About Us" section:

> This website is a place for Starbucks customers to give the company feedback on the quality of the coffee and service they received.

Light-level implementation may offer companies the occasional nugget, but it is unlikely to result in significant innovation because of the minimal amount of collaboration and customer empowerment. Further, as there is little to connect the customer with either the company or with other customers, customers may lack the motivation to contribute, or having once contributed, may not be motivated to continue contributing on an ongoing basis.[11]

Moderate-Level Implementation

Relative to the previous category, companies in this category invest more in listening to and engaging with their customers. The listening and engagement agenda is more likely to revolve around customer issues, not just company or product issues. Companies in this category are also more likely to use customer communities and dedicated physical spaces or digital arenas to connect with customers' ideas. Since digital listening, as a service category, is still in the early stages of growth, companies in this category are unlikely to have invested in full-blown, always-on digital listening programs. Additionally, value-creation activities are more likely to revolve around refining existing value, rather than co-creating new value. Companies in this category may also treat customers and customer communities as a virtual extension of company departments, seeking their formal review and evaluation of tactics and initiatives before they are implemented, as the following case study illustrates.

Mercedes Benz (MB): In Chap. 3 described MB's engagement of Gen Y customers in its proprietary, by-invitation only community, Generation Benz. Community members give MB their ideas and opinions on a variety of topics, such as dealership experiences, media consumption, driving habits, vehicle badging, and mobile-phone usage. Like companies in the light implementation category, MB also uses the community to partially augment and partially substitute its traditional marketing research efforts. Community members frequently take part in polls, discussions, and live chats with company executives.

In January 2010, for the first time, the marketing department at MB reached out to the year-old community to obtain its assessment on a proposed TV commercial for the SLS model. What's interesting about this is not that MB was seeking customer input, but the increased authority that MB was awarding the community. Since inception, MB's reliance on community members' advice and opinion has increased. It is this conspicuous integration of the community in everyday marketing decision-making that is noteworthy, as it represents a shift in the way MB refines marketing initiatives, and customer value, prior to implementation.

The ad in question was for the gull-wing SLS. Even though the absolute numbers of the 2011 SLS AMG projected to be sold in the United States are low, the car marks a big brand moment for MB. The company wanted to take advantage of that moment with emotional messaging and decided to rope the community members in a live chat to help refine the commercial. According to Steve Cannon, vice president of marketing, it was a win-win for both the community and MB. Involving the Generation Benz community was immensely helpful to both the company and the community; the company was able to emotionally fine tune its advertisement and the community loved having the opportunity to contribute.[12]

High-Level Implementation

In this category, collaboration between customers, and between customers and the company, takes place across the entire spectrum of value-creation. Both the Dell and Threadless cases studies discussed earlier are examples of high-level implementation. Companies in this category invest in sustained listening and customer engagement. They also invest in building dedicated spaces for ongoing interaction between customers and company staff. In this implementation category, companies approach collaboration and co-creation as a skill, a business competency that can be developed and nurtured through consistent effort and regular allocation of resources, much like any other business process, and not as one-off projects. Characteristics of the three levels of implementation on several key dimensions are summarized in Table 6.1.

Earlier, when introducing the three levels of implementation, we were careful to state that the implementation of collaboration and co-creation programs is not an all-or-nothing decision; it is more a question of degree. It reflects how companies commit their resources and which business models they wish to pursue. These choices can change, as a company's business situation changes. It is very possible for a company to start off with light-level implementation and gradually move to a high-level implementation, as the following example demonstrates.

Sun Microsystems launched Java, an object-oriented language, in 1995. Shortly afterward, the programming language caught the eye of the software community.

Table 6.1 Levels of Implementation: Summary of Characteristics

	Light	Moderate	High
Range of collaboration	Listen only	Listen + Engage	Listen + Engage + Respond
Scope of collaboration	Connect with ideas only	Connect with ideas + select ideas	Connect with ideas + select ideas + develop ideas
Customer empowerment	Low	Moderate	High
Customer ideas	Mainly invited	Invited and generated through engagement	Generated mainly through ongoing engagement
Selection of ideas	Company decides	Customers provide inputs, final decision rests with company	Customers vote and collaborate with the company in selecting which ideas to develop
Development of ideas	Company leads	Company leads; occasionally customers participate in refining value	Company and customers collaborate to co-create value
Collaboration platform	Company websites, occasionally customer communities	Company websites; occasionally dedicated physical collaboration spaces; customer communities	Company websites, dedicated websites and/or dedicated physical collaboration spaces, customer communities

Developers were quick to recognize and appreciate Java's versatility and power, which allowed them to develop numerous applications on multiple platforms. Unfortunately for the increasing number of devotees, the initial documentation on Java was scant and inadequate. Sun Microsystems was primarily a hardware-centric company and the scope of its software support and service was limited to software that could run on Sun hardware. Since Java was designed for cross-platform use, which included Windows, it meant supporting software in ways that were totally new to Sun. There was no Sun hardware support contract or service model in place that the company could use as a reference point. Java's biggest strength, cross-platform use, was beginning to give Sun big headaches.[13]

Phase I. Light-level implementation: Since Sun was interested in refining the software and expanding its application potential, it urged the developer community to get involved. The company wanted the developers to try Java and, based on their experience, fax recommendations for improvements and bug fixes to the company. The response to requests for bug reports and improvements was overwhelmingly enthusiastic. However, while Sun had been quick to get the community excited, it had been slow to respond internally. Investment in people and processes to deal with customers' ideas was lagging. Sun was not built on service. It didn't have enough internal resources to cope with the growing interest in Java among the developer community. At one stage, there were approximately 6,000 bug reports queued up in an inbox waiting to be read. Needless to say, there was virtually no collaboration between developers and the company. The emphasis of this stage of implementation was primarily on inviting and receiving ideas for improvement.

Phase II. Moderate-level implementation: Realizing the problem created by the lack of a service culture and inadequate resources, at the urging of company executives, Sun decided to launch an Internet help forum. The Java Developer Connection website was launched in 1996 and was patterned after Microsoft's Dr. GUI, which was an Internet site created specifically to answer customers' questions. Sun had two goals for the Internet initiative. First, Sun wanted someone to actually respond to the problems being experienced by developers. Second, it wanted to make money from the initiative; the company wanted customers to pay for the support. Consequently, the first version of the Java Developer Connection website was a pay-for-support service, and customers could access the site only if they had a current incident subscription.

The initial reception was lukewarm; the company sold only about 200 service subscriptions in the early going. However, there was a bigger problem than low sales. Customers tended to hoard the service units they bought. Their rationale: Why waste support dollars on routine, day-to-day events, instead of saving them for mission-critical incidents, when support is most critical? What made perfect sense from the customer's point of view was big trouble from Sun's vantage point. What if all Java customers with a current subscription called in at the same time? Sun would not be able to support them, regardless of how critical or urgent their need. The company just did not have enough capacity to respond if all Java customers made a simultaneous run on their support staff. Relative to the fax era, the Internet forum enabled greater interaction between the developers and the company.

However, the focus of the interaction still revolved around the product, fixing its limitations, not on enhancing customer experience. The agenda and scale of interaction was still controlled by the company.

Phase III. High-level implementation: Given the initial problems with paid incident support, Sun executives decided to gamble and make the service free. The company added new features to the website like a chat room, where engineers and developers could collaborate with one another, discuss problems and issues, and arrive at effective resolution in a timely manner. It seemed only logical, since developers were already offering advice to one another, independent of Sun, through emails. In addition to the chat room, Sun took another innovative step to accelerate collaboration. The company decided to offer incentives to the developer community to help answer questions. Developers who were more active in helping their colleagues were rewarded and publicly recognized. The results were astounding: approximately 85 percent of all questions and issues raised were addressed in one day. This was a far cry from the ever-increasing stack of unread faxes from a few years ago! Largely due to the program's success, the Java Developer Connection model was extended to the company's entire product line, leading to the creation of forums like the Sun Developer Connection.

The next innovative step in further accelerating customer collaboration was the open publication of the Java bug database. In 1997, there was hardly anything like this around. The concept of broadcasting bugs and sharing them with the developer community was entirely alien. Acknowledging limitations and defects of one's own product flew directly in the face of the preferred marketing model: tout the excellence and superiority of one's product and make the customer pay for service and support. However, the new collaboration among developers, Sun's engineers, and end users rewarded this authenticity and openness. The publicizing of bug reports, having end-users vote on which bugs should be fixed first, and inviting discussions on which new features to develop led to a spiraling cycle of product improvement and new product development. Developers and Sun were now collaborating across all phases of value-creation, which led to customers having a direct say in co-creating the new version of the software, namely Java 5. The community identified the top 25 features that needed to be added and the top bugs that needed to be eliminated. These suggestions formed the nucleus around which the new Java 5 was built.

Our motivation in describing Sun's journey from light to high-level implementation is not merely to chronicle corporate events leading up to the release of Java 5. It is to educate and inspire companies that are actively considering implementing customer collaboration initiatives, but feel overwhelmed at the thought of going from 0 to 60 in 4.2 seconds, to borrow a phrase from our friends in the automotive industry. As we have repeatedly stressed in this chapter, implementing collaboration and co-creation initiatives requires effort, organization, and resources. Sun's story is an excellent illustration of how transformation to being more open and collaborative does not have to occur in one giant step, but can instead take place in a series of small steps. Being open and collaborative is often more about organizational will and mindset than it is about availability of resources.

Innovation Intermediaries

The preceding discussion on levels of implementation rests on an important assumption: that the company makes collaboration happen on its own steam, or with the help of its partner service providers. However, doing it yourself (DIY) is not the only option. Another option is to use the services of specialized agencies that make collaboration and co-creation happen on behalf of a company: so-called innovation intermediaries. This is no different than what happens in other business processes, like advertising, where advertising agencies make all the investment in the infrastructure and processes to implement advertising campaigns for their clients. We have opted to discuss this option separately since the services of innovation intermediaries can be used as a stand-alone service, or in conjunction with collaborative activities being carried out by the company.

Innovation intermediaries, like TopCoder (Chap. 5), act like innovation bazaars, helping their clients implement collaborative innovation projects from start to finish. They are an important part of today's collaborative innovation landscape, as they often have the ability to connect companies to a global network of resources.[14] We will introduce a select group of these companies next, and examine how they are helping their clients become more open and collaborative.

InnoCentive (http: www.innocentive.com)

InnoCentive, is the poster child for innovation intermediaries; a pioneer, it gets frequent coverage in business books, case studies, and articles. Founded in 2001 by the venture capital arm of pharmaceutical giant Eli Lilly, InnoCentive is the world leader in prize-based open innovation (collaborators win prize money if their ideas and contributions are selected by clients). In 2005, InnoCentive was spun off from Eli Lilly, enabling the company to expand its offerings and serve clients in a variety of industries.

The company announces itself as the place where the world innovates, and for good reason. It connects its clients — companies, academic institutions, public sector, and nonprofit organizations — all seeking breakthrough innovations with a global network of more than 200,000 bright minds and creative thinkers from around the world: engineers, scientists, inventors, and professionals with expertise in life sciences, chemistry, math, computer science, and entrepreneurship.

InnoCentive works on a challenge and financial rewards system. Organizations, called Seekers™, post their challenges on the InnoCentive website, and offer registered Solvers™ — experts and solution providers — significant financial awards for the best solutions. Challenges are organized by discipline, such as Engineering and Design, or Food and Agriculture, or they are housed in Pavilions, such as NASA Innovation, Developing Countries, and Global Health. Both Seeker™ and Solver™ identities are kept confidential with InnoCentive managing the entire process of intellectual property (IP) development.

InnoCentive's clients include both large commercial companies like Avery Dennison, P&G, Eli Lilly, and Solvay, as well as philanthropic nonprofit organizations like the Rockefeller Foundation and Global Giving. A few challenges running on the company's website in the early March 2010 are presented below. Challenge descriptions, though abbreviated, are reproduced as they appear on InnoCentive's website.

- Design of a solar water treatment system based on TiO_2 nanoparticles: The Rockefeller Foundation is providing support to this Seeker for the design of a low-cost water treatment system based on solar radiation and titanium dioxide (TiO_2) (Challenge reward — US$15,000).
- Small-scale river turbines for the Peruvian jungle: A design is required for a robust and easy to assemble river turbine producing 6 kWh/24 period of operation from a river flowing at approximately 1 m/s. The turbines are for platform mounted use on the rivers of the Peruvian jungle (Challenge reward — US$20,000).
- Understanding the sensing of saltiness: Partners are requested who can aid the Seeker in better understanding the physiological mechanisms and technologies that could be used to influence the perception of salt taste from solid foods. The ultimate goal of the seeker organization is to decrease the salt (sodium chloride) content of foods, while maintaining the perception of salt taste and other organoleptic qualities of the food (Challenge reward — varies).

Innovation Exchange (http://www.innovationexchange.com/)

Like InnoCentive, Innovation Exchange (IX) is also a facilitated, challenge-based, open innovation marketplace for global for-profit companies and nonprofit organizations. However, it positions itself differently. Compared with InnoCentive, the company's mission is to enable on-demand innovation by tackling innovation challenges that have more to do with business than science. IX's web-based community of collaborators, or innovators, as IX calls them, is also comprised of smart people from the world over. However, due to the difference in the type of challenges that IX tackles, they are less likely to be highly technical or specialists in a single discipline.

The Toronto, Canada-based company follows a seven-step process in implementing open-innovation projects for its clients.

- Step 1. Brief creation: IX works with Sponsor organizations to develop Challenge Briefs and provoke high-quality thinking among Innovators in the IX community.
- Step 2. Review: Innovators from all around the world review the brief and decide if they want to respond to the challenge.
- Step 3. Search and Connect: Innovators who decide to respond to the challenge can search the IX site to connect with others who might want to work with them.

- Step 4. Collaboration: Innovators collaborate to develop a solution to the challenge, using the team's experience and talents.
- Step 5. Submissions: When satisfied with the quality of their response, teams submit their solutions.
- Step 6. Evaluation: Submissions are evaluated by sponsors to determine quality and fit with the specifications provided by the brief, in Step 1.
- Step 7. Selection: Sponsors determine which submission wins; upon being declared the winner a fee is paid to members of the winning team.

A few interesting challenges featured on the company's website in early March 2010 are listed below. A casual glance will reveal that these challenges are less technical than the ones hosted by InnoCentive. As in the previous example, challenge descriptions have been abbreviated and are reproduced as they appear on IX's website.

- Make laundry life more enjoyable and laundry space more inviting: The laundry process can be a chore from pre-laundering to washing, drying, then folding, stacking, hanging, storing and oh yes, ironing. These days, people are time-starved, looking for ways to simplify their lives and create order in their homes. The Fabric Care department of this company needs your innovative ideas for accessories to make the consumer's laundry life easier and more enjoyable, and at the same time, make the laundry space more inviting (Challenge reward — US$80,000).
- Help an alcohol beverage company move to the "green" side: The company is looking for new and innovative ideas for its North American business region that can help make it more environmentally friendly. These ideas can relate to the product itself, its production, its distribution, retail sales, consumption, packaging or disposal of their products (Challenge reward — US$50,000).
- Searching for a fun, new product idea or concept for holiday candy: The company is asking you for your innovative ideas or concepts for a new holiday candy that is unique, fun, exciting, which will get the retailers excited and consumers buying! (Challenge reward — 2 percent royalty continued over 4 years, est. min US$50,000, on ALL sales of your product idea or concept once it has been commercialized).

NineSigma (http://www.ninesigma.com/)

Founded in 2000, NineSigma advertises itself as one of the most experienced and advanced Open Innovation providers in the world. Like TopCoder, the company claims to have been offering open innovation solutions long before open innovation became accepted management practice. The company conducts open innovation projects across the entire innovation value chain, from front-end idea generation to back-end development. Its experience base spans a variety of sectors and industries, including health care, pharmaceuticals, energy, chemical, consumer goods, electronics, and utilities. This is reflected in its portfolio of clients, which lists companies like GlaxoSmithKline, Xerox, Kimberly Clark, Philips, and DuPont.

Based on the innovation needs of its clients, NineSigma invites Requests for Proposals (RFPs) by emailing project details to its global database of solution providers. Like its clients, NineSigma's solution providers are also a diverse group. They represent more than 135 different countries and span several different industries, and technical disciplines, including biotechnology, food technology, green technology, materials, and mechanical/industrial engineering. Unlike InnoCentive's Solvers™ and IX's innovators, NineSigma's solution providers don't compete for prizes; solution providers retain their intellectual property (IP) rights and negotiate their remuneration and contract terms directly with the companies interested in their solutions.

A sampling of live projects listed on the company's website in early March, 2010, follows; their description is as on NineSigma's website.

- Shelf-life extension for bread-enrobed sausage products: NineSigma, representing a global sausage manufacturer, invites proposals for extension of refrigerated shelf-life for bread-enrobed sausage products.
- Oxidation catalysts with reduced precious metal content: NineSigma, representing a Fortune 100 Automotive Company, invites proposals for novel catalysts that can oxidize hydrocarbons and CO with reduced precious metal content.
- Odor barrier technology: NineSigma, representing a major manufacturer engaged mainly in environment-related business, invites proposals for packaging materials or coating materials that can block the strong odor of dry sludge.

Appendix 6.1 provides names and web site addresses of other prominent Innovation Intermediaries not discussed above.

Culture and CEO: Inspiring and Enabling Collaboration

Adopting and implementing collaboration and co-creation programs, whether using a company's own resources, or working through innovation intermediaries, requires a change in the way companies think and behave. That's not always easy. A.G. Lafley, former CEO of P&G, was not the first CEO to proclaim, "The customer is boss." The importance of the customer to the long-term well being of a business has been known for years. Regardless of GM's woes today, Alfred Sloan, long-time president and chairman of General Motors, and "Buck Weaver," GM's first official marketing research director, were exchanging notes on the importance of understanding the customer as far back as 1933.

> Furthermore, we are passing through a kaleidoscopic era characterized by swift movements—social as well as economic—and such conditions cannot fail to bring more rapid changes in the tastes, desires and buying habits of the consuming public. So it becomes increasingly important that we provide the means for keeping our products and our policies sensitively attuned to these changing conditions.[15]

Neither is the expression not-invented-here (NIH) new. The importance and value of keeping an open mind has been stressed and celebrated in proverbs for thousands of years, as in "the frog in the well knows not the great ocean." No reason why it shouldn't apply to the business world as well.

Unfortunately, despite all the history and talk, most companies are still very insular, valuing their own talents, capabilities, and assets above what the rest of the world has to offer. The unspoken corollary of "Nobody knows more about our business than we do" is that "We are smarter than everybody else when it comes to our business." This culture and attitude of "We know best" or "What can our customers tell us that we don't already know" can't be overcome by rhetoric and slogan shouting alone. It requires the direct involvement and sponsorship of the CEO's office. Without the entire company lining up behind the transformation program, payoffs from collaborative and open programs are likely to be minimal. Nicolas Mirzayantz, Group President, Fragrances, at International Flavors and Fragrances, who has a sterling reputation for being a passionate supporter of collaboration and co-creation, likes to remind his associates: "You can't collaborate on the outside (with customers), without first collaborating on the inside (free flow of information and collaboration within and between departments)."

Two examples (we are sure there are others equally worthy) that epitomize how the CEO's office can inspire and facilitate transformation to a more collaborative and open way of creating customer value are Dell's IdeaStorm, and P&G's open innovation initiative, called Connect and Develop. It is fair to say that the results produced by both programs would not have been nearly as impressive had it not been for the personal investment and commitment of the two CEOs – Michael Dell and A.G. Lafley. What is impressive is the amount of effort that was spent inside, to prepare the company for collaborative innovation. Both Michael Dell and A.G. Lafley led a cultural renaissance to get their companies to first embrace collaboration internally so they could reap the rewards of collaborative and open innovation externally. Let us take a closer look.

Michael Dell Wanted Ideastorm

In August 2008, Vida Killian of Dell (readers will remember her as Vida K from Fig. 6.1) was interviewed by Ann All of IT Business Edge, an online source of news, knowledge, and information.[16] Responding to a question on whether Dell's history of interaction with customers helps IdeaStorm, Vida responds:

> Oh, absolutely. That culture comes from the way the company was established from Day One. One of the things I've read in a lot of the reports about communities is that companies don't have support from the top. Michael (Dell) wanted this community, and that's been instilled across the company. It goes back to the company culture.

Let's examine a few important ways in which this desire for a customer community, or the importance of listening to, collaborating with, and responding to customers' ideas, was instilled and communicated across the company.

- Dell will listen to customers' comments and opinions, and create for them a place to get together and talk to the company.
- Dell will not control, but will participate in, and be a part of, customer conversations.
- The company will be transparent and direct in its interactions with customers.
- Dell will not only invite customer suggestions, but also give customers the power to vote on which ideas should be developed and implemented.
- Dell will remain visible and respond to customers' ideas, and provide regular and periodic feedback on action taken on ideas implemented, partially implemented, under review, and reviewed.
- Dell will offer customers an explanation if no action is taken.

Strategic intent of this type is essential for an organization's culture — what people do on a daily basis without being told or watched — to internalize collaboration and co-creation. A big challenge for companies like Dell is to manage the implications of customer collaboration, especially responding to customers' ideas, internally. These are big companies, with professionals scattered around the globe, multiple departments, a large number of business groups, and consequently, a variety of business and personal agendas. Everybody has full-time jobs, and getting company personnel engaged with the customer is not always easy. Without an explicit investment in instilling a favorable and accepting culture, preferably sponsored and supported by the CEO, commitment to being open and collaborative is likely to be more symbolic than substantive (Box 6.2).

Connect-and-Develop Was A.G. Lafley's Baby

When A.G. Lafley took over as CEO of P&G, the consumer products giant and proud sponsor of moms, was, as the Brits would say, in a spot of bother. That would be putting it mildly. With lower-than-expected sales and earnings, profit warnings, and plummeting stock prices and market capitalization, Mr. Lafley had a lot to contend with in his early days at the helm. In *The Game Changer*, he very candidly discusses how he muddled through, and did not have all the answers the day he took over.[17] A vision that he communicated and shared with his senior management team in those early days is worth recounting:

> I encouraged them to compete like hell externally, but to collaborate like family internally. Just about every one signed on to this vision.

This perspective resonates exquisitely with the theme of this section and with Nicolas Mirzayantz's sentiments expressed earlier: namely, before you can collaborate with customers, you have to learn how to collaborate internally.

The arithmetic leading to Connect-and-Develop (C&D) was simple. As Huston and Sakkab reveal in their *Harvard Business Review* (HBR) article, P&G's R&D productivity had topped out in 2000, and was not in a position to meet the company's

---

Box 6.2 IBM's CEO, Sam Palmasino, Reflects on IBM's 2003 Values Jam

We've been spending a great deal of time thinking, debating and determining the fundamentals of this company. When IBMers have been crystal clear and united about our strategies and purpose, it's amazing what we've been able to create and accomplish. When we've been uncertain, conflicted or hesitant, we've squandered opportunities and even made blunders that would have sunk smaller companies.

It may not surprise you, then, that last year we examined IBM's core values for the first time since the company's founding. In this time of great change, we needed to affirm IBM's reason for being, what sets the company apart and what should drive our actions as individual IBMers. I don't believe something as vital and personal as values could be dictated from the top.

So, last summer, we invited all 319,000 IBMers around the world to engage in an open "values jam" on our global intranet for 72 hours. IBMers by the tens of thousands weighed in. They were thoughtful and passionate. They were also brutally honest. Some of what they wrote was painful to read, because they pointed out all the bureaucratic and dysfunctional things that get in the way of serving clients, working as a team or implementing new ideas. But we were resolute in keeping the dialog free-flowing and candid.

In the end, IBMers determined that our actions will be driven by these values:

- Dedication to every client's success
- Innovation that matters, for our company and for the world
- Trust and personal responsibility in all relationships

Clearly, leading by values is very different from some kinds of leadership demonstrated in the past by business. It is empowering, and I think that's much healthier. To me, it's also just common sense. In today's world, where everyone is so interconnected and interdependent, it is simply essential that we work for each other's success. If we're going to solve the biggest, thorniest and most widespread problems in business and society, we have to innovate in ways that truly matter. And we have to do all this by taking personal responsibility for all of our relationships — with clients, colleagues, partners, investors, and the public at large. This is IBM's mission as an enterprise, and a goal toward which we hope to work with many others, in our industry and beyond.[18]

---

growth objectives.[19] The counsel emanating from this realization, urging P&G to reinvent its innovation business model, was also relatively simple. What was not simple, though, was how best to implement the new and reinvented innovation model, which required P&G to bet its future on external connections and innovations. "It was a radical idea, one that required massive operational changes," explain Huston and Sakkab. Changes that would require transforming the company's culture, from resistance to innovations "not invented here," to enthusiasm for innovations "proudly found elsewhere."

What made perfect strategic sense — the more connections, the more ideas; the more ideas, the more solutions; the more solutions, the higher the company's sales and profits — also had to make organizational sense. Turning again to Mr. Lafley:

> And because what gets measured gets managed, I established a goal that half (50 percent) of new product and technology innovations come from outside P&G.

The execution of the chosen strategy required significant investment in enabling structures (organizational structure and processes that bring in and commercialize external ideas) and in developing a courageous and connected culture (an open learning culture that "applies and reapplies with pride," and that favors learning, and risk taking).

Programs like C&D are unlikely to succeed without accountability at the highest levels in the organization for its vision, day-to-day operations, and results. They touch too many aspects of the company and rely on too many hands to be cordoned off in a department, like R&D. To succeed, programs like C&D must be company-wide strategy. Having the CEO personally involved in steering the ship helps.

As the *Harvard Business Review* article reminds us: Never launch without a mandate from the CEO.

Appendix 6.1 Sample List of Innovation Intermediaries

Fellowforce (www.fellowforce.com)
InnoCentive (www.innocentive.com/)
Innoget (www.innoget.com/)
InnovationXchange (http://www.ixc.com.au/)
MillionBrains (www.millionbrains.com/)
NineSigma (www.ninesigma.com/)
One Billion Minds (www.onebillionminds.com/)
PRESANS (www.presans.com/)
Starmind (www.starmind.com/)
Tekscout (www.utekcorp.com/)
yet2.com (www.yet2.com/)
YourEncore (www.yourencore.com/)

Notes and References

1. Mason, B. & Thomas, S. (2008, 24 April). A Million Penguins Research Report. *Institute of Creative Technologies*. Retrieved March 5, 2010, from http://thepenguinblog.typepad.com/the_penguin_blog/2007/03/a_million_pengu.html
2. Adler, S. (2008, August 14). Trouble at the Office. *In Business Week*. Retrieved September 12, 2008, from http://www.businessweek.com/magazine/content/08_34/b4097030713566.htm?chan=magazine+channel_special+report

3. A Million Penguins Go to Sleep. *The Penguin Blog*. Retrieved March 5, 2010, from http://thepenguinblog.typepad.com/the_penguin_blog/2007/03/a_million_pengu.html?cid=6a00d8341c3b2653ef01310f4dab98970c

4. Jarvis, J. (2005, June 21). Dell Lies Dell Sucks. *BuzzMachine Blog- BusinessWeek*. Retrieved September 11, 2009, from http://www.buzzmachine.com/archives/2005_06_21.html

5. Jarvis, J. (2007, 17 October). Dell Learns to Listen. *BuzzMachine Blog- BusinessWeek*. Retrieved September 11, 2009, from http://www.businessweek.com/bwdaily/dnflash/content/oct2007/db20071017_277576.htm;

6. All, A. (2008, August 11). The Forecast is for Innovation at Dell's IdeaStorm. *ITBusinessEdge*. Retrieved September 11, 2009, from http://www.itbusinessedge.com/cm/community/features/interviews/blog/the-forecast-is-for-innovation-at-dells-ideastorm/?cs=23062&page=2

7. Inputs for the Threadless case study were obtained from numerous published sources and personal contacts and the company's website – www.threadless.com, Chafkin, M. (2008, June). The Customer is the Company. In Inc. Magazine (http://www.inc.com/magazine/20080601/the-customer-is-the-company.html), and Boutin, P. (2006, July 13). Crowdsourcing: Customers as Creators. *Businessweek*. Retrieved September 3, 2008, from http://www.businessweek.com/innovate/content/jul2006/id20060713_755844.htm

8. Owyang, J. (2008, November 25). Interview with Bob Pearson, VP Communities and Conversations: Why Dell Continues to Use Social Media. *Webstrategies*. Retrieved September 15, 2009, from http://www.web-strategist.com/blog/2008/11/25/video-interview-how-dell-is-benefitting-from-social-media./

9. Lafley, A.G. & Charan, R. (2008). *The Game Changer: How You Can Drive Revenue and Profit Growth with Innovation*. New York: Crown Business; Chesbrough, H. (2006). *Open Business Models: How to Thrive in the New Innovation Landscape*. Boston: Harvard Business Press.

10. Image and content reproduced with permission of Campbell Soup Company.

11. Rindfleisch, A. & O'Hern, M. (2008). Customer and Co-Creation: A Typology and Research Agenda. Working paper. School of Business, University of Wisconsin.

12. Halliday, J. (2010, January 25). Mercedes Panel Calls Shots on SLS ad. *Automotive News*. Retrieved March 10, 2010, from http://www.autonews.com/apps/pbcs.dll/article?AID=/20100125/RETAIL03/301259991/1286

13. All inputs for the Sun Microsystems case study were obtained from personal conversations with ex- Sun executives with knowledge Java's evolution, most notable among them being Calvin Austin.

14. Tapscott, D. & Williams, A. (2006). *Wikinomics: How Mass Collaboration Changes Everything*. New York: Penguin Group; Chesbrough, H. (2006). *Open Business Models: How to Thrive in the New Innovation Landscape*. Boston: Harvard Business Press; Prahalad, C.K. & Krishnan, M.S. (2008). *The New Age of Innovation: Driving Co-created Value Through Global Networks*. New York: McGraw-Hill.

15. Barabba, V. (2003, May 15). Henry Grady Weaver Hero, Thinker, Innovator, Practitioner or… Your Car as You Would Build It … Trust Me! *11th Conference On Historical Analysis & Research in Marketing (CHARM)* Michigan State University; Sloan, A.P. (1933). Quarterly Dividend Mailing to GM Common Stockholders. Detroit, Mich.: General Motors Corporation, Customer Research Staff document.

16. All, A. (2008, August 11). The Forecast is for Innovation at Dell's IdeaStorm. *ITBusinessEdge*. Retrieved September 11, 2009, from http://www.itbusinessedge.com/cm/community/features/interviews/blog/the-forecast-is-for-innovation-at-dells-ideastorm/?cs=23062&page=2

17. Lafley, A.G. & Charan, R. (2008). *The Game Changer: How You Can Drive Revenue and Profit Growth with Innovation*. New York: Crown Business

18. Excerpted from Samuel J. Palmisano's web address (IBM's Chairman, President, and Chief Executive Officer), *Our Values at Work*. (http://www.ibm.com/ibm/values/us/)

19. Huston, L. & Sakkab, N. (2006). Connect and develop: Inside Procter & Gamble's new model for innovation. *Harvard Business Review,* March, 84(3), 58–67.

Chapter 7
Rethinking Marketing and Innovation

At several places in this book, we have pointed out how the operating reality of collaborative organizations is very different from that of command and control, functional organizations. In doing so, we have resisted the temptation to make sensational and sweeping statements that predict the demise of the hierarchical-functional company. Nor have we likened collaboration and co-creation to a tsunami that will *forever change everything*. Collaboration and co-creation is still in its infancy. Where exactly it will settle between the two extremes of nothing will change to everything will change is still to be determined.

What has already been determined, though, is that the two worlds create markedly different outcomes for the company and customer. Revisiting the Sun case study introduced in Chap. 6 and examining the reactions of Sun's executives and developers to Java 5 will highlight the nature of this difference. Readers will recall that Java 5 was the outcome of collaboration between end-user developers and Sun's software engineers and developers.

- Executives who were around at Sun when Java 5 was co-created were unanimous in their praise for the collaboration that occurred within the Java Developer Community (JDC).[1] They also agreed that perhaps Sun could have ultimately arrived at Java 5 and developed it through the efforts of its own engineers and developers. But, they felt it would have taken Sun a lot longer and that the finished product would have been less satisfactory to both developers and end-users. Perhaps the most telling comment concerning why it may not have been as satisfactory as the co-created product was the admission that if Sun had relied on its own resources it would have given more weight to technical features and technological sophistication in building Java 5. Consequently, features deemed simple and unsophisticated from a technical/engineering lens would have been omitted, even if considered significant and valuable by customers. Collaboration and co-creation ensured that customer needs, not technological prowess, were given a higher weight in the development of Java 5.

G. Bhalla, *Collaboration and Co-creation: New Platforms for Marketing and Innovation*, 123
DOI 10.1007/978-1-4419-7082-4_7, © Springer Science+Business Media, LLC 2011

The Java 5 experience, along with the Dell, P&G, Threadless, and Marmite case studies before that, all point to an important conclusion: embracing collaboration and co-creation irrevocably changes how customer-value is created and how companies are run and managed. Two aspects are of special interest: marketing and innovation.

Rethinking Marketing

Let's agree on what we mean by marketing.

Before any serious rethinking on marketing can take place, it would be helpful to have a clear understanding of the nature of what we are trying to rethink. In short, it would behoove us to ask ourselves a simple question: What is marketing, especially in the context of collaborative and co-creation? Is it a department, is it an organizational function, or is it marketing communications (MARCOM)?

Business gurus, academicians, consultants, and practitioners have been reminding us for some time now that thinking of marketing as a department, or as an organizational function is incorrect.[2]

> Marketing encompasses the entire business. It is the whole business seen from the customer's point of view. Concern and responsibility must therefore permeate the entire organization — Peter Drucker
>
> From a philosophical point of view, marketing should be a focus of everyone in the organization, not a separate department — Frederick Webster, Jr.
>
> Marketing is everybody's business and companies need to move from marketing as a function, to marketing as a state of mind — Vince Barabba

David Packard's quip that "Marketing is too important to be left solely to the marketing department" best captures the soul of this entire category of objections. Dell incidentally agrees with David Packard, which is why a cross-section of the company supports the implementation of ideas identified for execution by the IdeaStorm community. Invisible to IdeaStorm customers is a team of approximately 40 people representing the many different departments of the company. This group, a miniature Dell, has one main job — to make sure that the company follows through and implements customers' suggestions. It's Dell's way of making marketing everyone's business and making sure that marketing is not just left to the marketing department (Box 7.1).

Since the culture and operating reality of companies are distinct and varied, each company needs to answer the question, "What is marketing?" for itself. In the absence of this exercise, different elements of the organization — R&D, Finance, and Operations — are likely to define marketing in self-serving ways and are unlikely to speak a common language that will resonate with the customer. Rather than force a perspective on the reader, we would like to do something different. In the spirit of collaboration and co-creation that this book stands for, we would like to offer a prototype that companies can play with, refine, and make their own,

---

Box 7.1 IFF Embraces Collaboration, Rethinks Marketing

International Flavors and Fragrances (IFF) is the world's leading creator and manufacturer of flavors and fragrances. On the fragrance side, the company has helped create such fragrance classics as White Linen, Beautiful, Youth Dew, Trésor, and Drakkar Noir. On the flavors side, IFF creates savory flavors for retail and food service processors, and has in-depth expertise in soups, sauces, and condiments, prepared meals, meat, poultry, and snacks.

Collaborating with customers and co-creating fragrances and flavors is one of IFF's strengths. Lately, the company has also been focused on pushing marketing thinking deeper within the company. Part of this effort involves getting the entire company, including R&D, to approach business opportunities from the perspective of customers' businesses, not merely from the perspective of technologies and ingredients.

So recently, when one of IFF's key accounts, a market leader in the ready meals category (IFF wanted to keep the client's name confidential) wanted to refresh and extend its offerings with current, on-trend recipes, IFF responded very differently than in the past. Rather than starting by showcasing its latest technologies, the company started by scanning flavors and eating trends. These trends were then mapped on to IFF technologies to develop concepts. Working collaboratively with the client, IFF flavorists developed several recipes, not just from a culinary perspective, but also from the point of view of market positioning and competitive differentiation.

The winning recipe, launched in Q1 2010, featured a new natural wok flavor that was specifically designed to deliver an authentic, pan-fried Asian taste. The client opted for a dry side-dish line extension with this new wok flavor and also commissioned development work for additional Asian style extensions.

Reflecting on the experience, IFF shared that in the past they would merely have shipped flavors to the client's product developers. However, since embracing co-creation and making marketing thinking a part of everyone's job, IFF is more concerned with developing whole solutions for clients, rather than merely shipping ingredients. Additionally, in developing whole solutions, IFF has two equally important concerns. IFF not only wants the innovative recipes to meet action standards set forth by the client's development team, it also wants the innovations to have a strategic fit with the client brand's marketing strategy.[3]

---

depending on their own unique histories and circumstances. A brief discussion of the components of this prototype follows:

- Marketing is a mindset and an orientation that compels a company to obsess about customer value. It is an innate characteristic of the entire company that motivates it to be continuously focused on creating, nurturing, and innovating customer value.

- The obsession with customer value must extend to all customers, not just those at the top of the pyramid who are able and willing to pay for products as configured today. It also must extend to those at the bottom of the pyramid who have unmet needs, but can't find products consistent with their ability to pay.
- Value is co-created with customers and other stakeholders and is derived through unique and personalized experiences that customers believe best meet their own individual needs.
- In order to implement value co-creation programs, companies need to energize the flow of information and knowledge-sharing within their own companies, and invest in connecting with a global network of knowledge, skills, and competencies outside the company. It is impossible to be open externally without first collaborating internally.
- Co-created customer value must do more than just meet short-term customer needs and do more than just benefit the company. Its must also benefit the community and the environment within which the company operates over a longer time period of time. Short-term good at the expense of longer-term harm is not an option.

To summarize, marketing is a mindset or characteristic of the entire company; it is an enduring obsession with customer value, not a department or an activity. As such, marketing represents a commitment: an *investment* in ensuring the ongoing relevance of a company to the unique and personal needs of customers, not merely an *expenditure* that can be adjusted at will to help the earnings picture of the company. The emphasis is on listening, engaging, and co-creating value and personalized experiences with customers; it's not on branding, selling, advertising, and promoting. The practice of marketing should benefit all key stakeholders, including the community and environment the company operates in, not just the company.

Customer Value: Not What It Was Previously

In his book, *Real Time*, Regis McKenna laments that "we still love our factories more than we love our customers."[4]

This is a smart way of asking: How do customers derive value from what we produce? It's also an effective way of asking: What drives a company's business — the product or the customer? Several years before McKenna's lament, Theodore Levitt had also warned companies against this tendency of falling in love with their own technologies and products. "Customers don't buy ¼" drills, they buy ¼" holes," is how he had phrased it in his landmark article *Marketing Myopia*.[5]

In the context of collaboration and co-creation, customer value is not a function of product features and attributes. It is a function of customer interactions and experiences. Value is not something that is built into a brand, product, or service. The potential value of products and services, or the value proposition they represent, materializes only through interactions among different stakeholders: between the customer and the company, or among communities of customers, or among networks of companies. The emphasis is on personalized and unique experiences and co-creation of value. The operative preposition is not "for," it is "with: then" companies don't create value for customers, they create value with customers.

World of Warcraft (WoW), for example, is about the co-creation of value and individualized experiences. Gamers don't derive value through the features of the game, but through their interactions with other gamers and the company's development personnel. In a manner of speaking, WoW is a platform. Blizzard provides it, but the gamers create characters and adventures to suit their own particular needs and personalities. The iPhone is also a platform. Its website claims, "Your iPhone gets better with every new app," an interesting admission by Apple that value is not something that is static, constant, and embedded in the device. Instead, value is variable and is an outcome of the solutions and experiences that iPhone customers co-create with the tens and thousands of apps available.

Additionally, the same physical product or service can offer different opportunities for value co-creation and personalization of experiences. For example, when IBM runs a "smart" urban transportation initiative to reduce urban congestion, the value derived by the city, commuters, and the transportation company is very different. The principal value for the city may be lower emissions and the provision of a better quality of life for its residents; for the commuters, less guilt and a chance to contribute to a greener city; and for the transportation company, a more sustainable business, resulting in higher revenues and profits in the future.

Customer Value Platforms, Not Products

The previous section mentioned how WoW is a platform; individual gamers decide how they will play the game. Are they going to compete? Are they playing for fun and adventure? Are they playing to exercise their creativity? The same is true for iGoogle. Google provides the platform, but individual customers decide which experiences to co-create and what value to extract — news, alerts, or learning.

When a company thinks about its offerings in terms of single products or product lines, its ability to offer greater value to the customer is limited by the physical format of the product or service. But when a company thinks of its offerings in terms of customer value platforms, its ability to offer greater value to customers increases. The company now has more opportunities for co-creating unique experiences with its customers, across multiple product formats and in different contexts, which also offers the company more opportunities to accelerate its own sales growth.

Crayola: In 1999, when Mark Schwab took over as CEO of Crayola, the company was in a slow growth phase. Like most other companies of that era, Crayola was organized around product formats. The company defined itself in terms of its physical offerings — crayons, pencils, markers, and paints — not in terms of consumer solutions or experiences.[6]

Mark Schwab and his team soon realized that slow growth was not due to a lack of ideas. The company had several very good ideas coming out of R&D, and some excellent proprietary technologies that were appealing to both moms and kids. One of these technologies, Color Wonder (CW), allowed Crayola to produce clear inks and paints, with colors appearing only when the inks and paints were applied to special CW paper. If applied by mistake to clothes or other surfaces, like walls, skin, or the floor, the product would not leave a mark, as the color would not appear. It was a magical way for kids to experience the colors appearing. It was a big boon for moms, too. They didn't have to worry about their children messing up or having to clean up after them.

Despite a stable full of wonderful technologies like Color Wonder, and despite having excellent customer insights, Crayola was finding it difficult to find the right formula for runaway growth. Mark Schwab and his senior management team soon realized that merely commercializing proprietary technologies was not going to produce the desired growth. They had to fundamentally rethink customer value, not as product offerings, but how they co-created fun experiences with children, moms, and teachers.

Around 2004, acting on the recommendation of the consulting firm Strategos, Crayola abandoned its old focus on physical product formats like crayons, markers, and paints, and organized itself instead around customer value platforms that corresponded to larger sets of consumer needs. One of these platforms was *No Mess*. Overnight, Crayola's ability to offer a greater range of co-creation opportunities increased. By focusing on customer value platforms, Crayola was able to liberate CW from just inks and paints and was now free to offer it in multiple formats, such as markers, magic light brush, and finger-paints. Moms, kids, and teachers, on the other hand, now had significantly greater opportunities for co-creating No Mess experiences. For example, consider children coloring or painting in the back seat of a car, with a product of their choice, while mom drives them to grandma's. The inks and gels used in the product would show only when applied to paper; they would not show if applied to car seats, clothes, or other materials, making spills and leaks a non-issue.

The power of customer value platforms to transform marketing — continuous obsession with customer value-creation — is further reinforced by the evolution of No Mess. Over time, No Mess evolved to *No Limits*. With No Mess, Crayola was able to liberate CW and embed it in multiple product formats. However, co-creation experiences were still limited to the special paper on which the ink appeared. With No Limits, Crayola wanted to liberate CW from this constraint too, so that co-creation experiences could occur any time, any place. New offerings like outdoor paint facilitated No Limits experiences. Outdoor paint was free of harmful chemicals. It could be washed easily by a garden hose or by rain, thereby increasing the quality of the consumer's experience.

Customer value platform thinking has altered the alchemy of growth and value co-creation at Crayola. Mark Schwab and his colleagues were able, in just a few short years, to take relatively small business lines, worth $15–$20 million, organized around physical products and technologies, and grow them into large business lines, worth more than $100 million, organized around customer value platforms.

Customer: Not Just Consumer, but Producer, Collaborator, Competitor, and More

The climactic scene of a number of Western movies evokes an eerie sense of déjà vu. The invincible hero has just shot the last bad guy, usually an evil gang leader, who, is lying in the sand, bleeding to death, hopelessly trying to force bullets out of the empty chamber of his six shooter, screaming uncontrollably — "Who are you?"

The same question can be heard echoing in corporate hallways. For the longest time, companies thought they had the customer all figured out. The climactic slides of most marketing and marketing research presentations invited a sense of déjà vu, serving to reinforce hubris concerning how well the company understood its customers. The eagerly sought after voice of the customer — have you ever wondered why its not voices of customers; after all there are many customers with different voices? — had lost its distinct timbre and as a result was no longer being heard. Then things changed. Enabled by technology, notably the Internet, a sometimes silent, sometimes noisy revolution confronted companies. Customers started behaving in strange, unpredictable, never-before-seen ways, leaving companies screaming uncontrollably, "Who are you?"

Previous chapters have discussed a number of examples that illustrate how today's consumer are multidimensional human beings who want to interact with companies in a variety of different ways. This chapter offers a few more examples to reinforce the importance of rethinking the customer in multiple and interrelated ways.

Customer as producer: Referred to sometimes by the portmanteau "prosumers,"[7] customers are a value-creation resource for the company. User Generated Content (UGC) — in the form of blogs, product and movie reviews, reports on crises and catastrophes, advertisements — is content that materializes when customers also act as producers. UGC informs, educates, influences, and mobilizes action, among other things.

According to Sir Mark Tully, former BBC Bureau Chief, New Delhi and now a freelance journalist and broadcaster, anyone with a cell phone and a camera — even better if built into the same device — is a journalist. He is right. BBC World Service reports that prosumers played a key role in breaking news to the outside world of the Haiti earthquake in January 2010. Ordinary citizens turned a range of networking tools — like microblogging on Twitter, video-sharing on YouTube, internet telephony through Skype, and sharing personal content on Facebook — into a steady stream of information, personal stories, and news updates. For over 24 hours after the quake, countless reports and images came not only from big, established news organizations, but also from ordinary people operating on the spot.[8]

Device manufacturers are responding. At the Mobile World Congress held in Barcelona, Spain, in February 2010, Sony Ericsson released "Creations," a new content publishing platform, where community members submit videos, pictures and other content for sharing. Others can also use, share, edit, or update the content, which is all covered under the Creative Commons license. The platform is Sony

Ericsson's attempt to ride the UGC wave and tap into the YouTube generation's user-generated mindset.[9]

Customer as collaborator: Case studies of Threadless, TopCoder, and Dell's IdeaStorm are first-class examples of customers acting as collaborators. Like Threadless and TopCoder, Ubuntu is also built on collaboration. The word "Ubuntu" has its origins in the Bantu languages and means "humanity to others" or "I am what I am because of who we all are." It is a free, open-source operating system for desktops or servers that can be used at home, school, or at work. The company offers a comprehensive suite of applications, from word processing and email applications, to web server software and programming tools.

Ubuntu thrives on collaboration and community. Since its inception in 2004, thousands of free software enthusiasts have joined the Ubuntu community. Called Ubunteros, these dedicated customers collaborate with Ubuntu's core development team on activities like identifying and fixing bugs, testing releases, writing documentation, and improving the look and feel of Ubuntu. They also do more. LoCo (local community) teams act as the company's marketing and advocacy arm, promoting awareness and usage of the company and its offerings in their local communities.[10]

Customer as competitor: In several case studies discussed previously, such as Hallmark and Sun's Java 5, customers also behave as competitors. In each case, not only do customers collaborate to co-create value, they also compete with the company to extract value for themselves. For example, consumers participating in Hallmark's greeting card contests are collaborating with Hallmark to expand the range of card offerings, but they are also extracting value (prize money, recognition) for themselves, in addition to competing with Hallmark's artists and writers. The large number of end-users and developers who were active in the Java Developer Community (JDC) are both collaborators with and competitors of Sun. So are the large number of Ubunteros and end-users active in Dell's IdeaStorm; they are both customers and competitors of Ubuntu and Dell, respectively.

Conversations, Not Communication and Promotion

Most companies are still managed as if they were stuck in an earlier era of mass markets, mass media, and impersonal transactions. They target their customers with one-way communications flowing outward from the company and its brands to the customer. But the era of pushing, interrupting, telling, and selling is over. Collaboration and co-creation is about listening, having conversations, answering questions, and cultivating relationships.[11]

Today's customers play a variety of different roles, as noted. One of these roles involves reversing and scattering the traditional one-way flow of communication. Customers are not waiting passively to receive marketing messages. They are actively creating their own messages, and sharing them with anyone who is interested in hearing — friends, strangers, communities, journalists, media, government, and yes, even companies.

An excellent example of how customers can create their own communication environment that may run counter to the company's intent is provided by Apple's iPad. Figure 7.1 features a brand promotion ad from Apple for its new iPad product. But that's not all that customers were hearing. They were also hearing one another. As Apple was exhorting customers to pre-order, customers were already in deep conversations with one another discussing the merits and demerits of placing an advance purchase order. One potential customer's recommendation from a set of live social media conversations captured on March 13, 2010 is representative.

> Decided to pass on pre-ordering an iPad. Past history has proven it is best to wait on the 2nd & 3rd generations of most Apple products.[12]

It can be argued that given the mad rush to get an iPad (at the time of writing, the product was in short supply), it didn't really matter whether Apple was clued-in and listening to customer conversations. Perhaps. But not all products are as fortunate as the iPad. Even if they are, customer enthusiasm and passion needs to be sustained; it can't be taken for granted. It is in the brand's best interests to evolve its communication and promotion agenda and take it to where the customer is, as the following example of Axe body spray demonstrates.

Unilever's Axe is the largest selling male body spray in the world, hugely popular with young guys. It is sold in over 80 countries as a fragrance body spray and

Fig. 7.1 Email from Apple Promoting the iPad

according to the tag line — The Axe Effect — helps guys get the girls. Launched in Japan in 2007, Axe became the number one-selling male deodorant in the market in just a few weeks. However, repeat purchase was lower than other markets. For high growth to continue, the company would have to convince young guys to increase usage and buy more often.

The traditional approach to addressing this marketing challenge would have involved developing a message — telling guys to spray Axe every day, or every morning, because they could run into girls anytime, anyplace, on the bus, on the train, or at work — producing an advertising campaign (TV commercials, radio spots, etc.), and airing it for a sufficient length of time. What Axe did instead was something different. The brand created an interactive mobile phone app. Rather than interrupting and intruding guys' routines, the brand actually allowed young guys to co-create unique experiences around their pre-existing routines.

Acting on the knowledge that most Japanese young guys use their mobile phones as alarm clocks, Unilever offered the opportunity to co-create a deep, immersive brand engagement first thing in the morning. Step 1, involved downloading a special Axe wake-up service mobile application; Step 2, choosing an Axe Angel to deliver the waking-up experience; and Step 3, setting the wake time for the alarm. Then every morning, the customer received a fun and sexy video wake-up call from his Axe Angel, who of course reminded him to spray Axe.

The application was developed like a Tamagotchi pet, meaning the waking-up experience was different every day. The more the guys used the service, the friendlier their Axe Angel became. If they ignored her, the Axe Angel would become sulky and upset, until the wake-up calls were reinstated. Axe also developed a wake-up service website to extend the range of co-created experiences, such as setting up a single wake-up call for the next day, downloading wallpapers, ringtones, and other mobile content. By reframing how Axe thinks about marketing, the brand was able to communicate differently and provide a truly engaging, entertaining, and relevant experience. Also, by situating the brand in context, from the bed to the shower, Axe was able to create an environment for the brand to communicate with young guys that neither TV commercials nor radio spots would have been able to achieve.[13]

Today, every brand or company wants to have conversations with its customers. They have realized that shouting messages at them won't help. Doc Searls and David Weinberger were among the early protagonists of *markets as conversations*. In their book, *The Cluetrain Manifesto*, they advise: "By listening, marketing will re-learn how to talk."[14] We agree strongly. It's no accident that Listening is Step 1 of our collaboration and co-creation framework, presented in Chap. 2. Throughout the book, we have stressed the importance of listening; before companies can have conversations with customers, they must first listen. We have also stressed the importance of authentic engagement in sustaining customer conversations. Several examples discussed in previous chapters — Susan G. Komen for the Cure, P&G's Beinggirl.com, Threadless, Dell's IdeaStorm, Hallmark's Circles of Conversation, and Nokia's Beta Labs — illustrate this new dynamic of communication that results in meaningful conversations with customers.

Pushing and selling products is old marketing. Listening to and engaging customers to generate opportunities for co-creating unique and individualized experiences is new marketing. This is not merely an academic perspective discussed only in business journals and books. It is a real discussion, taking place in the hall-ways of large and small companies, with significant implications for how these companies design, assess, and implement marketing and media programs. Consider Unilever's new marketing and media manifesto reproduced in Fig. 7.2. Inspired by *The Cluetrain Manifesto*, it looks at the outcomes of Unilever's marketing and media actions through the eyes of the consumer. According to Babs Rangaiah, Unilever's

Unilever Media Manifesto: From The People

Penetrate the Culture:
"We're immune to your tired "campaigns" and our eyes glaze over them…please spark our imagination with something interesting, meaningful and useful…for a change"

Be part of our World:
"We spend more and more of our time on the web and rarely see you. How can you be part of our world if you're never with us? We're not looking for you…"

Give us a Voice:
"We've got ideas about brands too..provide us with some tools, and the opportunities etc…and we'll make brands even better. Your org chart should include us and be hyperlinked."

Be Authentic:
"Brands can communicate with us directly now…but if you're too contrived or bs'ing us for that matter…we'll laugh at you and then abuse you relentlessly so everyone will see"…

Doing Good:
"If you want us to become your advocate, you have to get what we do, share our interests, be an active participant and show you care…like a real friend"…

Create more Value:
"You want us to pay? We want you to pay attention.. don't worry you can still make money…as long as you give us a real reason to buy."

Listen to us:
"We want you to take the 6billion of us as seriously as you take one analyst or one reporter from the Financial Times".

Don't be so Corporate:
"Speak to us in our language…then maybe we'd go to you instead of each other for answers."

Keep it Simple:
Why do you over complicate everything? Make things a lot easier for us."

Telling our Friends:
"We'd tell each other how great you are if you give us something to talk about…but if you do something to make us mad..we'll tell a lot more peeps…"

Fig. 7.2 Unilever Media Manifesto: From The People

Vice President of Global Communications Planning, "The intent is to reframe how we think about marketing and new media. We don't want to merely superimpose old models of advertising on to new media. Our goal is to *penetrate the culture*, not just interrupt with advertising, but provide engaging, entertaining, and relevant experiences through new media."

Rethinking Innovation

Yes, customers have changed. But so have companies and the environments within which they operate. In today's business environment, characterized by globalization, increased competition, rapid technological change, and the rising power of multiple stakeholders, most notably customers, the demands of value-creation are too complex and multi-faceted for any one company to handle on its own. Value chains have given way to value constellations, where companies are part of larger value-creation ecosystems, comprising a loosely connected group of companies, institutions, customers, and individuals.[15] In an ecosystem, gains due to collaboration and co-creation accrue only when innovation is approached and implemented as a team. The pipeline model of innovation, relying on the knowledge and resources of a company's internal R&D department, needs to give way to a value-creation system that proactively engages and utilizes the knowledge, skills, resources, and assets of the entire ecosystem.

To illustrate, innovations that comprise IBM's Smart Planet initiative don't just begin and end with IBM. They involve the knowledge and contributions of several different members of its ecosystem. Consider a specific initiative of the Smart Planet program called *Smarter Cities*. For several decades, rising urban populations have been stressing the infrastructure of the world's largest cities — transportation, water, education, policing, and power. With over half the world's population now living in urban centers, and with an estimated 70 percent of the world's population expected to live in cities by 2050, innovative solutions that can bring relief to large cities by easing traffic congestion, cleaning polluted rivers and waterways, and generating clean power are desperately needed. IBM has the technologies to make these cities better places to live. But it can't develop and implement these smart solutions on its own. It needs to engage and utilize the assets and resources of relevant organizations within the ecosystem, like city administrations and local government bodies. Put differently, IBM will need to innovate across the ecosystem to create meaningful and relevant opportunities for value co-creation, for itself, and for members of the ecosystem within which it operates.

Examples from two localities — Stockholm, Sweden and Galway Bay, Ireland — demonstrate how IBM engages and innovates across its ecosystem, to translate the vision of smarter cities into reality.[16]

Stockholm, Sweden: Working closely with the city of Stockholm and the Swedish Road Administration, IBM designed, developed, and implemented an innovative "congestion charging system." First piloted in 2006, the system has reduced traffic in the Swedish capital by 18 percent. It has also contributed to an increase in the proportion of green, tax-exempt vehicles in the area. The Swedish traffic authorities view these results very favorably, especially as they have been achieved against the backdrop of an overall increase in road traffic, residents, and jobs in Stockholm County. The program is helping the city meet its objectives of permanently reducing traffic to the inner city and improving the overall quality of the city's environment. Simultaneously, it has also improved access to the inner city for buses and for motorists willing to pay the congestion charge.

The innovative "congestion charging system," the largest of its kind in Europe, covers a 24-km^2 area of the inner city and was introduced after the Swedish National Parliament voted to permanently adopt it. For supporting enforcement, it has 18 barrier-free control points around the charging zone equipped with cameras and beacons to identify non-paying vehicles. Payment is accepted through multiple channels, like automatic direct debit, payment at banks, over the Internet, and at convenience stores like 7-Eleven. The congestion charge is a national tax; collections are used in the Stockholm region for investment in road infrastructure.

Galway Bay ("SmartBay"), Ireland: The SmartBay pilot, completed in 2009, is a marine research infrastructure of sensors and computational technology interconnected across Galway Bay. Its main purpose was to collect and distribute information on coastal conditions, pollution levels, and marine life. The monitoring services, delivered via the Web and other devices, benefit tourism, fishing, aquaculture, maritime industry, and the environment. The pilot also allowed researchers to respond in a more timely and effective way to critical challenges of bay management, such as pollution, flooding, fishing stock levels, green energy generation, and climate change threats.

The SmartBay pilot represents an extensive collaborative effort, involving several organizations that comprise Galway Bay's ecosystem. IBM and the Marine Institute of Ireland formed the nucleus of the collaboration. A select list of other collaborators included Galway Bay's Harbour Master, Bord Iascaigh Mhara (Gaelic for Irish Sea Fisheries Board), Irish Water Safety Council, the Hydraulics & Maritime Research Centre at University College Cork, and commercial fishermen and fishing organizations. Academic institutions like Dublin City University, University College Dublin, and the Tyndall National Institute in Cork also participated in the pilot.

The SmartBay project was showcased as an exemplary "smarter" initiative at the 2009 IBM "Smarter Cities" conference in Berlin. Yvonne Shields, director of strategic planning at the Marine Institute, who presented the SmartBay project to the conference, especially applauded the communication and collaboration triggered by the Galway project. In her assessment, the Galway project had contributed significantly to raising coordination, collaboration, and communication among Ireland's environmental monitoring agencies to a new and more efficient level.[17]

If Stockholm's congestion charging system has produced irreversible gains, and if SmartBay is an exemplary smarter cities project, it is largely because IBM engaged and innovated across the entire ecosystem. Any attempt to build solutions in isolation, independent of the key players in the ecosystem, no matter how brilliant IBM's technologies, would have missed the value-creation target by miles (Box 7.2).

Box 7.2 Sustainability: Innovation's Emerging Frontier

In September 2009, Unilever was named sustainability leader in the Food & Beverage sector of the Dow Jones Sustainability Index (DJSI) for the eleventh consecutive year. The company won with an overall score of 81percent for its social, economic and environmental contribution, measured across 22 performance criteria.

Launched in September 1999, the Dow Jones Sustainability Indexes are the first global indexes to track the financial performance of leading sustainability-driven companies worldwide. The indexes provide asset managers with reliable and objective benchmarks to manage their sustainability portfolios. The 2009 annual assessment, conducted by SAM (a Swiss sustainable asset management group), the Dow Jones Indexes, and STOXX (an investor information and market index company) was limited to the top 10 percent of the largest 2,500 companies worldwide that qualify as members of the Dow Jones Sustainability World Index (DJSI World). Unilever has participated in the annual assessment since its inception and has achieved "super sector" leader status in the Food & Beverage category every year since.

The company's achievements and plans for sustainable sourcing of palm oil are particularly noteworthy. The global market for palm oil is booming; it has doubled over the past 10 years and will double again by 2050. Unfortunately, meeting this demand has also produced significant negative environmental impacts, like deforestation and increased greenhouse gas emissions. To meet the growing demand, Indonesian and Malaysian growers, palm oil's largest suppliers, often encroach on peat lands and high conservation value forests. It is estimated that an area the size of Greece disappears every year.

As one of the world's largest users of palm oil, Unilever has made a public commitment to draw all palm oil from sustainable sources by 2015. The company has forged a partnership with Greenpeace, Oxfam, World Wildlife Fund, among others, and is using a variety of incentives and disincentives to transform the palm oil industry. The incentives are essentially financial. Unilever is buying certified sustainable oil coming on stream at a premium price. In 2009 alone the company purchased GreenPalm certificates covering 185,000 tonnes of this oil — representing 15 percent of its needs and 85 percent of available sustainable palm oil. The company is also helping lead the industry. Through a coalition it has built and leads, Unilever has persuaded over 20 global retailers and manufacturers to make public commitments, similar to its own, to draw all palm oil from certified sustainable sources by 2015.[18]

Platform Innovations Enable Greater Value-Creation

The traditional way of thinking about markets revolves around the following tenets:

- Customers and producers are different economic entities.
- They play fixed roles; the company provides value, the customer consumes it.
- Markets connect a buyer and a seller or a customer and a company.
- Markets exist to facilitate exchange of products and services that have value built in or added into them.

However, in the world of collaboration and co-creation, these perspectives don't hold. The lives and worlds of customers and companies collide, overlap, and often converge. Companies and customers don't play fixed roles; their roles evolve and change, especially the role of the customer, depending on the context within which collaboration and co-creation occurs. Further, markets are not simple exchange mechanisms connecting two domains of buyers and sellers. As discussed in the previous section, they are ecosystems where several sets of customers and companies interact and connect with one another to co-create and extract unique value.

Viewed this way, the focus therefore shifts from the simple act of fulfilling a need with a product, service, or solution to creating an infrastructure and environment within which the various members of the company's ecosystem can interact and co-create meaningful value for themselves, consistent with their unique needs, resources, and situational constraints. It is this new aspect of markets that makes rethinking innovation in terms of platforms an effective business strategy. Unlike a single product, a platform represents a core competence, or an asset base that is capable of supporting a family of products, services, and businesses. Platforms are able to extend the range of interactions with other members of the ecosystem into new domains, thereby significantly increasing the opportunities for co-creating new customer value and experiences, and consequently producing higher sales for the company.[19]

Crayola's Color Wonder (CW), discussed earlier in this chapter, effectively demonstrates the superiority of platforms over products. As long as the technology was buried in single products, such as paints, opportunities for co-creation were limited by what that particular product format had to offer. However, rethinking CW as a platform rather than as an embedded technology enabled Crayola to expand its range of interactions with consumers and significantly increase value co-creation opportunities for all members in the ecosystem: consumers, teachers, retailers, and itself.

IBM's SmartPlanet program is a platform and more; it's a system of platforms, capable of supporting other platforms like "Smart Grid," and "Smart Cities." Each of these platforms, like "Smart Cities," is capable of supporting other co-creation platforms, like "smart traffic systems," and "smart bays." This significantly increases IBM's ability to transport applications and solutions from one ecosystem to another. Consider this. IBM can leverage the same platform it used with the city of Stockholm to assist other cities, like London, Singapore, and Brisbane, to address their unique traffic management and congestion challenges. The co-created solutions finally implemented in London, Singapore, or Brisbane will be unique to the traffic needs of those cities, but they would have all originated from the same platform, or set of competencies, that helped Stockholm solve its unique traffic congestion problems. Apple's touch technology, Samsung's core competence in LCDs, and GE's "ecomagination" are other examples of platforms enabling these companies to co-create value with a diverse set of customers in different product or solution categories.

We Need More Meaningful and Substantive Innovations

Imagine receiving a birthday gift, attractively gift-wrapped with ribbons. You open it slowly, expectation increasing at every step. But to your horror, you discover the box is empty. No gift, just the promise of one. Several innovations fit this dark description. They are unable to transcend their packaging and have nothing meaningful or substantive to offer once the box is opened. The steady stream of new products, services, and line-extensions that we often encounter these days are rich in symbolism, but low on substance. They often find it difficult to answer simple questions like:

- Does what is created touch more people's lives? Does it benefit a greater number than before?
- Does it improve the quality of people's lives?
- Does it add meaning and substance in obvious, transparent ways?
- In the long run, does it do more harm than good? Does it sacrifice tomorrow's good for the sake of today's benefits?

If innovations need to be overhyped and oversold, then something is wrong. Somebody forgot the customer along the way. They forgot that value is created not by what companies do *to* products in their factories, but by what customers and other stakeholders are able to do *with* these products while living their daily lives. True innovations offer value co-creation opportunities that are personally relevant and valuable for customers, and other members of a company's ecosystem. They *invite* participation; the value created by innovation doesn't have to be *pushed* through telling and selling.

Marico: A leading Indian consumer products and solutions group, and one of eight Indian companies in S & P's list of emerging global challengers, Marico understands this. That's the reason why year-on-year it continues to be rated as one of Asia and India's fastest growing consumer solution providers. As Harsh Mariwala, Marico's CEO likes to point out, the main focus of innovation at Marico is not to push products out, but to invite customers in for conversations and for co-creating value.[20]

Marico's innovations have been particularly successful in co-creating healthy life-styles and eating habits. Unfortunately, India is the world's capital for heart disease. According to the World Health Organization (WHO), more than 50 percent of the world's cardiac patients are Indians. Several factors, like irregular eating hours, rich diet, increased stress due to urbanization, and inadequate physical exercise contribute to this unfortunate situation.

Marico's wellness business is built around Saffola, a brand that is widely recognized by Indian consumers to be "Good for the Heart." The Saffola product line includes edible oils, rice, salt, and functional foods (boxed mixes for preparing *roti* — Indian bread — that help manage cholesterol). The evolution of the brand reflects how innovations at Marico have engaged the knowledge and resources of various members of the brand's ecosystem, like doctors, dieticians, consumers, and pathology labs, to develop a sustainable customer value platform for co-creating healthier diets and healthier hearts. Two prime examples reflecting Marico's ability to listen, engage, and respond to its ecosytem with meaningful and substantive innovations are Saffola blended oils and Saffola functional foods.

Saffola blended oils: In the early 1990s, most packaged edible oil in the Indian market contained only one main ingredient, such as sunflower, mustard, or groundnut oil. Indian doctors were not impressed by this habit, as they felt persistent use of a single edible oil increased the risk of cardiovascular disease. They favored switching and rotating between different oils to mitigate this risk. This medical opinion prompted Marico to experiment and innovate with blended oils, resulting in the launch of New Saffola, which contains safflower oil (known as Kardi in India — 60 percent), and rice bran oil (40 percent). New Saffola also contains Vitamin E, a popular and potent antioxidant.

Saffola functional foods: Consumers provided the inspiration and knowledge for this innovation. *Roti*, a traditional Indian bread, that resembles a Mexican flour tortilla, but is thicker and fluffier, is a staple food for most Indians. Made from wheat flour (*atta* to most Indians), it is eaten with a wide variety of foods, like lentils, cooked vegetables, and curries. It can be eaten dry or spread with *ghee* (clarified butter), like butter on toast. In conversations with Marico, consumers revealed that they were adding soy and other ingredients to the *atta* before preparing the *rotis*, to increase their nutritive value. Saffola followed up by creating and launching boxed *atta-mixes*, convenient, functional foods that can be added to wheat and contain soy but other nutrients that are good for both reducing cholesterol and managing diabetes.

Think Reverse Innovation

In the world of collaboration and co-creation, country boundaries count for little. They didn't in the nineteenth century, when people living in the English-speaking world collaborated to co-create the Oxford English Dictionary, and they don't in the twenty-first century, when IBM collaborates with countries like Sweden to build smarter cities. Examples shared in previous chapters also point to the no-boundaries aspect of co-creation. Innovation intermediaries like TopCoder and Innocentive co-create value for their clients using a global pool of collaborators.

However, while ideas and resources have traveled freely between countries of unequal economic power, products and services created by innovation have generally tended to flow only from West to East. This too is changing. In an article in the October 2009 issue of *Harvard Business Review* (HBR), Jeffrey Immelt, Vijay Govindrajan, and Chris Trimble discuss how GE is reversing this flow, by actively developing products in China and India for global distribution.[21] Two examples of reverse innovation discussed by the article are a $1,000 handheld electrocardiogram device developed originally for rural India and a $15,000 portable, PC-based ultrasound machine developed for rural China. Developed by GE initially for local market use, both these products are slated for global distribution and form part of GE's ambitious plans to create at least 100 health care innovations in the next six years that will increase patient access, lower costs, and improve quality.

Like collaboration and co-creation, reverse innovation is also the new old. It has been alive and kicking for a number of years, in areas such as microfinance, education, outpatient surgery, energy conservation, and social entrepreneurship. Giants like Grameen Bank (microfinance), Aravind Eye Hospitals (ophthalmic surgeries, both paid and free), and Mumbai's Dabbawallas (social entrepreneurship) have been at the forefront of this movement for several years. They continue to provide hope and ideas to companies and organizations in other regions and sectors. What is new is the adoption of reverse innovation as a core business practice by countries and companies considered best in class until now, as the reverse innovation example in community health care from Haiti illustrates.

Community Health Care: In March 2010, Vijay Govindrajan built on his reverse innovation ideas presented in the Harvard Business Review article by blogging about *How Haiti Is Helping America*. The blog discusses how Dr. Paul Farmer, Dr. Jim Kim, and their colleagues at Partners in Health (PIH) are doing "whatever it takes" to bring medical care to the poor in Haiti. When PIH first started, it was virtually impossible to treat multi-drug resistant tuberculosis in poor countries. Today, not only does PIH know how to treat the disease, but it has protocols to treat it, and it has driven the prices of drugs down by more than 90 percent.

In effect, PIH has created a laboratory for medical innovations in poor countries that has potential for application in rich countries. Its community-based model of care is being examined and adopted by leading health care delivery providers in the developed world. For instance, Boston's Prevention and Access to Care and Treatment (PACT) bases its delivery of home-based medical care to HIV/AIDS patients on the PIH model of fighting drug-resistant tuberculosis in Haiti.

Adapting the *accompagnateur* model developed in Haiti, PIH's only domestic healthcare program trains and employs community members to check in on HIV patients on a daily or weekly basis, making sure they attend medical appointments, take their medications and have access to other essential needs and social services.[22]

As noted, reverse innovation has both rational and emotional appeal. However, for reverse innovation to become a strong and enduring force, companies and organizations in developed countries will need to develop genuine respect for ideas and value co-creation experiences of people in less developed countries. The not-invented-here (NIH) syndrome will need to be aggressively reigned in, if all ideas, individuals, companies, and organizations, regardless of country of affiliation or origin, are to merit equal consideration.

Doing Well by Doing Good

Reverse innovation, reversing the flow of innovation from poorer countries to more developed countries, effectively sets the stage for passing the baton to the next chapter. The current chapter has focused mainly on persuading companies to rethink marketing and innovation because the dynamics of value-creation have changed. The key point is that for value-creation to be effective in today's complex world, it needs to be inclusive; inclusive of customers and other stakeholders in a company's ecosystem. Companies need to involve and engage the creativity, passion, and production potential of empowered customers, not just their wallets. Further, they need to share the value created with all stakeholders, not just with a select few.

This way of thinking raises several important questions. Which customers: those who can afford to pay, or also those who live in poverty, and can't afford products and services the way they are currently produced and packaged? If all stakeholders, not just a select few, then should companies use their global infrastructure and resources to tackle social problems like hygiene, water shortage, and lack of economic opportunities, previously considered to be the preserve of governments?

While these questions are provocative and capable of generating heated discussions, a few things are beyond debate. Companies can no longer approach their own growth agendas — and value - creation is about growth — by ignoring the interests of those customers who live at the bottom of the pyramid, or by compromising the interests of the communities and environment within which they operate. "Sustainability is not the only new frontier of growth and innovation," as Harish Manwani, President Asia, Africa, Central and Eastern Europe Region, Unilever, and Chairman, Hindustan Lever, recently pointed out. "The new sweet spot is doing well by doing good. In future, business success will belong to companies and brands that can successfully integrate a socioeconomic agenda into their innovation and development strategies, and into their relationships with consumers, especially those described as living at the bottom of the pyramid."

But its not just companies that are concerned with growth; countries are also concerned with growing their economies. They too live in a world of scarce resources, global competition, and empowered citizens. Additionally, value-creation is not undertaken by commercial organizations alone. Nonprofit organizations, like hospitals and city governments are equally concerned about creating value for their patients and residents. Some of them are experimenting with the new platforms of collaboration and co-creation to shape socioeconomic outcomes differently than they have done in the past — much like their counterparts in the private sector, Marmite, the Phoenix Suns, Dell, Blizzard Entertainment, and Threadless. Let's travel beyond the business world and get acquainted with some of these experiments now.

Notes and References

1. Based on conversations and a recounting of events by Calvin Austin, who was at Sun during the period covered by the case.
2. Webster, F.E. Jr. (1994). *Market-Driven Management.* New York, NY: Wiley; Drucker, P.F. (1954). *The Practice of Management.* New York: Harper & Row; Barabba, V.P. (1995). *Meeting of the Minds.* Boston, MA: Harvard Business School Press; Lusch, R.F. and Vargo S.L., Editors (2006). *The Service-Dominant Logic of Marketing: Dialog, Debate, and Directions.* Armonk, NY: M. E. Sharpe.
3. Materials for the IFF case study were provided by Sherry Irizarrya and Hernan Vaisman.
4. McKenna, R. (1999). *Real Time: Preparing for the Age of the Never Satisfied Customer.* Boston. MA: Harvard Business School Press.
5. Levitt, T. (1960, July–August). Marketing Myopia. *Harvard Business Review*, 38, (4).
6. All materials for the Crayola case-study were obtained through telephone conversations with Mark Schwab, Sharon DiFelice, and Michelle Powers.
7. Usage of the word "prosumers" — a blend of proactive, or professional, or producer, and consumer — has increased significantly in the last several years. According to the Wikipedia and other sources, usage of this word can be traced back to the writing of Marshall McLuhan and Alvin Toffler. More recently, books like *Cluetrain Manifesto, Wikinomics, and We-Think* have discussed how Prosumers are a source of collaboration and co-creation.
8. Macleod, L. (2010, January 22). New media vital in breaking Haiti earthquake story. *BBC News Online.* Retrieved March 20, 2010, from http://www.bbc.co.uk/worldservice/worldagenda/2010/01/100122_worldagenda_haiti_monitoring.shtml
9. Duryee, T. (2010, February 14). Sony Ericsson Announces User-Generated Content Platform and Three New Phones. *MocoNews Online.* Retrieved March 22, 2010, from http://moconews.net/article/419-sony-ericsson-unveils-user-generated-content-platform-and-three-new-pho/
10. Website: Ubuntu. (n.d.). The Ubuntu Community. Retrieved March 20, 2010, from http://www.ubuntu.com/community
11. Rust, R., Moorman, C. & Bhalla, G. (2010). Rethinking marketing. *Harvard Business Review*, January–February, 88, (1).
12. Website: Spyappspot. (2010, March 13). Comment. Retrieved on March 14, 2010, from http://spy.appspot.com/find/iPad?latest=25
13. Text for the Axe Wake-up Service case study excerpted from insights and materials provided by Babs Rangaiah, Vice President, Global Communications Planning, Unilever, and from http://campaignlive.co.uk/news/926148/APG-Creative-Strategy-Awards — Axe-wake-up-service-BBH-Singapore. Additionally, readers interested in receiving more information on Tamagotchi pets should visit http://www.tamagotchi.com
14. Locke, C., Levine, R., Searls, D. & Weinberger, D. (2001). *The Cluetrain Manifesto: The End of Business as Usual.* New York, NY: Basic Books.
15. Normann, R. & Ramirez, R. (1998*). Designing Interactive Strategy from Value Chain to Value Constellation.* Hoboken, NJ: Wiley; Moore, J. (1997). *The Death of Competition: Leadership & Strategy in the Age of Business Ecosystems.* New York, NY: Harper Paperbacks; Iansiti, M. & Levin, R. (2004). *The Keystone Advantage: What the New Dynamics of Business Ecosystems Mean for Strategy, Innovation, and Sustainability.* Boston, MA: Harvard Business School Press.

16. All materials on IBM's Smart(er) Planet and Smarter Cities programs obtained from conversations with Ed Bevan and Cary Barbour and from materials shared by them.

17. Scally, D. (2009, June 26). IBM sees smarter side of urban life. In *Irish Times*. Retrieved March 7, 2010, from http://www.irishtimes.com/newspaper/finance/2009/0626/1224249571652.html

18. Text for "Sustainability: Innovation's Emerging Frontier" obtained from the following sources: Unilever's website (http://www.unilever.com/mediacentre/pressreleases/2009/UnileverleadsDowJonesSustainabilityIndexfor11thconsecutiveyear.aspx); Dow Jones Sustainability Index website (http://www.sustainability-index.com); SAM's website (http://www.sam-group.com/htmle/about/portrait.cfm); STOXX (http://www.stoxx.com); and CEO Unilever, Mr. Paul Polman's speech given at a conference organized by the Economist (speech provided by Gavin Neath, Senior Vice President Global Communications, for Unilever).

19. Laurie, D.L., Doz, Y.L. & Sheer, C.P. (2006). Creating new growth platforms. *Harvard Business Review*, May, 84, 5; Gawer, A. and Cusumano, M.A. (2008). How Companies Become Platform Leaders. *MIT Sloan Management Review*, Winter, 49, (2).

20. All materials for the Marico case study were provided by their CEO, Harsh Mariwala, and their Head of Strategy, Ameya Naniwadekar.

21. Immelt, J., Govindrajan, V., Timble, C. (2009). How GE is disrupting itself. *Harvard Business Review*, October, 87, (10).

22. Website: The Prevention and Access to Care and Treatment. USA/PACT. (2006). About PACT. Retrieved March 20, 2010, from http://www.pih.org/where/USA/USA.html

Chapter 8
Beyond the Business World

This book started by discussing how the forces of collaboration and co-creation are transforming traditional firm-centric activities like marketing and innovation. What is important, though, is to recognize that the relevance of these platforms is not limited to the business world. Their relevance extends beyond the business world to fields such as education, health care, energy, alleviation of poverty, and sustainability. Their usage in non-business environments is gaining momentum, as countries, regions, and cities experiment with collaboration to co-create more promising futures for their people and the environments in which they live.

In this chapter, we would like to go off the beaten path and travel beyond the business world. We would like to introduce the reader to organizations and people that can be referred to as "silent revolutionaries." Silent, because they don't generally thump their chests on YouTube or celebrate victories on Facebook. Revolutionaries, because the collaboration and co-creation programs they are working on are significant agents of change. We were filled with awe and excitement by what we learned about these organizations and their programs during our discussions with them. We felt we were in the presence of tall people who were aiming for even taller achievements. We would like to share some of their wonderful stories with you.

Denmark: Co-creating a More Vibrant Future

Our first example comes not from an organization but from the country of Denmark. Part of a larger region known as Scandinavia, the Kingdom of Denmark, which includes Greenland, has approximately 5.5 million people. It is the only country in the world with a national collaboration and co-creation program.[1]

Readers familiar with the management culture and business practices of the region will probably not be surprised. Led by pioneers like Professor Jacob Buur, Scandinavian nations have a rich heritage in participatory design. Both private and public sector organizations in the region are known for involving stakeholders in innovation and design processes. Denmark elevated co-creation to a national priority when it launched the Program for User-Driven Innovation (UDI) in 2007. As the world's first government-sponsored user-driven innovation program, UDI exemplifies

G. Bhalla, *Collaboration and Co-creation: New Platforms for Marketing and Innovation*,   145
DOI 10.1007/978-1-4419-7082-4_8, © Springer Science+Business Media, LLC 2011

Denmark's belief in collaboration and co-creation as a core component of its strategy for economic growth and for competing globally. The program also reflects the country's resolve and commitment to increase its stock of innovations and innovating capabilities.

By way of background, the foundation for a national-level co-creation initiative was laid in 2006, when the Danish government articulated a new strategy for elevating Denmark's status in the world economy and reshaping the country's national identity. Four initiatives form the backbone of this strategy:

- Premier education system
- Robust and innovative research
- Increase in high-growth start-up companies
- Renewal and innovation.

In order to execute this new global growth and leadership strategy, the Danish government realized it needed an unconventional and distinctly Danish approach to innovation. The government decided to focus on two factors — scope and cost-effectiveness — because it believed these factors would give the country a unique competitive advantage. In terms of scope, the government decided to support both technological and non-technological initiatives, whether new or supplementing existing innovation, in both public and private sectors. On the cost-effective front, Denmark realized that its high-wage structure would make it impossible for it to compete effectively against low-wage/low-cost countries. The only way it could be cost-effective was if it focused on innovation efficiency. This was fine-tuned to hitting the market with precision, which meant meeting end-user needs accurately by formally and consistently involving them in the innovation process.

The User Driven Innovation (UDI) Program

Denmark's Enterprise and Construction Authority (DECA), a branch of the Danish national government, manages the UDI program. A twelve-person Board, comprising individuals from both the public and private sectors, oversees the initiative. The Board's responsibilities include determining overall strategy for the program, selecting themes for UDI's strategic effort, and evaluating and prioritizing new project applications.

DECA initiates projects to deliver outcomes at both the national and regional levels. Across both categories, the UDI program had initiated 83 co-creation projects by the end of 2009. A majority of these projects address contemporary economic and social issues, such as education, social welfare, and sustainable energy. Case studies of a few UDI funded projects follow:

- Minimum configuration home automation: This project created a prototype for a more efficient home energy system to increase people's awareness of their energy consumption, so that they could modify their behavior to conserve energy. It covered all of a building's energy-consuming installations. Inputs to the project were obtained by observing the daily routines and consumption habits of two test families over a one-year period. Based on these observations, the project team was able to determine end-user preferences, in terms of which aspects of the home energy system they wanted to manage directly and which they preferred to be managed remotely and automatically. The project also developed an inventory of factors to motivate end users—in this case homeowners—to conserve energy. An engineering school led the project. Other companies and organizations that partnered in the project included a manufacturer of windows; two electronic surveillance companies; and a knowledge broker, Alexandra Institute, responsible for knowledge diffusion between universities and businesses.

- E-Trans: The road to success with electric cars in denmark: The goal of this project is to help Denmark move further away from transportation dependent on fossil fuel. Significant technical uncertainty surrounds the future of electric cars, in terms of their design and technical specifications. A new e-car system must address these technical issues; it must also address and evaluate commercial issues, such as customer willingness to switch to electric cars, commercial potential, and market size. Lastly, the overall economic value to the economy of switching energy platforms from fossil fuels to electricity also needs to be assessed. Project E-Trans addresses these interrelated issues using user-driven innovation methods. The focus of the innovation methods is on designing interrelated systems that will produce the highest rate of adoption of electrical cars in Denmark. A major Danish design school, Design Kolding, is the project leader; twelve other private and public organizations also partnered on the project.

- Innovation center Copenhagen: This is a platform for collaboration between the public and private sectors for the co-creation of welfare services. It focuses entirely on the Danish welfare system, which faces a number of challenges, including an aging workforce and continuous demand for high-quality services from users. The center works with communes (the smallest unit of a local community in Denmark) in Copenhagen that are seeking new and better ways to provide welfare services in child, school, and elderly care settings. The program matches public sector institutions with companies, invites participation from a broad group of interested parties and facilitates projects that involve end-users.

- Bringing the hospital closer to citizens: This initiative focuses on co-creating wellness. The fundamental goal of the project is to motivate patients to take a more active role in their own treatment by providing them with appropriate tele-medicine solutions. It hopes to achieve this goal by identifying user needs that can be effectively met by tele-medicine solutions and by developing new and appropriate tele-medical services to effectively meet these needs. The project is led by Herley Hospital, one of Copenhagen's largest hospitals. A leading IT company and a tele-solutions provider are also involved in this collaborative effort. Pregnant women and patients with heart conditions were among the first groups on which the project was tested.

As of early 2010, many of UDI's projects, including some discussed above, are still ongoing. Consequently, the full range of results and outcomes has yet to emerge. However, based on activities completed so far, DECA does have some initial performance indicators to track success against overall program goals:

- Innovation activity: 72 percent of participating companies have developed, or were expected to develop, new products or services by the end of 2009.
- Cross-sector participation: 75 percent of projects involve public-private sector partnerships.
- Private sector involvement: 66 percent of participating organizations are private sector companies.
- Small organization involvement: Over 50 percent of participating companies have fewer than 50 employees.

Based on the original plan, UDI was slated to run for three years, through 2010, which it has done successfully. Going forward, the original UDI program has been discontinued and replaced by a new program called the Business Innovation Fund. The new fund will also run for a period of three years, until 2012. UDI will be a part of this new fund. However, the new fund will also support large, mature projects developed and implemented with relevant collaborators in the business sector. In both cases, the Innovation Fund will focus on primarily supporting projects that aim to develop Welfare and Green solutions. A visual depiction of the goals and focus of the new Business Innovation Fund is presented in Appendix 8.1.

Scotland: Co-creating Quality of Life for the 50+ Age Group

The next example is from Scotland and centers around co-creating quality of life for Scotland's aging population. (NESTA) National Endowment for Science, Technology and the Arts is the UK's single largest endowment focused exclusively on innovation. Its charter is to help solve economic and social challenges by funding research and start-ups and by implementing new programs.

The demographic shift toward an aging population, common to many Western countries, including Scotland, creates specific demands for health, economic, and social services. In response to its own aging population, Scotland's government has created a strategic initiative called *Reshaping the Future Care of Older People*. The main goal of this program is to prevent social isolation, so that the quality and prosperity older individuals enjoy in the later years of their lives can be improved. Scotland's government sees this initiative as a critical component of its national priority of sustainable economic growth.

Age Unlimited Scotland, a part of the Reshaping the Future Care program, went live in December 2009. The program is designed to mitigate social isolation by involving Scotland's senior citizens in shaping their own quality of life. It aims to sponsor and nurture approximately 20 socially motivated start-ups or community ventures that will address the issue of social isolation among elderly citizens.

The program's beneficiaries are also the innovators; the target age group, 50+, that benefits from services to prevent social marginalization and isolation also helps co-create and develop them. Consequently, these ventures are led by teams of individuals from local communities who seek to make aging a more "fulfilling, healthy and socially inclusive experience."[2]

NESTA has specified three criteria for projects and ideas to be considered. Ideally, projects should:

- Be scalable and replicable
- Be cost-neutral, preferably cost-saving
- Demonstrate genuine innovation and avoid replicating existing community initiatives.

The agency considers all adults living in Scotland, especially those in the 50+ age group, to be its primary collaborators. NESTA is aware that individuals in this age group often have valuable business experience and first-hand involvement with caring for the elderly. They are also aware that the ideas and contributions of this group often go overlooked, as older adults tend to be pushed aside and feel marginalized in today's world. Just as Professor James Murray appealed for readers in May 1879 to help co-create the Oxford English Dictionary (see Chap. 1), Age Unlimited too appeals directly to its potential collaborators:

> Maybe you have experience as a caretaker or volunteer with older people and have skills and experience you'd be willing to share? Maybe you are approaching retirement, are recently retired or have been made redundant and are looking for a new challenge? If so, we want to hear from you. In return we've got support and funding to make your idea become real.[3]

NESTA plans to build its pipeline of ideas and projects by following a multi-stage process that covers submission, selection, refinement, and implementation. The program promises to support chosen ventures with funding and training, offering £10,000 in staged payments and a 10–12-week incubation process involving:

- Group training: One day per fortnight in marketing, finance, and presentation skills
- Telephone coaching: To help participants take more intelligent risks
- Mentoring: Assistance in developing the venture from a volunteer mentor, who will act as a critical friend and ally.

Age Unlimited Scotland is still in the early stages of conception and implementation. However, NESTA and those guiding Age Unlimited Scotland need to be complimented for their bold thinking. The creation of the program itself has helped the program achieve part of its overall goals. Not only does the program offer potential innovators a proving ground for testing and refining their ideas, it also offers them a chance to build community. Social connectivity — the ability to connect and network with peers — offers potential entrepreneurs and innovators a chance to both refine their ideas and reverse their sense of isolation and marginalization. Age Unlimited Scotland benefits because it gets to build a pipeline of ideas and projects.

Simultaneously, the pool of collaborators and co-creators in the 50+ age group benefit because they are now more immersed in their communities.

Early results have been very promising. The first Age Unlimited Scotland challenge drew 115 entries from individuals and/or teams with the seed of an idea for a social or community enterprise. In a press release issued in July 2010 to celebrate the winners, Jackie McKenzie, NESTA's Head of Innovation Programs in Scotland commented: "The Age Unlimited Scotland program has shown that there is a wealth of innovative ideas amongst local people to help improve services in their own community for older people. With intelligent support and appropriate funding, they can make a significant difference in tackling one of Scotland's biggest social challenges." Appendix 8.2 presents a list of Age Unlimited Scotland challenge winners, and a link to the press release.

Chicago: Co-creating a Greener City

Popularly known as the Windy City, Chicago is also one of the greenest cities in the United States. Under the leadership of Mayor Richard Daley, the city has undertaken major initiatives like protecting waterways, preserving green spaces, and promoting alternative transportation, to earn and protect its green badge.

Emission reduction as a means of stemming climate change is a key priority of the city's administrators. A special council, the Chicago Council on Climate Change, the only legally binding carbon reduction program of its kind in the United States, was created to help Chicago meet these goals. To implement carbon reduction activities, the Council developed and launched the Chicago Climate Action Plan (CCAP).[4]

CCAP is a highly collaborative initiative and is designed to involve and benefit multiple stakeholders. According to the program's vision, every Chicago resident and business has a role to play in implementing the Chicago Climate Action Plan. In addition to improving the quality of life by improving the city's climate, the program also hopes to contribute to the city's economy, to job creation, and to new technology development. In order to ensure that the program is actionable, CCAP has developed a system of interrelated program goals, specific strategies, and supporting activities.

First are the emissions reduction goals:

- Reduce 1990(1)-level greenhouse gas (GHG) emissions by 80 percent by 2050
- Reduce1990-level GHG emissions by 25 percent by 2025
- Prepare for the effects of climate change.

Next are the strategies that support the overall emissions goals:

- Increase energy efficiency of buildings
- Transition to clean and renewable energy sources
- Improve transportation options
- Reduce waste and industrial pollution
- Adapt to climate change.

Finally, the five strategies are supported by a portfolio of over 30 specific activities and projects.

Where does collaboration and co-creation enter the picture? From start to finish: from goal setting through implementation. CCAP goals were developed through a collaborative partnership among the city government, local businesses, and environmental science leaders. This cooperation helped ensure that the goals were challenging, yet attainable. CCAP intends to directly engage all stakeholders in implementing a variety of emission reduction activities. Collectively, the program will offer all Chicago residents, from businesses, to community organizations, to individual residents, an opportunity to co-create a greener city and do their bit to help fight climate change.

Two examples of these collaborative projects are shared below:

- Chicago Conservation Corps (C3): This is an environmental volunteer program and is run by the city's environment department in collaboration with community partners. C3 volunteers work to improve the quality of life in the community through environmental service projects like water protection, land restoration, and energy conservation. C3 seeks collaboration and co-creation participation at three levels: leadership, student clubs, and explorers. Collaborators participating in the C3 leadership track are community members who receive training and resources to implement environmental service projects in their neighborhoods. The C3 student clubs offer an opportunity for students and teachers to collaborate by facilitating participation and involvement in environmental activities in their schools. The C3 explorer track allows ordinary residents to get involved with short-term environmental volunteer opportunities in projects led by partner organizations and C3 leaders.[5]
- The $800 Savings Challenge: This project aims to educate and motivate individuals to make small environmentally friendly contributions. In spirit it is similar to Denmark's Minimum Configuration Home Automation project. Using checklists, it demonstrates how by taking small steps Chicagoans can benefit the environment and their wallets. Individuals log in to the program's dedicated website, where they can receive information on small changes that they can make in their energy consumption habits, such as adjusting home thermostat settings. The website also helps individuals compute the monetary impact of their efforts. By aggregating the impacts across several participants, individuals participating in the program are able to develop a big-picture understanding of their grassroots contributions. Getting people to change their energy consumption behavior is an important aspect of combating climate change (Box 8.1).[6]

These activities are a token indicator of CCAP's expansive plans to co-create a greener Chicago. They are designed to mobilize the entire city of Chicago so all stakeholders, from individuals to large organizations, feel empowered to collaborate and contribute. By all accounts, CCAP has been very successful in making significant contributions toward helping Chicago meet its overall emissions reduction goals. A progress report published in 2010 applauds the achievements of

Box 8.1 Next Frontier in Sustainability: Getting People to Change Their
Behavior

Washington, D.C. hosted the third annual Behavior, Energy and Climate
Change Conference in November 2009. The conference focused on the critical
role of individual and organizational behavior and decision making in accelerating society's transition to an energy-efficient and low-carbon future.[7]

The conference brought together a diverse group of energy experts, social
scientists, and policymakers to discuss practical implementation issues, like
reducing energy use through the adoption and application of more energy-
efficient technologies, energy conservation activities, and lifestyle changes.
An important outcome of this meeting was to demonstrate that technology
alone can't help a household, organization, community, city, or country
achieve its reduced energy consumption and sustainability goals.

There will always be a choice component to human behavior that technology alone can't address. Decisions related to recycling, composting, cycling
to work, walking to the store, unplugging electrical components not in use,
turning off lights, buying from local farmers, and using daylight rather than
incandescent or fluorescent light while working are essentially human decisions. To influence these decisions requires a deeper understanding of human
beings, of behavioral economics, and the dynamics of social change.

Grassroots efforts like the $800 Savings Challenge attempt to achieve this
change one human being at a time. The platforms of collaboration and co-
creation help accelerate this change within communities and countries, by
using the power of technology to connect individuals with one another and to
worthy causes.

CCAP and provides a comprehensive list of impact highlights for the first two years
(2008–2009). Appendix 8.3 lists the key achievements and provides a link to the
progress report.

Norway: Co-creating Health Care Innovations

Outpatient clinics are a common complement to hospital health care in most
urban centers. But the outpatient Clinic of Innovation at Oslo University's
Ullevaal Hospital is literally one of a kind. Unlike traditional outpatient clinics
that augment inpatient hospital care, the Clinic of Innovation builds a bridge
between research and innovation on one side and socially useful services and
products on the other. Instead of catering to patients with illnesses, the Clinic of
Innovation caters to individuals with ideas. Though designed to operate like a
traditional outpatient clinic, it is not in the business of creating physical well

being, but in the business of facilitating innovation through the creation of new technologies and services.

The clinic is the brainchild of Andreas Moan, MD, Ph.D., and Kari Kværner.[8] It was launched in 2007, on Dr. Moan's return to Ullevaal Hospital following an eleven-year stint with the pharmaceutical industry. On his return, Dr. Moan observed that the entrepreneurial and innovative mindset that he had experienced in the private sector was lacking in the hospital environment. The scientific process seemed to stop with the publication of research. There was little interest in moving from research to developing practical, useful solutions for patients or for society. He and Kari Kværner were convinced that more could be done to foster innovation by soliciting ideas from end-users and putting them into practice.

The Clinic of Innovation

The overall purpose of the Clinic of Innovation is to increase the volume of ideas generated and facilitate their conversion to new commercially viable products and services, that benefit both patients and society. In addition, the Clinic also sees itself as a forum for advancing the cause of innovation in society. The Clinic believes that it has an obligation and the ability to inform and educate society at large on the importance of innovation and on its positive economic impacts. Because the Clinic is a joint venture between one of Norway's leading hospitals and a major technology transfer firm (Medinnova), the Clinic of Innovation has legitimacy and the strength of voice to achieve this higher-order purpose.

To fulfill its purpose, the Clinic of Innovation works with two sets of important stakeholders (or customers):

- Professionals working within the health system: the Clinic helps them develop new ideas on how services, treatments, processes, or products can be improved or developed.
- Individuals, commercial parties, and biotech and other research-intensive companies that are external to the hospital: these parties are but interested in collaborating on specific ideas with experts within the health care system.

So, how does it work? Very much like a normal outpatient clinic, except that its procedures are applied to ideas rather than illnesses:

- The process begins when collaborators or customers refer themselves to the Clinic with an idea for a product or service innovation. Ideas can also be submitted online or by telephone for initial vetting. The Clinic has weekly intake meetings to review ideas. Collaborators who have referred ideas usually receive a response within two weeks. On occasion, the Clinic may contact the customer before the intake meeting to obtain more information on the submitted idea. The Clinic guarantees full confidentiality and signs a confidentiality agreement with the client during the first appointment.

- Next, the idea is diagnosed. Diagnostic work-ups at the Clinic involve evaluating an idea's potential, using both research and commercial criteria. External experts are called in to assist with the evaluation on an as-needed basis. Based on the diagnosis, the Clinic offers various treatment options for the idea, such as:

  1. Direct problem solving: The Clinic works one-on-one with the owner of the idea.
  2. Development as a joint venture: Sensing synergy, the Clinic may suggest getting other parties and collaborators involved.
  3. Expanding inputs by networking with other individuals or groups: In cases where the Clinic feels that the idea needs further development, it may recommend inputs from a network of individuals or groups.
  4. Group therapy: The Clinic may connect the idea owner with other innovators facing similar problems.

- Occasionally, the Clinic may also offer follow-up consultation, if an idea requires additional attention, or if it requires support in the implementation process.

By its first birthday in 2008, the Clinic had reviewed forty ideas, eight of which became technology projects. In addition, patent applications were filed for three new inventions, including a support technology that informs doctors/nurses whether they have properly intubated a patient. More ideas have been submitted since then, and by early 2010, the Clinic had received approximately eighty ideas. To cope with increased flow of ideas, the Clinic upgraded its current system of manual registration to an online, open access system for soliciting and treating ideas in March 2010.

One particularly successful idea generated from the clinic, which has also resulted in the launch of a new venture, involves using stem cells to grow corneal eye tissue. Developed by two Oslo University Hospital ophthalmologists, the innovation overcomes the major limitations of today's know-how related to variation in quality, problems with storage, difficulty of transportation, timing of elective surgery, and feasibility of large-scale production. The proposed innovation, because of its new technological properties, opens up an entirely new realm of treatment possibilities:

- Corneal tissue can be stored for up to a week.
- Storage makes it possible to transport the tissue.
- Transportation makes treatment available in different parts of the world, including developing countries.

In addition, the new technology helps deliver better clinical results through enhanced quality and sterility of transplants. Finally, the innovation makes large-scale production feasible and economically attractive, in one or a few centers.

The Clinic has recently established a collaborative partnership with Harvard University for scientific and commercial development of the corneal tissue cultivation technology. Three scientists from Oslo University Hospital have been invited to Harvard to further develop the technology. Institutions like the U.S. Department of Defense have also shown significant interest in collaborating to further develop the technology. Private investors have funded a venture to help develop the technology in which Harvard University, Oslo University Hospital, and the ophthalmologists who developed the innovation will all be shareholders.

The next stage in the Clinic's evolution as an innovation accelerator is to shift a portion of the responsibility for disease prevention and treatment to people's homes. In short, the Clinic would like to co-create well-being with customers of health care in their homes, not just in the hospital. Online medical services are likely to play a central role in this effort. By empowering health care customers with digital tools, the Clinic would like customers to engage in behaviors like entering relevant information about themselves and their disease online, recording specific behaviors and daily practices, and monitoring the health-related consequences of their behavioral choices. Using these tools, customers and Clinic staff can collaborate to generate data and knowledge that can be applied toward the care of the specific individual, as well as other health care customers. The Clinic would like customers to reset their thinking and migrate from being mere consumers of health care services to being enlightened contributors, responsible for co-creating their personal well-being.

Visionaire 42 and 47: Co-creating a Unique Sensory Experience

What do you get when leading perfumers, chefs, and artists collaborate with one another to co-create an entirely new aesthetic experience — one that combines the senses of taste and sight? The sponsors of this unique experiment, Visionaire, an exclusive multi-format album for fashion and art, and International Flavors and Fragrances (IFF), a global leader in creating some of the most famous scents and tastes, were not sure, but they had a strong hunch on what to expect — a unique sensory experience![9]

They had good reason. Their previous collaboration had been very successful, culminating in Visionaire No. 42, a limited edition, boxed, forty-page booklet with twenty perfume bottles, devoted exclusively to the exciting world of *Scent*. The collaboration exercise, conducted in 2003, asked some very interesting questions:

- What does cold smell like? What does it look like?
- What about heat? Electricity? Softness?

Leading image-makers from the world of fashion and art were asked to visually interpret an innovative roster of never-before conceived modern scents, mixed by some of the best noses in the perfume industry. For example, Mario Sorrenti, a successful fashion photographer was paired with a fragrance developed by Yves Cassar to interpret *Cold*. Karl Lagerfeld, a versatile man of many interests including fashion, antiques, and photography, was paired with a fragrance developed by Sandrine Malin to interpret *Hunger*. The outcome was an exclusive issue consisting of individual vials of exclusive scents to be enjoyed over time, with a complement of full-color images, housed in a customized case.

In Visionaire 47, produced in 2005, the two companies wanted to explore the realm of *Taste*. Leading artists such as Jenny Holzer, Yoko Ono, Maurizio Cattelan, and Bruce Weber, as well as other accomplished cultural figures like chef Ferran Adria and rock star Elton John, teamed up with IFF's professional flavorists and perfumers, such as Kevin Miller, Cathianne Caiazzo, Guinevere de la Margarite, Marion Sudol, Mauricio Poulsen, and Christophe Laudamielto, to break new ground in the exploration of taste. The co-created experience consisted of twelve original flavors produced exclusively for Visionaire, in the form of fast-dissolving breath-strips in individually marked, custom-designed cases, with images corresponding to each taste printed in an accompanying hardcover book. True to Visionaire's custom and style, the limited edition of 4,000 numbered copies was housed and presented in an innovative, eye-catching package.

This groundbreaking collaboration produced a stunning result. Featured at the international art show in Miami, *Taste* elevated flavor to a pure art medium and co-created yet another unique sensory experience. *Taste* features twelve themes such as *Mother, Guilt, Youth, Luxury,* and *Adrenaline*. As in the case of *Scent* (Visionaire 42), each theme is interpreted by selected artists collaborating with a flavorist, to co-create a unique sensory experience around that theme (Box 8.2).

For IFF, both *Scent* and *Taste* were important experiments: forays into new areas where flavor, art, and emotions converge. Both experiments resulted in new value for IFF's customers.

- The *Scent* experiment resulted in two new products: Liquid Karl (Karl Lagerfeld) and New Dior Fragrance for Men.
- The *Taste* experiment resulted in an enhanced understanding of the role of emotions in taste, expanding the domain of flavors to include both gustatory and emotional aspects. The fast-growing category of comfort foods is a good example of a category where both emotions and taste interact to deliver value to consumers.

IBM's Habitat Jam: Solutions for Pressing Human Problems

Habitat Jam is the celebration of three remarkable days in history. A collaboration between the United Nations (UN) and IBM, it offered 40,000 individual citizens from around the world an opportunity to be heard as equals. We can't think of a better way to end this chapter than on this note of hope and inspiration.[10]

Held in 2005, Habitat Jam was a 72-hour online global event. The Jam invited participants from all walks of life to share their ideas on issues critical to their communities, like sustainability, governance, poverty, and peace. The event's lofty goals included:

- Fostering collaboration on a global level
- Involving individuals who typically would not have the opportunity to participate in a formal social policy forum

- Jump-starting the change process for critical social welfare issues
- Generating actionable ideas for implementation
- Creating new networks for global collaboration.

In the words of Charles Kelly, Commissioner General of World Urban Forum III:

Habitat Jam is the first time that citizens of the world have the opportunity, without the filters of national governments or repression, to share their points of view.

Box 8.2 The Flavor of Luxury and Youth

Luxury[11]

- Inspiration: Chef Ferran Adrìa's famous dish of pinecone tips was served in a sweet acidic syrup. Adrìa says that the pinecone tips are more exclusive than white truffles or caviar. They are picked in May and June from the pine trees that surround his renowned El Bulli restaurant in Spain.
- Flavor: Flavorists John Wright and Guinevere de la Marguerite combined the flavors of pine needle, nuts, fat, and freshness to convey sophistication.
- Art: Photographer Sølve Sundbø captured an up-close view of a woman's lips and tongue, coated in a rich syrup and preparing to eat a single, savory pine nut.

(continued)

Box 8.2 (Continued)

Youth

- Inspiration: Photographer Bruce Weber wanted to capture the essence of youth and happy emotional memories from childhood.
- Flavor: Flavorist Kevin Miller crafted a cherry licorice flavor to convey youth. He calls it a "sweet, intoxicating, complex berry blend" with a depth of flavor that triggers childhood nostalgia.
- Art: Photographer Bruce Weber captured a young man rubbing his eyes, in the process of waking up, probably reluctantly, since the photo is portraying youth.

Chapters Five and Six discussed how Jams — large-scale online collaboration and co-creation efforts — pioneered by IBM are used by companies to address complex issues, such as agreeing on company values, developing innovation agendas, and setting three-to-five-year strategic priorities. The 2007 Habitat Jam was the first time IBM used its Jam expertise outside the walls of its own company. In addition to IBM and the UN, other significant participants included the Global Dialogue Center, World Urban Forum, and the Government of Canada. Most significant, however, was the participation of close to 40,000 individuals from 158 countries. They included architects, activists, urban planners, teachers, representatives from NGOs, bankers, women, young people, poor, slum dwellers, and government leaders.

Collaboration helped the Habitat Jam achieve its first goal: it gave individuals and groups that are not traditionally invited to global policy discussions a seat at

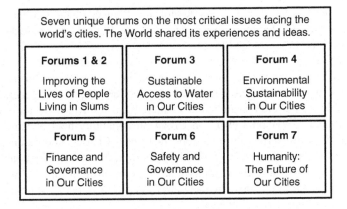

Fig. 8.1 Habitat for Humanity Discussion Forums

the table and a voice. The online forum was a great equalizer. It put participants on the same footing, regardless of background, qualifications, or social status. As described in Chap. 6, achieving this goal required organization and advance planning. Organizers used viral marketing techniques to solicit worldwide participation. In addition, they used a network of local partner organizations for grassroots marketing. Local partner organizations also ensured an adequate supply of computers, so that non-ownership of computers or lack of Internet availability would not limit participation of the poor or those from rural communities.

The remaining goals were addressed during the 72 hours of the Jam's life. Fig 8.1 lists the seven forums sponsored by the event to organize conversations and channel ideas. Participants' ideas submitted online were captured by the Jam database. Multiple modes of interaction, such as focus groups, chat rooms, virtual cafés, and online rallies, were used to stimulate conversations and share ideas.

A good example of the productive conversations that occurred during the Jam was Forum 7, which dealt with the theme "humanity and the future of cities." Working with moderators, participants identified the top ten issues the group wanted to discuss. One issue that captured the group and the world's attention was: "What does it mean to be a good neighbor?" The goal was to define the attributes and qualities of a good neighbor at various levels, at the level of individuals, communities, and countries. Participants co-developed a list of qualities that good neighbors possess:

- They help one another
- They value each other unconditionally
- They stand up for one another
- They do not rip you off or leave you stranded
- They do not hurt you or blow up your house
- They care for your animals, pets, and children as if they were their own.

The group also explored the idea of creating a charter for cities, based on "good neighbor" attributes that it had identified. A small group of participants continued the work after the forum, to ensure that *good neighbor* ideas would get implemented.

Debbe Kennedy, a key Forum 7 moderator and founder of the Global Dialogue Center, continues to champion this issue and keeps it alive on her organization's website and blog.

The Habitat Jam succeeded astoundingly on several dimensions — inclusiveness, global reach, and the number of actionable ideas generated. During the jam, 4,000 pages of discussion and ideas were recorded, 600 ideas were generated, and 70 actionable ideas were researched and summarized for World Urban Forum III, an international UN Habitat event on Urban Sustainability held in Vancouver in June 2006. It is not surprising, therefore, that when Charles Kelly addressed the Vancouver audience at the UN World Urban Forum, it was with a palpable air of exultation. That's because the commissioner general of the forum had achieved a feat never before accomplished: he had literally *"consulted the world* on the themes to be addressed during the conference."

The true significance of Habitat Jam goes beyond a single meeting. It reinforced the value of dialogue and conversation. It laid the technological and ideological foundation for global collaboration and co-creation to address some of humanity's most pressing problems. There were no governments, no flag-waving officials — just enthusiastic citizens from all over the world, eager to share their ideas and their voices. Ideas and voices that are typically suppressed when hierarchical bureaucratic structures take center stage and push collaboration and co-creation aside. The Jam demonstrated that it was possible for groups of people who had never met or worked with one another before, to generate approximately one actionable idea per hour: 70 actionable ideas in 72 hours.

The work started by the Habitat Jam endures. Actions, both big and small, are underway in numerous cities. Above all, a new threshold in human collaboration and communications was crossed during the Jam, clearing the way for even more innovation to follow.

Appendix 8.1 Business Innovation Fund Focus

Appendix 8.2 Winners of NESTA's Age Unlimited Scotland Challenge

A press release by NESTA stated that six social ventures established by entrepreneurs aged over 50 will share a £100,000 pilot fund as part of NESTA's Age Unlimited Scotland challenge.[12] The purpose of the Age Unlimited Scotland project is to radically transform public services in Scotland by involving people aged 50 plus to help to tackle social isolation in the very old.

The six winners are:

- **Volunteer Gold in Forfar**: The purpose of the venture is to enable older people to have access to a range of physical, creative, and learning activities that maintain or improve their physical health and wellbeing.
- **Third Age Fun and Games**: Based in Edinburgh, this venture will enable older people to learn to play computer games and have fun.
- **The Big Event**: This venture is a one-day festival that will bring together all the local work, volunteering, and social support initiatives in South Lanarkshire interested in the over-50 age group.
- **Better Balmedie**: This venture is a voluntary gardening group that wants to improve the appearance of the village with a particular focus on making gardening accessible to older people.
- **Book Exchange**: Based in Argyll, this venture will provide a way for sections of the older population to enjoy, swap, and discuss books in an interactive way.
- **Dragon's Tooth Golf Course**: Located in Spean Bridge, this venture provides a choice of physical and creative activities which all have a direct connection with the Dragon's Tooth Golf Course, and in particular with the mystical Dragon Monkeys that live there. The project aims to be self-sustaining through sale of the Dragon Monkey items and associated fund raising activities.

Appendix 8.3 Chicago Climate Action Plan Progress Report: First Two Years

The Chicago Climate Action Plan issued a progress report for 2008–2009 to document its achievements for the first two years of the program.[13] Impact highlights for this period are listed below.

- 456 initiatives developed through 16 City departments and sister agencies to reduce emissions and adapt to change
- 13,341 housing units retrofitted to be more energy efficient
- 393 commercial and industrial buildings retrofitted to be more energy efficient
- 30,542 appliances traded in
- 20 million more Chicago Transit Authority rides annually
- 35 million gallons of water conserved per day

- 1.8 million square feet of additional green roofs installed or under construction
- 120 green alleys installed
- 636 new car share vehicles available
- 208 hybrid buses added to Chicago Transit Authority fleet
- 508,000 gallons of alternative fuel used
- 83 percent of construction and demolition debris recycled

Notes and References

1. Inputs for this section were obtained from a vast amount of information and materials shared by organizations and individuals associated with Denmark's User Driven Innovation Program. Key among them were Anna Helene Mollerup, of Danish Enterprise and Construction Authority (DECA), Professor Jacob Buur, University of Southern Denmark, Anna Kirah, who was with CPH Design at the time of writing, and Karin Wall and Lars Andersson, of Innovation Management. (continued) Additionally, an interview with the Director of DECA published in Innovation Management was also helpful in shaping the contents of the section — (2009, September 22). Is Denmark a Lead User of User-Driven Innovation? *Innovation Management.* http://www.innovationmanagement.se/index.php?option=com_content&view=article&id=255:is-denmark-a-lead-user-of-user-driven-innovation&catid=140:article&Itemid=289

2. Website: Age Unlimited Scotland. (n.d.) About NESTA. http://www.nesta.org.uk/areas_of_work/public_services_lab/ageing/age_unlimited_scotland

3. Ibid (Ref. # 2)

4. Website: Chicago Climate Action Plan. (n.d.) About Chicago Climate Action Plan. Retrieved 2 April, 2010, from http://www.chicagoclimateaction.org/pages/chicago_climate_action_plan/45.php

5. Website: Chicago Climate Action Plan. (n.d.) About Residential Programs. Retrieved April 2, 2010, from http://www.chicagoclimateaction.org/pages/for_residents/55.php

6. Website: Chicago Climate Action Plan. (n.d.) Take the $800 Savings Challenge. Retrieved April 2, 2010, from http://www.chicagoclimateaction.org/pages/savings_challenge/39.php

7. Website: American Council for an Energy Efficient Economy. (2009). 2009 BECC Conference Leadership. Retrieved April 4, 2010, from http://www.aceee.org/conf/09becc/09beccindex.htm

8. Subject matter for this section were obtained from information and materials shared by Dr. Andreas Moan. At the time of inception of The Clinic, Kari Kværner was the Director of Innovation at Medinnova; at the time of writing she was the Director of Research and Innovation at Ullevaal. Additional materials also used for this section include — The Official Norwegian Trade Portal. (2009, December 11). Clinic for the Conversion of Ideas for Use in Socially Useful Services and Products. from http://www.nortrade.com/index.php?cmd=company_presentation&companynumber=261234&page=profile; 2008, April). Clinic of Innovation Uses Health Care Metaphors to Win Staff Over to Tech Transfer. *Technology Transfer Tactics.* Vol. 2, No. 4, pp. 49–64. Retrieved April 2, 2010, from http://www.medinnova.no/filestore/2008aprilIdepoliklinikkeniTechTranssfTactics.pdf; Be Well Stanford, Healthcare Industry and Policy Community. Moan, Andreas. (2008, October 21). Outpatient Clinic of Innovation." Retrieved April 3, 2010, from http://stanford.wellsphere.com/healthcare-industry-policy-article/outpatient-clinic-of-innovation/435664

9. Inputs for this section were obtained through information and materials shared by Carol Brys of International Flavors and Fragrances, by Javier Bone-Carbone of Visionaire, from Visionaire's website — http://www.visionaireworld.com, and from www.artworld.com, a website that specializes in new books on art, photography, architecture, design and critical theory

10. Inputs for this section were shared by Liam J. Cleaver of IBM, from Knowledge Gallery. (2006). Habitat JAM Podcast. Retrieved March 30, 2010, http://www.globaldialoguecenter. com/exhibits/backbone/index.shtml, and from Manfield, L. (n.d). A New Collaboration System Lets Anyone, Anywhere Voice an Opinion. *Backbone Magazine*. Retrieved 27, April, 2010, from http://www.backbonemag.com/Magazine/CoverStory_10270601.asp
11. Please see reference 9 for acknowledgment of text inputs. Photographs reproduced with explicit permission from Visionaire. Reader's interested in exploring images associated with all twelve tastes covered by the special issue should visit — http://www.visionaireworld.com/ issues.php?id=47— and click the images to experience each specific taste
12. http://www.nesta.org.uk/areas_of_work/public_services_lab/ageing/age_unlimited_scotland/ assets/features/third_age_entrepreneurs_win_nestas_age_unlimited_challenge
13. http://www.chicagoclimateaction.org/filebin/pdf/CCAPProgressReportv3.pdf

Epilogue

It is natural for questions like "What's next?", "Where do we go from here?", and "Where is collaboration and co-creation headed?" to arise after reading a book like this. Each time a new business practice gathers momentum, its strongest protagonists are quick to predict the demise of competing incumbent practices. In this case the contest could be advertised as "collaboration and co-creation versus traditional firm-centric methods of value-creation."

But we know that's not how the world operates. Reality is far more sticky and stubborn. New media has been predicting the demise of broadcast TV for several years now. But broadcast TV is still alive and kicking. Or take the concept of customer-centricity, a mainstay of collaboration and co-creation. Ben Shapiro's rather feisty article "What the Hell Is Market Oriented?" first appeared in the November–December issue of *Harvard Business Review* in 1988. Two decades later, customer-centricity is still struggling to make it to the top of the strategic agenda of most companies. Conversations about brand equity and maximizing shareholder value still take preference over listening, engaging, or responding to the customer. Probably that's the reason why the special issue of Harvard Business Review (January–February 2010), "Reinvent," carried two articles on the importance of customers — "Rethinking Marketing" and "The Age of Customer Capitalism" probably to remind companies that they have been falling significantly short in meeting their commitments to customers.

So, making sweeping generalizations will not help. Rather than play soothsayer and write a lengthy essay predicting in which round the knockout will occur, we would prefer to do what we have done throughout the book. We would like to discuss a few telling case studies and use them as a guide to determine in which direction the adoption and usage of collaboration and co-creation is headed. Do the examples point to a future with increasing rates of adoption and usage, or do they suggest a more ambivalent future, with a lot of ifs, buts, and question marks?

Let's continue where we left off in the previous chapter, with a macro example: global collaboration among governments, state organizations, and everyday citizens, a first-time application by an organization new to collaboration and co-creation.

Global Pulse 2010

In his landmark speech delivered in Cairo, in June 2009, President Barack Obama pledged to engage the global community, especially the Muslim world, in shaping his administration's approach to foreign assistance in the areas of entrepreneurship, education, science, technology, and health.

> All these things must be done in partnership. Americans are ready to join with citizens and governments, community organizations, religious leaders, and businesses in Muslim communities around the world to help our people pursue a better life.

In order to follow through on the promise, the U.S. Agency for International Development (USAID), in partnership with the Departments of State, Education, Commerce, and Health and Human Services, organized Global Pulse 2010. A 3-day online collaboration and global conversation, the event was held from March 29 to March 31, 2010. It attracted thousands of participants from over 155 countries and resulted in close to 10,000 ideas, reactions, opinions, and perspectives. I am pleased to share that I was one of those voices.

Global Pulse 2010 was powered by IBM's jam technology and implemented by Liam Cleaver, IBM's Program Director for Collaborative Innovation, and his team, the same team that helped implement the United Nations-sponsored Habitat Jam in 2005, discussed in Chap. 8. According to Hanna Jung, USAID Program Manager for Global Pulse, the program had two main objectives. The first was to demonstrate that the US government is truly committed to the president's vision for global engagement. The second was to "create an opportunity to engage with people, and obtain ideas through a collaborative dialogue process that hopefully would identify more innovative ideas than we could develop on our own." Global Pulse 2010 succeeded handsomely on both counts.

The Global Pulse website (http://www.globalpulse2010.gov/) is inactive, since the event is over, though registered jam participants can still log in and review the ideas and suggestions made by jam participants on topics such as *Empowering Women and Girls*, *Advancing Entrepreneurship, Trade and Economic Opportunity*, *Enabling Essential Education*, and *Supporting a Sustainable Planet*. The landing page (post log-in) carries an extremely pertinent message from Raj Shah, USAID Administrator:

> By listening to each other and collaborating, each of us can become an agent of change and contribute to innovative and sustainable solutions to local and international challenges. We take all these ideas, suggestions, and opinions seriously, and we strongly encourage you to help us carry this conversation forward after the close of Global Pulse 2010 by becoming a fan on Facebook.

Let us now consider another example, of a company growing its business, not by using the traditional pushing and selling model, but by using the new co-creation and personalization of experiences model with a new market segment: consumers living at the bottom of the pyramid.

Swasthya Chetna (Hindi for "Health Awakening")

Swasthya Chetna is the largest rural health and hygiene education program ever undertaken in India. It is not a government initiative, but is sponsored instead by Hindustan Lever – more specifically by its leading soap brand, Lifebuoy. The goal of the program is to educate 200 million people in India, approximately 20% of the population, on the importance of hand washing with soap. Health education teams, children, and health clubs co-create this educational, health, and hygiene experience. Health education teams visit thousands of schools and communities to teach children about the existence of germs and the importance of washing hands with soap. Children put on shows about fighting germs, and health clubs organize community events to ensure long-term change in hygiene behavior. The process of engagement, from initial contact to self-supporting health clubs, takes two to three years. In order to help consumers on low incomes effectively participate in *swasthya chetna*, the company has introduced a smaller, 18-gram bar of Lifebuoy, enough for one person to wash his or her hands, once a day, for 10 weeks.

Just to assure the reader that the preceding example is not about philanthropy, but about marrying social responsibility with hard issues of growth, let us review one more case study, this one from Denmark, a country with a very different socioeconomic climate than India.

I Do 30 (http://www.ido30.org/)

"Rethink Tomorrow" is what Novozymes, the world leader in bioinnovation, with businesses in industrial enzymes, microorganisms, and biopharmaceutical ingredients, urges us to do. Its mission is to help companies make more from less, through solutions that use less energy and raw materials.

One way in which the company is asking its customers to rethink tomorrow is by reconsidering how they wash clothes. Life cycle assessment of laundry habits shows that if every household in Europe changed from washing at 40 to 30°C and from 60 to 40°C, and every household in the United States changed from "hot" to "warm" and from "warm" to "cold" washes, the world could save up to 32 million tons of CO_2, which is equivalent to taking eight million cars off the road. To promote this agenda, Novozymes launched "I do 30" in June 2009, a campaign that encourages consumers in Europe to make a difference by turning down the temperature on their washing machines to 30°C, thereby reducing CO_2 emissions (readers are encouraged to watch the video on the "I do 30" website- www.ido30. org). The campaign was also a way of exerting pressure on political decision-makers to support strong climate policies at the UN Climate Change Conference (COP15), held in Copenhagen in December 2009. Novozymes handed over 16,000 signatures from people from all over the world to Danish Prime Minister Lars Løkke Rasmussen, who was the host of COP15.

Like Unilever's industry leadership, in connection with sustainable palm oil (Chap. 7), Novozymes is also leading an industry group in connection with sustainable detergents. In December 2009, the company hosted the Copenhagen Detergent Sustainability Summit to shape actions toward a more sustainable future for the industry. To equip the industry with the tools to translate sustainability into business growth, Novozymes brought key representatives together from organizations and companies, such as World Wildlife Fund, Marks & Spencer, Unilever, Reckitt Benckiser, Henkel, McBride, Whirlpool, and P&G.

All three case studies discussed above, —Global Pulse 2010, *Swasthya Chetna*, and "I do 30," —point to an expansion of the demand for collaboration and co-creation. If, as Hanna Jung and Raj Shah of USAID remind us, collaborative dialogue can identify more innovative ideas than organizations, like USAID, can on their own, and if socioeconomic agendas are going to be an integral part of business growth strategies, then we should witness an expansion in the adoption of collaborative value-creation platforms in the future. More companies and organizations are likely to experiment with collaboration and co-creation to support new causes and co-create new experiences with new market segments.

Additionally, current users, companies that have tasted success, like Frito-Lay Dell, and Unilever, will in all likelihood increase their usage of these platforms for value-creation. That's clearly the case with user-generated content (UGC) and brand communications. Organizations like MOFILM (described in Chap. 5) are a clear indicator that the share of UGC ads will continue to increase, as more companies adopt and begin to use this model. The same applies for co-creating new products with passionate customers, as exemplified by Marmite XO, Electrolux, and several other examples featured in this book. Following the successful launch of Marmite XO, David Cousino, Global Consumer and Market Insight Director at Unilever, told UK's online *Marketing Magazine* "This (collaboration and co-creation) is not a fad or fleeting tool which will get abandoned. Consumers will have a real voice with manufacturers through a real platform. This is going to be the future of marketing."

Our thesis that more organizations will adopt and use collaboration and co-creation, while those currently using will increase their usage, should not be interpreted to mean that everything is hunky-dory. A few issues will continue to nag and harass.

- Resistance by incumbents: Change is resisted because it threatens incumbents. Earlier in the book we discussed how a company's R&D personnel often suffer from the not-invented-here syndrome (NIH), causing them to resist the adoption of collaboration and co-creation initiatives. *Marketing week*, UK, reports that Unilever UK's Peperami brand caused a furor in the ad world when it terminated its relationship with Lowe advertising and used a consumer prize-based contest instead to create the Peperami "Animal" advertising character. In the words of one infuriated ad agency executive, "a rich, deep, and long-lasting client relationship is worth much more than a scattergun approach to ideas." Needless to say, the client, Unilever, disagrees.

- Intellectual property (IP): This is another vexing problem. In Chap. 6, we discussed how different Innovation Intermediaries handle the question of IP. Hallmark requires all consumers participating in its communities to sign a release document which states that any and all ideas that arise as a result of their interaction with Hallmark or other community members are Hallmark's property. Issues related to IP are complex and can't be solved through formulaic prescriptions. It is possible, that in the future, certain types of collaborators like lead users, may expect to share in revenue streams resulting from innovations they helped co-create, so they too can benefit from the fruits of their creative efforts.
- Monetary compensation: currently, recognition is the currency of collaborative innovation. That may prove insufficient as customers give more time and effort to collaborative innovation programs. As the McKinsey report (Chap. 5) suggests, money is important, and prize-based competitions are best for mobilizing creativity and resources. Companies seem to be listening, and the incidence of prize-based competitions is increasing. Beyond a critical threshold, it is difficult to imagine customers participating in collaborative innovation projects without monetary compensation.
- Motivation: in any collaboration and co-creation project, only a finite number of collaborators can participate. Only a handful of ideas are selected and even fewer ideas are implemented or win contests. The majority of the people participating in these programs may never have an idea accepted, leave alone win a prize. Over time these customers may lose their motivation to participate. It is also possible that these customers may lose some of their passion and affection for the company and its brands where they couldn't break through, gain recognition, or win.
- Creative capability: if customers are a source of ideas and if the usage of this resource is likely to increase, whose responsibility is it to invest in increasing the creative capability of everyday customers? Should it be the company's responsibility? Etsy (http://www.etsy.com/), a digital bazaar to buy and sell all things handmade, believes it is. Etsy Labs hosts a free weekly skill-sharing craft night in Brooklyn, NY, where attendees can learn to sew their own clothing and tote bags, make their own jewelry, bind books, embroider, knit, and crochet. Consumers can then take these newfound skills, open a digital shop, and do business on Etsy.

By all accounts the adoption and usage of collaboration is poised to expand in the coming years. The issues listed above may slow the pace at which co-creation practices are adopted, but they can't arrest its growth.

Collaboration and co-creation is an emerging and growing business practice. We expect conversation and opinions concerning its pros and cons to increase as its adoption and usage increases. We invite you to participate in this conversation and share your opinions, experiences, and case studies with fellow readers from around the world at www.gauravbhalla.com/co-creation.

Acknowledgments

A book is like an expedition: difficult to undertake and complete without the help of sponsors. Several generous individuals, companies, and organizations have graciously sponsored the completion of this book through their gifts of time, materials, ideas, opinions, attention, and love. Without their lavish support, this book would still be what it was several months ago: a concept.

I would like to begin by first thanking all the individuals, companies, and organizations that shared their stories, materials, and case studies. Their contributions provided substance to the book.

- Unilever: A special thanks to Paul Polman for graciously agreeing to write the Foreword. Harish Manwani, who I have known since my high school days, was instrumental in connecting me with the organization; thank you Harish for your support, perspective, and insights. Gavin Neath, Matt Burgess, Tom Denyard, and Babs Rangaiah — all wonderful people gave ungrudgingly — thank you for your time and willingness to share a rich array of exciting case studies.
- The Decker Family: A very deep and heartfelt thank you to John Decker and his lovely family for their very valuable and courageous contribution; listening to John's story and writing about it was a true growth experience.
- Hallmark: Tom Brailsford and Ann Nelson deserve special thanks for getting the book off to a great start. Thank you, Ann, for connecting me with Tom, and thank you, Tom, for the history, the wealth of detail, and insights that only you could have provided. Thank you also for connecting me with Mark Schwab.
- Denmark: The warmth and generosity of our Scandinavian friends made writing Chapter 8 a joyous experience. To Anna Helene Mollerup I owe special thanks; for her patience, effort, and time spent educating us on Denmark's user-driven innovation program. Interacting with Prof. Jacob Buur was like reading an encyclopedia; sincere thanks for your historical perspective, and your rich and deep insights. Anna Kirah's enthusiasm is infectious; thank you for your insights, and above all for connecting me with Andreas Moan. Last, but not least, thank you, Karin Wall and Lars Andersson, for connecting me with tall people with warm hearts, and handsome ideas.

- Norway: Andreas Moan and Kari Kværner are rare individuals who specialize in medicine and innovation; the book is richer for their contributions. Thank you, Kari and Andreas, for sharing your one-of-a-kind Clinic of Innovation case study with the readers.
- IFF: Nicolas Mirzayantz wears his passion for collaboration and co-creation on his sleeve. Sincere and heartfelt thanks, Nicolas, for sharing your penetrating insights and personal philosophy on collaborative innovation. Hernan Vaisman and Sherry Irizarry were very indulgent of my many requests and provided me with a ringside view on IFF's collaborative approach to marketing and innovation. Carol Brys deserves sustained applause for her tireless coordination and constant support.
- IBM: A very special thanks to Liam Cleaver and his IBM Jam team, Kristine Lawas, Richard Nesbitt, and Kevin Vaughan, for educating me and admitting me as a participant to Global Pulse 2010. Thank you for sharing a wealth of information and unique case studies. Special thanks to Cary Barbour for her "on demand" support, for getting me the required approvals, and for sharing the Smart Cities' case studies; thanks also to Ed Bevan, Sharon Nunes, and Rajesh Radhakrishnan for their vivid explanations on how IBM approaches marketing and innovation in an open, collaborative world.
- Crayola: Thank you, Mark Schwab, for vividly reliving your collaboration and co-creation journey while at the helm at Crayola; very instructive to be able to see it from the Captain's perch; thanks also to Sharon Difelice and Michelle Powers for augmenting Mark's contributions with contemporary insights on collaboration with consumers at the Crayola Factory and the Consumer Insight Center.
- Pitney Bowes: Sincere thanks to Alexandra Mack and Austin Henderson for combing through PB's rich portfolio of co-creation examples and recommending one that offered the best fit with the scope and objectives of the book; your patience and ungrudging support was a boon.
- Mercedes Benz: Thank you, Kristi Steinberg, for your valuable contributions and for sharing MB's collaboration and co-creation journey in *Generation Benz*.
- Passenger: Sincere thanks to Steve Howe and his team for sharing relevant case studies and examples of how clients are using the company's platform to engage with customers.
- Marico: Thank you, Harsh Mariwala and Ameya Naniwadekar, for so willingly sharing Saffola's inspiring collaboration and co-creation journeys; a very worthy addition to the book. Co-creating healthy hearts, diets, and lifestyles is a truly unique application of collaborative innovation.
- Campbell Soup: Thank you, Bette Steele, Aby Elu, and John Faulkner, for permission to use the web image from Campbell's website.
- Visonaire: Thank you, Javier Bone-Carbone, for answering my questions and for your generous permission to use photographs from Visionaire 47.
- Electrolux: Thank you, Frederique Pirenne and Tom Astin, for connecting me with the Electrolux Design Lab, and for sharing information on current and previous competitions.

Amy Jo Martin (formerly with the Phoenix Suns) and Calvin Austin (formerly with Sun Microsystems) were among the first to share valuable insights and personal co-creation experiences with us; my sincere thanks to them for their support and sponsorship and for embracing the book's vision and goals. In addition, Richard Binhammer of Dell and Kristen Studard of Threadless were unstinting in their willingness to answer our questions and help us master complex details; sincere thanks to both of them.

Several individuals from the consulting and academic worlds were very forthcoming with their time, effort, and thoughts. They helped us brainstorm ideas, made us aware of alternate schools of thought, and proofread early versions of the chapters without grimacing. Thank you for taking a personal interest in the contents, flow, and focus of the book.

I would like to thank Vince Barabba for his guidance, insights, and story-telling; sessions with him were highly informative and entertaining. In particular I would like to thank him for introducing me to Buck Weaver's work — an invaluable education. Sincere thanks also to Vijay Govindrajan (VG), one of my very first professors at the Indian Institute of Management, Ahemdabad, for continuing to educate and inspire more rigorous thinking. Karen Mulvahill, former CMO, Comerica Bank, is a long-time friend and business associate. Her willingness to immerse herself in the early drafts was immensely helpful in improving the quality of thinking and writing. Thank you, Bernie Jaworski, Roland Rust, Page Moreau, Aric Rindfleisch, and Robert Gunther, for provoking deeper thinking and for helping proofread the text. Sincere thanks also to Ronnie Maineri, a brilliant physicist and good friend, for reading early drafts and for recommending improvements.

In the world of academics, I would like to thank Marietta Baba, Lucy Suchman, George Day, John Lastovicka, Hope Schau, Narayan Janakiraman, Robert Lusch, Albert Muniz, Sue Brown, Carl Mela, Michelle Weinberger, Jeff DeGraff, P.K. Kannan, and Yogesh Joshi. In the consulting and corporate world, sincere thanks to John Hagel, Lisa Jabara, Jeanne Glasser, Venkatesh Narayan, Sanjiv Chawla, Brian Bishop, Andrew Leary, and Justin Cooper for their ideas and contributions at various stages of the book. A personal thanks to Arun Bewoor and Bharat Patel, my early bosses at Vicks, who have remained friends, for their encouragement, and for connecting me with all the right people at IFF and Marico, respectively.

Rabyia Sheikh, Julie Kennedy, Anna Tulchinskaya, and Nancy Morrison deserve special mention. Rabyia has been my executive assistant for several years and, as always, she was rock solid with her help and support — creating figures and charts, proofing, and making sure all loose ends were tied up. Rabyia and Anna also deserve thanks for creating several interesting cover design prototypes; Anna never stopped pushing the envelope; thank you, Anna. Thank you, Julie, for your diligent and thorough research, and for creating early drafts of case studies. Thank you, Nancy, for your superb editing skills, your sustained support, and your calm, collaborative spirit.

Every organization has heroic executive assistants, without whose help life and work would not flow as smoothly. I have already expressed gratitude for my own, but I was also very fortunate to have interacted with some of the finest in other companies. I owe them a special thanks; they helped the book meet its publishing commitments through their contributions. Angela O'Mahony, Yaw Nsarkoh, and Natalie Parr (Unilever), Dana Debidin (IFF), Heather Irvine (formerly with Passenger), and Laurie Friedman (IBM) — thank you all, for your help in setting and rescheduling appointments and getting me case studies and company materials in a timely fashion.

All expeditions need the services of expert navigators. We had the services of two of the best. Our editor Nicholas Philipson was an absolute joy to work with. Candid, focused, with an infectious sense of humor, he balanced encouragement and realism, as only accomplished professionals can. Thank you, Nick, for your trust and confidence, and for helping transform an idea into reality. We would also like to thank our perennially pleasant editorial assistant, Charlotte Cusumano, for her patience and infectious "Don't worry, we'll get it done" attitude. We couldn't have asked for a better editorial team.

Every expedition also needs someone and someplace to come back to. To my wife, Dilnavaz, and my daughter, Panah – thank you, ladies, for your love, encouragement, and support. Dilnavaz deserves an additional round of applause for reading and re-reading the drafts without ever complaining.

Finally, I would like to thank you, dear reader, for your willingness to spend your valuable time reading this book.

Acknowledging the Collaborators

This book is about collaboration and co-creation. It is also the output of a lyrical collaboration between Gabriela Head, based in Tucson, Arizona, Deanna Lawrence, based in Temparance, Michigan, and yours truly, based in Reston, Virginia. The most noteworthy aspect of this story is that I did not know Gabriela and had not met her when we agreed to collaborate. I still have not met her and the book is written. Neither has Deanna for that matter, barring a one-hour skinny café latte (nobody ever drinks coffee anymore) tête-à-tête during a visit to Phoenix. Deanna, I have known and worked with for several years.

It is safe to say that we all grew during this collaborative venture. Words are necessary to express gratitude and salute this spirit of collaboration, but they are not sufficient. Gabriela and Deanna played different, but complimentary, roles. Deanna was the quintessential generator, a popcorn machine, connecting with people and case studies at a rate often far in excess of the capacity of our email inboxes. Gabriela was the accomplished alchemist, harnessing the pull and energy of all the research and client conversations and converting them into smart, intelligent content and case studies.

Thank you, Gabriela, thank you, Deanna, for your dedication, commitment, and contribution. The book is infinitely richer for it.

Subject Index

Name Index

Company Index

About the Collaborators

Deanna Lawrence is a research strategist in the fields of social media and peer-to-peer collaboration. She is especially passionate about advancements in digital media technology and measurement, online observation, and the ability of consumers to play a stronger role in influencing brand performance.

Gabriela Head is a budding marketing professional with a keen interest in collaboration and co-creation, especially as it applies to technology products and services. She received her MBA from the Eller College of Management, University of Arizona, where she developed an abiding appreciation for collaborative innovation.

About the Author

Gaurav Bhalla is an innovation, strategy, and marketing professional who has experienced the business world as a corporate executive, business consultant, entrepreneur, and educator. His global experience spans corporate positions in business strategy, brand management, and sales management at companies such as Nestle and Richardson Vicks, now a part of P&G, and consulting assignments with Fortune 500 clients in Pharmaceuticals, Technology, Finance, and Fast Moving Consumer Goods sectors.

He is currently the CEO of Knowledge Kinetics, an entrepreneurial venture that focuses on customer value innovation and co-creation. Knowledge Kinetics is his second entrepreneurial venture: his first, G. Bhalla & Associates, merged with TNS, a large market information and customer insight company in 2003.

Prior to launching Knowledge Kinetics, he was the Global Innovation Director at TNS. He also has extensive experience conducting executive education seminars and workshops around the world. In this capacity, he has held adjunct faculty positions at the Fuqua School of Business, Duke University, and at the Robert H. Smith School of Business, University of Maryland, where he also serves on the Department of Marketing's Corporate Advisory Board.

He blogs regularly on issues related to collaboration and co-creation at www. gauravbhalla.com, and can be reached through either his blog or his company's website — www.knowledgekinetics.com.

CPSIA information can be obtained
at www.ICGtesting.com
Printed in the USA
LVOW13*1619301017

554317LV00008B/289/P